I0876852

EX AUDITU

An International Journal of Theological Interpretation of Scripture

Volume 16 2000

Ex Auditu is published annually by Pickwick Publications, 215 Incline Way, San Jose, California, 95139-1526, USA.

Subscriptions
- Individuals:
  - U.S.A. - $17.00
  - Canada - $15.00 (in U.S. Funds)
  - All other countries - $18.00 (in U.S. Funds)
  - Students - $12.00
- Institutions:
  - U.S.A. - $30.00
  - Canada - $25.00 - (in U.S. Funds)
  - All other countries - $30.00 (in U.S. Funds)

This periodical is indexed in the *ATLA Religion Database*, published by the American Theological Library Association, 250 S. Wacker Dr., 16th Flr., Chicago, IL 60606, E-mail: atla@atla.com, WWW: http://www.atla.com/; *Internationale Zeitschriftenshau für Bibelwissenschaft*; *Religion and Theological Abstracts;* and *Old Testament Abstracts.*

Please address all subscription correspondence and change of address information to Pickwick Publications.

© 2001 by Pickwick Publications
ISSN 08883-0053

EX AUDITU

An International Journal of Theological Interpretation of Scripture

KLYNE R. SNODGRASS, *Editor*

NORTH PARK THEOLOGICAL SEMINARY
3225 WEST FOSTER AVENUE
CHICAGO, ILLINOIS 60625-4987
USA

Tel: (773) 244-6209
Fax: (773) 244-6244

e-mail: ksnodgrass@northpark.edu

web site: http://www.northpark.edu/sem/exauditu

EDITORIAL BOARD

Dikran Y. Hadidian, *Pickwick Publications, San Jose, CA*
Jack Dean Kingsbury, *Union Theological Seminary in Virginia, Richmond, VA*
John E. Phelan, Jr. *North Park Theological Seminary, Chicago, IL*
Peter Stuhlmacher, *University of Tübingen, Tübingen, Germany*
Geoffrey Wainwright, *The Divinity School, Duke University, Durham, NC*

THE EDITORIAL BOARD MEMBERS AND CONSULTANTS represent various disciplines and denominations. Theological Interpretation of Scripture is a task to be taken seriously by scholars who are committed to the Christian faith and tradition. However, as one editorial consultant stated: "let people gradually get used to the idea that a sane hermeneutics is both oriented in advance toward agreement/consent and is simultaneously exigent, discriminating, critical."

EDITORIAL CONSULTANTS

C. K. BARRETT
University of Durham
Durham, England

FRANÇOIS BOVON
Harvard Divinity School
Cambridge, MA

RONALD H. CRAM
Columbia Theological Seminary
Decatur, GA

JAMES D. G. DUNN
University of Durham
Durham, England

JAN du RAND
Rand Afrikaans University
Johannesburg, South Africa

ROLAND MUSHAT FRYE
University of Pennsylvania
Philadelphia, PA

ALASDAIR A. I. C. HERON
University of Erlangen
Erlangen, Germany

ROBERT K. JOHNSTON
Fuller Theological Seminary
Pasadena, CA

NICHOLAS L. A. LASH
Cambridge University
Cambridge, England

I. HOWARD MARSHALL
University of Aberdeen
Aberdeen, Scotland

JAMES L. MAYS
Union Theological Seminary
in Virginia, Richmond, VA

EUGENE H. PETERSEN
Regent College
Vancouver, Canada

MARTIN RUMSCHEIDT
Atlantic School of Theology
Halifax, N.S. Canada

HAROLD P. SCANLIN
United Bible Societies
New York, NY

SANDRA SCHNEIDERS
The Jesuit School of Theology
at Berkeley, Berkeley, CA

GRAHAM N. STANTON
The Divinity School
Cambridge, England

DAVID C. STEINMETZ
The Divinity School
Duke University
Durham, NC

ROBERT D. TAYLOR
School of Law
Duquesne University
Pittsburgh, PA

ANTHONY C. THISELTON
University of Nottingham
Nottingham, England

STANLEY D. WALTERS
Rosedale Presbyterian Church
Toronto, Ontario, Canada

N. THOMAS WRIGHT
Canon Theologian of
Westminster Abbey,
London, England

EX AUDITU

Volume 16 2000

CONTENTS

Announcement of the 2000 Symposium v

Abbreviations vi

Introduction
Klyne Snodgrass vii

Body-Piercing, the Natural Sense and the Task of Theological Interpretation: A Hermeneutical Homily on John 19:34
Kevin J. Vanhoozer 1

Response to Vanhoozer
David S. Cunningham 31

Ex Akoēs Pisteōs
James D. G. Dunn 35

Response to Dunn
David P. Moessner 47

On the Interpretation of the Old Testament by the Church
Rolf P. Knierim 55

Response to Knierim
Stephen Chapman 77

God in Human Form
Ulrich Mauser 81

Psalm 33 Interpreted of the Triune God
Geoffrey Wainwright 101

Toward Recovering Theological Exegesis
Brevard S. Childs 121

Only a Distant Memory: Old Testament Allusions to Joshua's Days
Robert L. Hubbard, Jr. 131

Mary Goes to Reform School: A Reformer, A Reformed and Reforming Meet Mary
Kathryn Greene-McCreight 149

Response to Greene-McCreight
Vincent Bacote 165

"You Who Were Far Off Have Been Brought Near": Reflections in the Aid of Theological Exegesis
R. R. Reno 169

Response to Reno
Todd E. Johnson 183

Sermon: A Brazen Faith (John 3:14-15)
Stephen Chapman 187

Annotated Bibliography on Interpreting Scripture Theologically 193

Presenters and Respondents 203

Persons in Attendance 205

Ex Auditu - Volumes Available 207

Announcement of the 2001 Symposium

North Park Theological Seminary in Chicago, Illinois, is pleased to announce that the seventeenth Symposium on the Theological Interpretation of Scripture will take place September 27-29, 2001. The Symposium will start at 7:00 p.m. on September 27 in Nyvall Hall and will extend through a Saturday evening worship service on September 29.

The theme in 2001 will be Biblical Ethics. The following persons have agreed to make presentations:

Iain Provan, Regent College	Old Testament
Daniel Carroll R., Denver Seminary	Old Testament
Graham Stanton, Cambridge University	New Testament
Marion Soards, Louisville Presbyterian Seminary	New Testament
John F. O'Grady, Barry University	Theology
Sondra Wheeler, Wesley Seminary	Ethics
F. Burton Nelson, North Park Theological Seminary	Ethics
Geffrey Kelly, LaSalle University	Ethics
Claretta Dupree, University of Wisconsin	Nursing
Peter Rhea Jones, McAfee School of Theology, Mercer University	Preaching

Persons interested in attending the sessions should write before September 1 to:

Ms. Guylla Brown
North Park Theological Seminary
3225 W. Foster Avenue
Chicago, Illinois 60625

Meals may be taken at North Park and assistance can be provided in finding nearby lodging.

ABBREVIATIONS

Adv. Haer. *Adversus haereses*

A. H. *Against Heresies*

BBR *Bulletin of Biblical Research*

CBQ *Catholic Biblical Quarterly*

CD *Church Dogmatics* (Karl Barth)

CSEL Corpus scriptorum ecclesiasticorum latinorum

DtH Deuteronomistic History

GCS Die griechisches christliche Schriftsteller der ersten [drei] Jahrhunderte

Hist. eccl. Eusebius' *Ecclesiastical History*

Interp *Interpretation*

LW *Luther's Works*

LXX Septuagint

NEB New English Bible

NJB New Jerusalem Bible

NIV New International Version

NRSV New Revised Standard Version

NTS *New Testament Studies*

PG Patrologia graeca (J.-P. Migne, ed.)

PL Patrologia latina (J.-P. Migne, ed.)

REB Revised English Bible

SJT *Scottish Journal of Theology*

TDNT *Theological Dictionary of the New Testament*

TS *Theological Studies*

ThTo *Theology Today*

W. A. *Weimar Ausgabe* (of Luther's Works)

INTRODUCTION

This the sixteenth issue of the journal *Ex Auditu* offers an opportunity to revisit the reason for the journal's existence, i.e., to promote the theological interpretation of Scripture. The planners sought to offer an opportunity to focus on method, on models of theological interpretation, and on an assessment of current trends. Like all the symposia that stand behind the journal, this symposium brought differences and angles of view that the planners did not anticipate. Disagreements were not unexpected, but the differences about the nature of the task and the desired goal were quite deep, although congenially discussed.

The differences compel reflection about what we are doing with Scripture. What is the theological interpretation of Scripture? The differences at least partly stem from whether the word "theological" or the word "interpretation" is given priority and from how the two words are understood. How large is the task of theological interpretation? Is it concerned to discover the theology expressed by the text, the theology that stands behind and as a foundation for what is in the text, the theology that we devise from our meditation on the text, or all the above (and more)? How does the theological interpretation of Scripture relate to the task of reading, and indeed, what does reading include? How much of the task is tied to the intent of the author of the biblical text, and does that include the divine author, and if so, how does one get at divine intent? Does our language presuppose we do interpretation and then do theological interpretation? Robert Morgan suggests that biblical theology is all theologically motivated interpretation of the biblical texts. [*Journal of Religion*, 76 (1996), 210.] If that is true, then all interpretation is biblical theology, for no interpretation takes place that is not motivated theologically in some way, even if by an anti-theology.

Do we need a special hermeneutic for theological reading, one that prioritizes if not presupposes theology, and a different hermeneutic for other kinds of reading? Is a theological hermeneutic one that we can use only in the community, or can we use it in inter-faith dialogue as well? Is there a difference between reading and meditating? Is theological interpretation of Scripture different from interpretation of Scripture? Do we only have this issue of theological interpretation because some have tried to avoid it, even if they have only hidden their theologies (or anti-theologies)? Is there a difference between theological interpretation of Scripture and the theological adaptation of Scripture? Is praying the Psalms the same as reading them? We need clarity about what we are doing and how the stages of our process differ from and relate to each other. Further, we need to establish ways to determine the legitimacy of a theological interpretation. None of us will say that just anything goes in interpretation, but how may an interpretation in the tradition or in our own time be falsified? How can we value tradition without repeating its mistakes? Without careful determination of such issues theological interpretation is left vulnerable to the charge of eisegesis, and interpreters will retreat once again into so-called "scientific" exegesis. Two major issues often dogged the discussion at the symposium: 1) the relation of the testaments and the use that the NT makes of the OT—quite possibly the most crucial and most poorly understood arena of theological interpretation; 2) an assessment of the tradition of the church's—often allegorical—theological interpretation. Lurking behind the discussion were issues of the authority of Scripture and of tradition. As announced previously, the authority of Scripture in the postmodern world will be the subject of the symposium in 2003.

As always the opinions expressed are those of the authors and not necessarily of the planners and publisher. Readers should be aware that the authors were given the opportunity to edit their papers, whereas most of the responses are as they were given originally.

Expressions of thanks must be extended to all the presenters and the respondents for their contribution to the journal and to North Park. In particular, Russell Reno and Stephen Chapman are to be thanked for agreeing quite late in the schedule to make presentations after others orignally scheduled were forced to withdraw. We also thank Brevard Childs and the editors of *Pro Ecclesia* for permission to reprint Childs' helpful article "Toward Recovering Theological Exegesis." The decision to reprint this article was made even before planning of our symposium had been completed. A word of special thanks must be expressed to Linda Forbes who has assisted with running the symposia since their inception at North Park. This is Linda's last year of service. We are grateful for all she has done; she will be missed.

The bibliography obviously could have been expanded considerably, but we sought to focus on works that would help understand method and procedure or that provided particularly helpful models.

Klyne R. Snodgrass
Editor

PUBLISHER'S NOTICE

Since its inception in 1985, *EX AUDITU* subscriptions have remained unaltered. In January 2001 the US Postal Service made drastic increases in the postal rates, both domestic and international. Hence, we are obliged to increase our subscriptions. The increases are listed on the Title Page of this issue.

BODY-PIERCING, THE NATURAL SENSE, AND THE TASK OF THEOLOGICAL INTERPRETATION: A HERMENEUTICAL HOMILY ON JOHN 19:34

KEVIN J. VANHOOZER

INTRODUCTION: TWO TYPES OF THEOLOGICAL INTERPRETATION OF SCRIPTURE

Paul Tillich famously distinguished two types of philosophy of religion by comparing the experience of meeting a stranger with the experience of overcoming estrangement. Reflecting on these two experiences gives rise to two very different types of theology: to theism (God as supreme Being) and to panentheism (God as Being-itself) respectively. This essay explores a similar parallel with two types of theological interpretation of Scripture: between receiving a person hospitably as a stranger into one's community, on the one hand, and socializing a person into a set of authorized communal practices on the other.

How does the distinction between "meeting a stranger" and "overcoming estrangement" bear on our consideration of the task of theological interpretation? In the former case, the stranger (read "text") retains a certain individuality, a degree of over-againstness with regard to the community. A stranger can say things that shock us, things that lead us to view our own community in a different way. In the latter case, a person (read "text") is defined and identified in terms of his designated role and contributes, by performing his designated function, to the good of the whole community. In this respect, socialization resembles "totalization," where the "other" is not allowed to retain its integrity, particularity, or difference, but is instead forced into the mold of the "same." At issue is whether the text of Scripture has a "meaning" independent of the community's own culture and language—whether Scripture has a "voice" of its own, and the power to shock and disturb us.

Now this is an over-simplified picture of the contemporary options in theological interpretation. Its purpose is not to give a comprehensive survey, however, so much as to highlight an important area of disagreement concerning the aims and the norms of theological interpretation of Scripture. The "socializing" approach lays stress on the priority of the aims and purposes of the reading community. On this view, theological interpretation is a church practice governed by the end of building up the body of Christ in worship and spiritual formation. This contemporary approach is significantly strengthened by an appeal to the ancient Rule of Faith, which acts as a hermeneutical rule—a rule for reading. According to this position, the theological interpretation of Scripture makes edifying use of the Bible—namely, to "form Christians"—in ways that are compatible with the Rule of Faith. The chief purpose of theological interpretation is building up the body of Christ.

The other approach focuses on the author as a significant, sometimes strange, "other," and continues to speak of the "meaning" of the text, however difficult a notion that is to define. Must these two aims—to edify the interpretive community and to recover the author's intended meaning—necessarily conflict? Not if, as I shall propose, we view the concept of meaning as an interpretive *norm* rather than as an interpretive aim. Theological interpretation, on this view, is a matter of discovering the divinely authored message in Scripture. This approach draws upon church history too, particularly upon the wide consensus concerning the authority and priority of the literal sense. As we shall see, the concern for interpretive norms need not lead to a neglect of interpretive aims, though I shall argue that the latter must be tested by the former.

In a somewhat related fashion, Robert Morgan posits a basic dichotomy of interpretive aims between, on the one hand, the academic community, with its concern with historical reconstruction and literary composition, and the ecclesial community, with its interest in reading the Bible as faith-forming Scripture on the other. Is it indeed the case that the aims of scholars and saints must ultimately conflict?

We are, clearly, in a dichotomized situation. What is needed, I believe, is an approach to theological interpretation of Scripture that includes both aims and norms, an approach that attends both to edification and to textual meaning. One promising way forward is to focus on what I shall call "the *theological* natural sense" of Scripture. By "natural sense" I refer to what authors are doing with just *these* words in using them in just *this* way in just *this* literary context.[1] By "theological" I refer to what God, as divine author, is doing with just these human words in just this canonical context. The category of the "natural" is, of course, a much-disputed topic in postmodernity. For it is a common postmodern reflect to demythologize talk about the "natural" into talk about the "social." For many postmoderns, all talk about "the way things are" translates into "the way we *think* things are" or "the way *we will* things to be." For better or for worse, then, the term "natural" highlights the specific area of disagreement over the theological interpretation of Scripture in a postmodern, community-oriented context, namely, whose aims will have the upper-hand: authors' or readers'?

The goal of this paper is to proffer a strategy for the postcritical retrieval of something like the classic theological interpretation of Scripture. Crucial to this attempt will be the rehabilitation of the natural sense, as well as a correction of certain distortions that have crept into this notion.[2] I begin by examining certain analogies between "bodies" and "texts" and suggest that the "natural" itself is susceptible of theological interpretation. I then return to a consideration of the two types of theological interpretation: the one which relies primarily on the Rule of Faith (and the socialized or ecclesial sense); the other which relies primarily on a reconstituted concept of the natural sense (the author's intended sense). I then examine John 19:31-37 as a practical example of what is involved in theological interpretation. Finally, using vv. 34-36 as a springboard, I make some summary suggestions as to the nature, necessity, and norms of theological interpretation of Scripture. The conclusion draws some implications of my thesis for the church as the community of theological interpreters. The metaphorical red thread running through it all is, improbably enough, body-piercing.

THE POSTMODERN CHALLENGE: "NATURAL" BODIES?

The basic premise of this essay, as indicated by its title, is that the contemporary fad for body-piercing symbolizes the postmodern concern for identity construction, and that something similar takes place in biblical interpretation when the aim of the interpretative community is likewise identity construction. To begin with, however, I turn to the very notion of "natural" bodies and the parallel with the "natural" sense.

"Natural" as an essentially disputed concept

In contemporary ethics and hermeneutics alike, appeals to categories such as the "natural" or the "proper" often evoke suspicion and distrust. Such suspicion can be either mild or radical. The milder suspicion points out that what often passes as "natural" is actually something culturally and historically relative. It may be "natural" for us to think of marriage in terms of a legally ratified monogamous relationship between a man and a woman, but a mild hermeneutics of suspicion will point out the cultural and social contingency of such an arrangement. The more radical postmodern version of this suspicion, however, insists that what passes as "natural" is never anything but a social convention.[3]

When it comes to postmodern biblical interpretation, nurture is a clear winner over nature. According to Stanley Hauerwas, "There simply is no 'real meaning' of Paul's letters to the Corinthians once we understand that they are no longer Paul's letters but rather the Church's Scripture."[4] Interpretations do not tell us about the plain or natural sense of the text; they tell us rather about the culture and sociopolitical location of the reader and about the way the reader has been nurtured. Hauerwas's point is that the church should not be made incidental to the process of biblical interpretation. When he denies that Scripture does not make sense apart from a Church that gives it sense, however, he imperils the very distinction between textual meaning and community interpretation.

Many postmoderns are happy to deny the text/commentary distinction. There is no natural sense of words or texts, only senses that have been socially constructed. Interpretation, like knowledge more generally, has become a thoroughly political affair, a matter of power, a matter of what individuals or interpretive communities *will* texts to mean. Postmodernity stands for the crisis of legitimation in interpretation, for the suspicion of hermeneutics, and for the rejection of the very concept of "correct interpretation." Richard Rorty, for instance, suggests that we give up trying to "get it right" and concentrate on "making it useful." Is it possible that some of the current proposals that favor reading the Bible in the church for the church may in fact owe more to secular philosophy than to a Christian ecclesiology on which they claim to be based?

Once one abandons the concept of the natural sense the question of criteria for legitimate interpretation immediately arises. Postmoderns want to know whose reading counts, and why. Why should one prefer the reading of the Christian community to interpretations produced in the secular academy? Why should one prefer a Lutheran interpretation to a Reformed, a Pentecostal to a Puritan? Can we say anything more than, "Because I belong to this community"?

Some postmoderns contend that our interpretations, of Scripture or of any other text, are at best relative to the standards of particular interpretive communities, and at worst wholly arbitrary. Reading always serves some purpose or other. Interpretation is shot through with ideology and power interests. One's reading is shaped by interpretive interests of gender, race, class, and so forth. It has been said that since there is no such thing as an innocent reading, we must say what reading we are guilty of. Christians can agree with this. Human interpreters are finite and fallen; what we presently know we know as through a glass, darkly (1 Cor 13:12).

A. K. M. Adam offers a more neutral definition of ideology: "a description of all the social interactions that ascribe 'significance' to our behavior."[5] On this view, the Christian ideology is learned by participating in ecclesial practices, for it is here that we learn what "divine," "holy," "evangelical," "salvific," and "liberating" mean.

An honest survey of church history—a history that Gerhard Ebeling identifies with that of biblical interpretation—surely leads one to conclude that interpreters in the church are not immune to the temptation of ideological criticism. There are numerous—far too numerous!—examples of communities forcing their own theological interpretations onto texts that often seem reluctant to accept them. Indeed, reading the Bible to "discover" the theology of one's confessional tradition is but another example of what Derrida calls "ethnocentrism," the attempt to equate "*our* way of reading" or "what *we* see in the text" with "the natural sense." It is an open question, however, whether one should infer from the fact that Christians sometimes pervert the natural sense that the very concept of the "natural sense" has nothing to commend it.

Heavenly bodies—Gen 1:14: "and let them be for signs. . ."

"Nature" includes both the heavens and the earth. Let us begin with the heavens. It would be reasonable to think that there could be little dispute over the category "natural" when applied to phenomena such as the stars and planets. Not only are they far removed from human life and culture, but their movements, as Galileo discovered, are susceptible to mathematical explanation and objective measurement. Surely if there is a candidate for a non-socialized natural, it would be these heavenly bodies.

In fact, the conflict of interpretations is all too apparent with regard to heavenly bodies as well. One has only to contrast the approaches of astronomy and astrology. The astronomer (like the historical critic!) wants to distinguish reality from appearance, to state "what actually happens." Astrologers, on the other hand, provide "edifying" interpretations of the celestial bodies. Horoscopes represent ample evidence that it is all too easy to read more into celestial bodies (e.g., into the positions and alignment of the stars) than is really there. From the perspective of the astronomer, astrology is an example of gross eisegesis.

Christian theologians have had to debunk astrology throughout church history. Augustine's refutation in *The City of God* is both sophisticated and decisive, even appealing to twin studies to refute the premise that heavenly bodies determine human behavior. For our purposes, it is interesting to note that Calvin's objections to astrology are virtually identical to his objections to allegory: both interpret "signs of certain things" to be whatever their fancy dictates. When Gen 1 was composed, however, the author was writing about the order of nature. Calvin concludes that both astrology and allegory read signs "unnaturally."[6]

While a Christian theological interpretation of celestial bodies will include a good dose of demythologizing, it would be a mistake to depict Moses as a naturalist. For it is a mistake to confuse the natural with the naturalistic (i.e., with the *only* natural), just as it is to confuse the literal with the literalistic.[7] Christians may reject astrology, but it does not follow that the sun, moon, and stars have *no* semiotic value. On the contrary, according to the Bible, "the heavens declare the glory of God" (Ps 19:1). Nature is God's work, and a complete description of nature requires not only scientific laws, but the doctrine of creation. A "theological natural" interpretation, then, is one that evokes God as an explanatory hypothesis or factor.

The human body

While disputes over how to interpret heavenly bodies preoccupied a good number of precritical theologians, the more divisive interpretive disagreements have shifted in recent times to something altogether more earthly, namely, the human body. The current craze for body-piercing is, I submit, an apt metaphor for how texts, including the Bible, are often treated in the postmodern world. Body-piercing is, in one sense, a flagrant violation of the "natural." The body of the biblical text is similarly "pierced" by those who are concerned less for its natural sense than for its role in constructing personal or communal identity. The question is whether such piercing is ultimately not an act of violence on "the natural": on flesh, in the one case; and on authorial intention, in the other.

T*he body as cultural construct.* At first blush the human body would seem to stand solidly on the side of nature rather than culture. After all, the body is a biological entity whose various systems work involuntarily according to physical and chemical laws. Philosophers and cultural theorists, however, insist that the body is a social, even political, construct. They are not oblivious to the body's cellular composition, but their main interest is in conceptualizing the body as the site of multiple, often contesting, discourses. For example, social constructionists like Michel Foucault examine the ways in which society has "shaped" and "disciplined" the body in order to make it meaningful. In itself, the body is an underdetermined space, waiting to be written.

Biblical genealogies sketch one type of relation between human bodies, namely, that of begetting. There is, of course, more to begetting than biology. The purpose of the biblical genealogies is not simply to chart the history of a particular set of human genes. They are also evidence of the faithfulness of God across the generations. In postmodern theory, however, genealogy refers to an attempt to "deconstruct" or undo what appears to be something natural by tracing its lineage back to the moment of its social construction.

What does body-piercing mean? The body is the physical link between our deepest selves and the outside world, the medium through which we project ourselves into social life. Perhaps nowhere else does the body more clearly appear as the site of identity construction than in the contemporary craze for body-piercing. To be sure, body-piercing is a global phenomenon that has been practiced for millennia. In many non-Western societies, for instance, tattoos and piercings define one's social status, they "mark" people in long established social positions. In these tribal contexts, body-piercing serves an integrative purpose.

In the social context of the late twentieth and early twenty-first centuries in the post-industrial West, however, the practice of body-piercing may well be of an entirely different order than its function in tribal or primitive societies.[8] In the West, body-piercing is a much more deliberative and reflexive process, often bound up with a person's desire to stand out from society. During the 1970s, body-piercing was associated with an aesthetic kerygma that proclaimed one's individuality and *apartness* from society. For many, tattoos and piercings were marks of dissatisfaction with conventional society. Body-piercings communicate messages both about identity construction and about the culture in which they circulate. What, then, does body-piercing mean?

If there is a language of the body, then body-piercing is a peculiarly graphic speech act. According to one recent study, body-piercings are "acts that ask to be witnessed."[9] Anthony Giddens argues that, as the dominant discourses of religion and family lose their currency, people are attempting to construct a "narrative of self" upon the only tangible material left: their physical bodies.[10]

Some social theories see the body as an unfinished biological phenomenon that is transformed as a result of its participation in certain social practices.[11] Body-piercing can be viewed as an attempt to "write the meaning" of the body over and above its biology. One's body and one's self-identity are viewed as aesthetic projects, underdetermined phenomena that invite further construction, not just passive reception. There is apparently some satisfaction in the feeling that one has a degree of power over the project of constructing one's identity.

Postmoderns like Foucault see the human body not only as the site of identity construction, the canvas with which one expresses one's individuality, but as the site of a power struggle. Whose interpretive community will be allowed to determine the body's meaning? Whose reading of sexuality, for instance, will prevail? In our present situation, marked as it is by the conflict of interpretations, body-piercing represents an assault on the very notion of a "natural" sense. The postmodern assumption, again, is that human identity is not received but achieved, and body-piercing is viewed as a strategy for "augmenting" body language. Sex-change operations, perhaps the most radical form of body-piercing, go far beyond commentary and would be better construed as radical attempts to "rewrite" the body. Such manipulative operations, I suggest, are wholesale rejections of a person's particular bodily "text." As we shall see, such rejections of the natural have their counterparts in hermeneutics and in biblical interpretation.

A theological interpretation of the body. I have no wish to side with "naturalistic" social theorists who reduce the complexities of social life to some basis in biology. Yet neither do I agree with the social constructionists who contend that the body is a primarily social phenomenon either. If the category "natural" has any application to discussions concerning the human body, then, it must be determined by something other than biology on the one hand or sociology on the other. A non-reductionistic understanding of the natural requires nothing less than a theological interpretation. Let us therefore introduce the concept of the "theological natural": nature and the natural as interpreted by the word of God revealed in the narratives of Israel and the church, and preeminently in the narratives concerning Jesus Christ.

From a theological perspective, the natural is precisely that which accords with the creator's intention, with what Plantinga calls the "design plan." Our embodied identity as male or female, for instance, is something we are to receive with gratitude, not something arbitrary that can be made into something else. To reject the natural sense, to rebel against nature construed theologically in terms of the created order, is thus to rebel against God. Further, our bodies are not our own but "were bought with a price" (1 Cor 6:20). The body, says Paul, is not meant for immorality, but for the Lord (1 Cor 6:13). A complete theological interpretation of our natural bodies would include the following points: that they are created by God; are members of Christ (1 Cor 6:15); and finally, temples of the Holy Spirit (1 Cor 6:19). These theological indicatives lead to a theological imperative: to present our bodies as living sacrifices (Rom 12:1).

What we do with our bodies creates a particular shape of life. Nevertheless, the true or theologically natural meaning of our bodies is more a matter of divine rather than human construction. Our true identity—as creatures of God, men and women in Christ, temples of the Holy Spirit— is something we receive and realize, not something that we develop or construct. Note too that what the celestial bodies do involuntarily—glorify God—should also be the voluntary aim of human bodily action. While celestial bodies invariably perform their natural function, humans do not. We humans have the terrible capacity to reject the natural, to refuse our divine author's intention.

The body of the text

The body, then, is like a text. Instead of writing one's own meaning onto the body, Christians, I have suggested, should see the body as already inscribed with meaning, with a "natural sense" as it were, by the triune God. Conversely, the biblical text is like a body. We turn now to the parallel assault on the category of the "natural" by some theological interpreters of Scripture. Again, my working hypothesis is that there is an important parallel between the idea of identity construction that underlies the practice of body-piercing and the idea of social formation that lies behind a certain practice of theological interpretation of Scripture.

In common parlance the "body" of the text refers to the main part of a text. In the hands of some contemporary readers, however, the text appears as an inert, lifeless body, on which the interpreter performs various operations. Both bodies and texts can be victims of violence. To anticipate the biblical passage that we will examine below, we may compare what interpreters do to inert texts to what the Roman soldiers did to Jesus on the cross: "The body as object is already being treated as mere flesh, a consumable, a dead, unwanted, discardable thing, before Jesus breathes his last."[12] Similarly, "Texts, like dead men and women, have no rights, no aims, no interests. They can be used in whatever way readers or interpreters choose."[13] Dead bodies make no gestures. They do nothing. They are passive, not active. To the extent that the text has no aims or life of its own, it is at the mercy of the reader. It would appear that there is only one active agent in interpretation—the reader. Mark Taylor therefore only slightly exaggerates when he characterizes interpretation as "a *hostile* act in which interpreter victimizes text."[14]

In the context of text interpretation the notion of body-piercing can actually be applied in two very different ways. On the one hand, one can look at the text, like the body, as the site of identity construction. *This predilection for identity construction is precisely what contemporary body-piercers and postmodern interpreters have in common.* There are two problems, however, with viewing interpretation as a means of identity construction: 1) if what gets constructed depends less on the nature of the text or the natural sense than the sense nurtured in the interpreting community, how can the interpretive community's treatment of the text be defended as something more than an (arbitrary?) social convention, especially given the plurality of interpretive communities? 2) to the extent that the community uses the text to construct or reinforce its identity, how can it avoid the charge that its interpretation is nothing more than an imposition, perhaps even a violent one, onto the body of the text?

On the other hand, one can pierce the body (or the text) in the sense of getting beneath the surface and discerning what lies beneath (e.g., its "soul" or message). As we shall see, this latter sense of body-piercing views the body of the text not merely as a passive object but also as something active—a *communicative* act, to be precise.

WHAT IS THEOLOGICAL INTERPRETATION?

It is both curious and ironic that recent dictionaries of biblical interpretation are virtually silent on the subject of the theological interpretation of Scripture. The new two volume Abingdon dictionary (ed. John Hayes) has entries on "psychoanalytic biblical interpretation," "ideological criticism," "inner-biblical interpretation," and even "Ethiopian biblical interpretation," but nothing on "theological biblical interpretation."

What, then, is the force of the qualifying adjective "theological" when it comes to biblical interpretation? Obviously, such interpretation has something to do with God, but what? There are several possibilities, but I will consider only the two options mentioned above in my introductory remarks. The one view sees *theological* as qualifying the *object* of interpretation (viz., Scripture as the Word of God); the other sees it as qualifying the *process* of interpretation (viz., the socialization or identity construction of the people of God). For the first, what makes biblical interpretation theological is the appeal to God as in some sense Scripture's author; according to the latter view, what makes biblical interpretation theological is more a matter of the aim and outcome, namely, living faithfully with others before God.

At present there seem to be two major fault lines that prevent the two approaches from appreciating fully the other's potential contribution. One fault line has to do with the nature of the hermeneutics undergirding the theological interpretation of Scripture (namely, general vs. special); the other pertains to contrasting emphases (namely, norms vs. aims). I believe that the way forward for theological interpretation of Scripture lies in a fusion of both these horizons.

Between general and special hermeneutics

Theological interpretation and hermeneutics in general: the meaning of meaning. General hermeneutics concerns the principles of text interpretation as such. Many biblical scholars seek to use the best general principles in interpreting Scripture. Benjamin Jowett, for instance, speaks for many historical-critics when he exhorts interpreters to read the Bible "like any other book," namely, for "the meaning," which has traditionally been associated with the sense the historical author intended. However, numerous studies have documented how historical critics became side-tracked by attempts to reconstruct either the history of the text's composition (i.e., the text's "pre-history" in source, form, and tradition criticism) or the real rather than the apparent historical events referred to, or thus spending more energy on what lay behind the text than in what lay in it.

Theological interpretation and Scripture in particular: ecclesial interests. This preoccupation with the history *behind* the text has led other biblical interpreters to relegate the question of authorial intention to secondary status. They argue that textual meaning should not be equated with authorial intention, nor should the quest for "the meaning" define the project of theological interpretation. On the contrary, what makes biblical interpretation *theological* is the specific interpretive interest in using the Bible to build up the community in faith, hope, and love. General theories of meaning and interpretation are of little use to these theological interpreters. Of the definitions of meaning and the approaches to interpretation, there is no end. Christians should focus instead on the goal of interpretation: fostering communion with God and others. To put the point slightly differently, according to this view the theological interpretation of Scripture is less an epistemological project of coming to know determinate meaning than it is a political project of trying to shape a particular communal form of life: "The aim of faithful living before the Triune God becomes the standard to which all interpretive interests must measure up."[15]

Theological hermeneutics: towards a Christian theory of interpretation. Is it enough to know the ends of theological interpretation? Although often overlooked, there is an alternative to general (often secular) theories of meaning on the one hand and the notion that Christian communities read the Bible in their own way on the other. A number of recent writers—myself included—argue for a theological hermeneutics, i.e., a theory of interpretation—of the Bible and of texts in general—that is itself formed, informed, and reformed by Christian doctrine.[16] This strategy combines the concerns of both general and special hermeneutics by offering a properly *theological* account of "the meaning" of a text.

Interpretative aims: the Rule of Faith as a hermeneutical rule

According to a growing number of community-oriented interpreters, it was only thanks to the ancient church's Rule of Faith that early Christians read the Bible, Old and New Testaments, as a unified canon. While scholars in the academy may read the "Hebrew Bible" in isolation from the NT, Christians cannot; for the Rule insists that we make a theological connection between the God of Israel and the Father of Jesus Christ, and hence a hermeneutical connection between the two choirs of witnesses. Proponents of "ruled reading" contend that classic Christian hermeneutics never approached the text with methods only, but always with certain rules, rules that ultimately function to aid Christian formation. Such "ruled reading" is the best means for arriving at the end of theological interpretation, namely, a deeper communion with God and others. The connection between "ruled reading" and "socializing" interpretation (e.g., the type that seeks to overcome estrangement) should now be clear. Ruled reading—reading in communion with other saints for the sake of spiritual formation—is a matter of learning authorized community interpretive practices. The *telos* of these practices, we may recall, is to build up the community, not to discover something about the message of the text.

Many who commend ruled reading see theological interpretation of Scripture more in terms of politics than of epistemology. The point, they say, is not to develop general principles for coming to know texts, but rather to foster a certain shape of community life. The Rule of Faith performs three hermeneutical functions in pursuit of this community end: 1) it helps determine the plain sense of the text; 2) it unifies the Scriptures; 3) it serves as a criterion for interpretation.

The plain sense. Origen famously rejected the literal meaning of certain OT narratives precisely because he found them unedifying. Is ruled reading simply another name for allegorizing? What happens to the plain sense on this view?

It is common for proponents of ruled reading to assert the priority of the plain sense of Scripture. However, upon closer inspection it becomes evident that they do not consider the plain sense to be a property of the text. The plain sense is rather the sense the text has when read in the context of the believing community.[17] This fits in with the general theme that texts have no intrinsic aims nor interests and with the idea that theological interpretation is primarily a matter of the aims and interests of the interpretive community. According to Kathryn Greene-McCreight, the concept of the plain sense means something slightly different depending on which theologian is speaking about it, but in general she sees two constraints on interpreting for the "plain sense": the verbal sense of the text, and the Rule of Faith. The Rule of Faith functions as the sanctioned "preunderstanding" of the subject matter of Scripture and basically sets forth the story of what God was doing in Christ.[18] The Rule's shape is essentially narrative, its substance Trinitarian. This ecclesial preunderstanding of what the Bible is fundamentally about, based on the centrality of the narratives of Jesus, enables the church to "rule in" some interpretations and "rule out" others. What is noteworthy is that the plain sense may or may not coincide with the explicit *verbal* sense of the text.

As to the unity of the Bible, here too it is primarily a matter not of some textual property but of the way in which Scripture is read in community. Unity is less a matter of the coherence of its parts than the by-product of a habit of reading. Finally, the Rule of Faith functions as a criterion with which to determine which readings are appropriate for the Christian community, since the interpretations are finally tested not by the text but by the Rule. This is precisely what one would expect of those who follow Stanley Fish, for whom authority in interpretation is vested in the practices of the interpretive community, not in some alleged inherent textual properties. To the cry "Exegesis! Exegesis! Exegesis!" one wonders whether ruled readers might rejoin "Tradition! Tradition! Tradition!"[19]

Whose use? Which grammar? A catholic rule. The suggestion that theological interpretation of Scripture take the form of ruled reading is a powerful one. It carries the venerable weight of ancient tradition and also appeals to postmodern sensibilities (e.g., the authority of interpretive communities; interpretation as a mode of identity construction). The main thrust of the proposal is that one view the aims of the interpretive community, that is, the church's interest in spiritual formation, as constitutive of the practice of theological interpretation of Scripture. How should we evaluate this proposal? In particular, what should we make of the eclipse, at least a partial eclipse, of the natural sense of the text itself in favor of the community's aims and rules for reading Scripture?

To begin with, we may note a certain tension, or irony, built into the claim that ruled reading caters to the specific aims of the believing community to the detriment of general theories of meaning. In fact, the notion that one should look "not to the meaning but to the use," is easily traced back to Ludwig Wittgenstein, who is neither Fish nor Fowl, but the philosophical presence behind both.

Let us assume, for the sake of the argument, that Wittgenstein is correct in his assumption that we need to attend to the particular uses of words. The question then becomes: to whose use should theological interpreters of Scripture look? Possible answers to this query fall into three types: 1) to the persons (authors, redactors, canonizers) responsible for producing the final form of the text; 2) to readers seeking to use Scripture for the sake of edification in accordance with the Rule of Faith; 3) to God as the ultimate author or appropriator of the biblical text. The first option, favored by historical critics, gets us only as far as the history of religion; we shall therefore consider it no further. The third option will be considered below. Given its prominence, it is the second option, ruled reading (the method of "socialization" referred to in the opening paragraphs of the present essay) that requires further scrutiny.

According to a ruled reading approach, the aims of the biblical text, which is to say the aims and interests of the individuals and communities responsible for producing it, appear to be subordinate to the aims of the present interpretive community. After all, it is argued, the community, together with its Rule of Faith, preexisted the NT. What books we find in the NT are there only because they cohere with the core beliefs of the church's christological confession "Jesus is Lord." The church canonized certain texts "because (when used and used properly) these writings agree with the Rule of Faith in content and consequence.[20] Indeed, as we have seen, the "plain sense" itself is a result of the verbal (potential) sense and the community's ruled reading. While it is true that Fowl and Jones refer to the importance of critical biblical scholarship and to "virtuous" interpretation in the context of reading the Bible "over-against ourselves," it is not altogether clear how this can be done in the absence of any stable or determinate textual meaning (e.g., the natural sense).

Does the Rule of Faith indeed derive not from Scripture itself but from certain patterns of the believing community's reading of Scripture? Ruled readers apparently agree with Wittgenstein that "interpretation" is a matter of making grammatical remarks about the ways in which texts are used. What sense, then, does it make to speak of the Bible as "canon" (e.g., measuring rod, rule)? For ruled readers, the Bible is canonical only when its texts play a certain role for a particular group of people. To be "canonical," then, is less a thing (e.g., a list of books) or a property of books than it is a function or dynamic relation between certain texts and a certain interpretive community. As with "plain sense," so with "canon": neither is a textual property or phenomenon. Rather, both are concepts that refer to the *interaction* of text and community.

The Rule of Faith, then, is the "grammar" implicit in the community's interpretive practice. This grammar stipulates the following rules: read the two testaments as a single book; read the story of Jesus as the fulfilment of the story of Israel. The conclusion follows inevitably: "the canon that measures the legitimacy and efficacy of the Bible's interpretation is the church's Rule of Faith."[21] What is Christianly adequate is measured by the Rule of Faith, not by Scripture. The point is that the Rule of Faith becomes a "canonical" rule, the chief criterion for adjudicating between legitimate and illegitimate theological interpretation.

Is it not somewhat disingenuous both to claim that the Christian community reads Scripture in a manner that is *sui generis* and to rely (at least tacitly) on a general theory in support of this claim? Ruled readers say they are not interested in theories of meaning, yet current formulations of ruled reading fit in perfectly with the contemporary turn to reader-oriented approaches in secular criticism, and some of these theorists (e.g., Stanley Fish) are explicitly cited in support. To say that the interpretation of texts is inseparable from the history of their reception is just to take sides in contemporary debates about textual meaning.

Whose use of Scripture is authoritative, and why? Whence come the grammatical rules of Christian faith? The pressing question is just this: *whose* Rule is it? Ruled readers invariably answer: the catholic church's. "A critical theological hermeneutic requires that every rule of faith must bear close family resemblance to the catholic Rule of Faith."[22] The Rule of Faith is a catholic rule, a summary of how the ecumenical church has, through its history, read the biblical texts. This catholic rule thus affords an anchor in the sea of interpretive possibilities.

At this point we must pose two critical questions: First, just how catholic is the Rule of Faith? How do we know the church got the doctrine of God right, or should we simply accept that might, in this case relative catholicity, makes right? Is it simply a contingency of church history that the Rule is Trinitarian rather than Unitarian?

Second, quite apart from the all too obvious present problem of there being a plurality of ecclesial communities, the ruled reading approach fails to ascribe supreme authority to the Scriptures because it fails adequately to recognize Scripture as the result of divine authorship. Authority is vested in reading practices and, therefore, in reading communities. Francis Watson has recently suggested that this approach owes more to postmodernity than to patristic theology. He argues that this hermeneutic actually works against theology by substituting the being of the community for the communicative agency of God. The community must not become the basic principle in hermeneutics.[23] The church itself is derivative; it owes its being to God's prior evocation. I submit that we must recognize the ecclesial and hermeneutical priority of God, specifically, the priority of his speech agency or "authorship" of Scripture. To interpret the Bible theologically is to interpret it as the verbal communicative action of God that bears witness to God's historical communicative action in the history of Israel and of Jesus Christ. There are indeed many possible interpretive aims and interests, but the people of God must above all concern themselves with what God is saying, and doing, in and through the Scriptures.

Interpretative norms: the natural sense

In his important article on postcritical canonical interpretation, George Lindbeck comments that Childs' canonical approach, which reads the Bible as an authoritative witness to the Word of God, fails to provide adequate guidance to the Christian community. Lindbeck makes a similar point about reading Scripture in order to participate in its narrative world. He worries that the canon risks becoming a grab-bag for ecclesial interpreters: "The choices tend to range between the three poles of ecclesiastical magisterium, unchanging communal tradition, and private interpretation or, more concretely and inaccurately expressed, Rome, Constantinople, and Wittenberg/Geneva."[24] The first two approaches are unable to lodge an appeal to the text as a basis for preferring one interpretation to another: "For both, choices between alternative patterns of canonical construal are intratextually arbitrary; one must exit the text in order to find grounds for decision; and as to how one does that they seem to have no hermeneutically usable answers."[25]

What Lindbeck's comments bring to light is the need, not for another interpretive aim, but rather for an interpretive *norm*. Interestingly, Lindbeck himself is intrigued by Wolterstorff's authorial discourse model, which represents the required exit from the text that alone can ground one's preference for one reading rather than another. While I applaud Lindbeck's openness to the notion of the author's intentional action—a notion I now intend to develop myself—I do not accept that an appeal to the author is an exit from the text. On the contrary, the text just *is* an intention (communicative) action. This leads me to privilege not Wittenberg but *Gutenberg*, for this norm reflects not some community interest but the texts', or rather, their *authors'*—human and divine—communicative interest which the written discourse enacts.[26]

Five theses on theological interpretation of Scripture: the role of communicative action. I have argued elsewhere for the cogency of the following theses. Here I will limit myself to a short exposition, in order then to turn to an extended exegetical example. It is worth observing, however, that I have sought to derive these theses from Christian doctrine; the use of speech act philosophy is merely ancillary to my theological purpose.

1. *The ultimate authority for Christian theology is the triune God in communicative action.* Theology is a human response to a divine initiative: communicative action. God makes himself known in word and deed. God is the initiator of

this action (agent), the Word or content of this action (act), and the Spirit or power of its reception (consequence). It is imperative, insofar as we seek to preserve the integrity of the gospel, to respect the difference between the Word of God embodied and enacted in Scripture on the one hand, and human commentary on the other. This fundamental intuition—that the gospel of Jesus Christ does not change at the behest of our interpretations—requires nothing less than a distinction between true and false religion, as well as a distinction between right worship and idolatry.

2. *A text's "plain meaning" or "natural sense" is the result of a person's communicative action* (e.g., what an author has done in tending to his or her words in this way rather than another). It is the *author's* use of words in communicative action that determines their particular sense. True, words have a range of verbal or conventional senses, but the way in which authors employ linguistic and literary conventions usually indicates which of the many conventional senses (and there may be more than one) are intended. The natural sense, in short, is the authorially intended sense: the sense the words bear when used in *this* context by *this* author. While it is possible to say what readers make of a text, this is not the same as interpreting it. To read Galatians as if I rather than Paul had authored it is to engage in a new act of composition, not commentary.[27]

3. *To call the Bible "Scripture" is to acknowledge a divine intention that does not contravene, but supervenes on, the communicative intentions of its human authors.* Nicholas Wolterstorff has recently shown how God could be said to "appropriate" human discourse. That is one way to associate a divine communicative intention with one that is human. There are two other ways: the traditional insistence on the dual-authorship of Scripture, an insistence that ultimately presupposes a doctrine of providence; and the more recent insistence that the divine intention comes into its own when the parts of the text are read in light of the canonical context.[28]

4. *The theological interpretation of Scripture requires us to give "thick descriptions" of the canonical acts in the Bible performed by both the human and the divine authors.* The task of literal interpretation is to say what authors have done with their words. If one takes divine authorship of Scripture seriously, then literal interpretation must have recourse to the canonical context, for the meaning of the parts is related to the whole of Scripture. The literal sense of Scripture as intended by God is the sense of the canonical act (e.g., of the communicative act when seen in the context of the canon). We may recall that the norm of interpretation—the natural sense—is a matter of an author's intentional action. What is important to remember is that some features of an action only emerge against a certain context of description. There are many ways to describe what someone has done: we may say that a person moved his index finger, fired a gun, killed someone, assassinated a political figure, and precipitated the First World War. All of these descriptions are true as far as they go. But the higher level description—he precipitated the First World War—gives a "fuller" sense of the act than "he moved his index finger." It is only against the larger canonical backdrop that we can discern what God may have intended in particular biblical texts.[29]

5. *The norm of theological interpretation (namely, what an author has intentionally said/done), generates an interpretive aim: to bear competent witness to what an author has said/done.* A certain interpretive imperative follows from

the above indicative, that is, from the notion that the text just *is* an intentional communicative act. "Thou shalt not bear false witness" is only the negative version of this interpretive imperative. The positive version is "Do unto the texts of others as you would have them do unto yours."

A canonical rule. "The aim of reading Scripture, to build up Christian faith and practice, should always order decisions about which methods and approaches to adopt."[30] This is a laudable aim. I have argued, however, that this aim needs a norm. There is indeed a rule or norm for theological interpretation, but it is *canonical*, not (at least, not primarily) catholic.

What constitutes a theological interpretation of celestial bodies, of the human body, and of the body of the text? A theological interpretation, if it is to be authoritative, not to mention true, must involve more than the church's say-so, more than a set of community conventions. It is God's say-so that enables the Church's say-so to be properly theological. To give a theological interpretation of celestial, human, and textual bodies, therefore, is a matter of articulating the Creator's intention, an intention realized preeminently in the life and fate of Jesus Christ as attested in the Old and New Testaments.

It is important not to overdraw the distinction between the catholic and canonical rules. Greene-McCreight's suggestion that the community's Rule of Faith is in fact a canonical rule is particularly helpful in this regard. The Rule of Faith—that prior understanding as to what the biblical texts are fundamentally about—is taken from Scripture itself: "Since these rules are drawn from Scripture itself, they are not considered extratextual interpretative devices."[31] This particular account of ruled reading is most congenial to my own approach, insofar as it acknowledges that the community's rule is in fact regulated by the two testament canon itself, especially inasmuch as it entails the assumption of the divine authorship of Scripture. There are even indications that her version of ruled reading is compatible with a *sola scriptura* approach: "Ruled reading thus allows scripture to interpret itself."[32] All this is to the good, particularly insofar as it makes room both for interpretive aims and an interpretive norm in the theological interpretation of Scripture.

If the above re-reading of what is involved in ruled reading is correct, then we may say that the *catholic* Rule of Faith makes explicit what is already *implicit* in the canonical Scriptures. In this regard, we may note in passing that each of the rules of "traditional hermeneutics" often cited by proponents of ruled reading is already implied by Paul's use of the OT Scriptures. The rules for theological tradition, I submit, have their origin not in the "Great Tradition" but rather in the *apostolic* tradition embodied in the Scriptures.

BODY-PIERCING AND THE BODY OF JESUS: INTERPRETING JOHN 19:31-34

Earlier in this paper we examined the contemporary phenomenon of body-piercing as a metaphor of sorts for the eclipse of the natural sense in contemporary biblical interpretation. Body-piercing, we claimed, is a means to the end of identity construction. We now turn to an ancient example of body-piercing and seek to interpret it in such a way that we do not victimize the body of the text of the Fourth Gospel. Our goal is to pierce the biblical text, not in the sense of inflicting a wound by violently imposing our interpretive will, but in the sense of discerning its true intent in order to penetrate its "joints and marrow."

"But one of the soldiers pierced his side with a spear, and at once there came out blood and water" (John 19:34). The account of the piercing of Jesus' side is an appropriate case study for several reasons: 1) it occurs at a climactic place in the most theological of gospels, and it is the only part of the passion narrative that has no parallel in the Synoptics; 2) it involves the relation of both testaments; 3) it raises questions about the extent, and the complexity, of the author's intention, about how determinate it is, and about how definite we can be about its determinacy; 4) it touches on a number of theological doctrines, including incarnation, soteriology, ecclesiology, pneumatology, and divine providence; 5) historically, it has generated a rich tradition of theological interpretation; 6) it touches on the postmodern concern for the textuality of the body and the bodiliness of the text.

Of the many aspects of the text that could be examined, I wish to focus on just one: how to interpret the natural sense of the result of Jesus' body-piercing, namely, the flow of blood and water. Just what is the author of the Fourth Gospel saying/doing at this point? Is the evangelist describing something that actually happened? If so, does he think it is a natural event or a miracle? If it is a natural event, why is it important to mention? Most importantly, what does the task of theological interpretation mean when it comes to making (natural!) sense of the blood and water?

History of interpretation: the catholic rule

A number of church fathers understood the blood and water to refer to the "two baptisms": of water (cleansing) and of blood (martyrdom). More commonly, patristic commentators saw the double flow as referring to the two chief sacraments of the church: baptism and Eucharist. It is this latter reading that will interest us most, for it raises the issue of whose interest assumes priority in theological interpretation of Scripture: the author's or the interpretive community's. Clearly, there is nothing *contrary* to the Rule of Faith in interpreting the blood and water as an anticipation of the sacraments that nourish and give life to the church. On the contrary, such a reading admirably serves the goal of community formation (e.g., social identity construction). The issue, however, is whether this "socialized" reading may legitimately claim the authority of Scripture. Is the text speaking of baptism and Eucharist or is the interpretive aim of the community (interest in ecclesial edification) here trumping the interpretive norm (the natural sense)? Just what is the Word of God for the church in John 19:31-37?

Augustine. Augustine's interpretation is based on a Latin mistranslation of the Greek. Augustine read 19:34 as "One of the soldiers with a spear *opened* his side." To compound matters, Augustine chose to focus on the significance of this errant term, commenting that the evangelist used a "wide awake" or suggestive word. Augustine even makes a special point of saying that the evangelist did *not* say "pierced" or "wounded"! No, the evangelist said "opened" in order to speak of the door of life that was flung open and from which the sacraments of the church flow. Augustine saw a foretelling of this in the Noah narrative, for Noah was ordered to make a door *in the side of the ark* where those animals that were not going to perish in the flood could enter. (These animals, we may note, prefigured the church).

The idea of an opening in the side suggests another episode from Genesis to Augustine as well. Eve, the mother of the living, also came forth from an opening in Adam's side. The crucified Christ is indeed a second Adam who "slept on the cross in order that from there might be found for him a wife—that one who flowed from the side of the One sleeping."[33] Other church fathers work the analogy even more. Since sin came from man's side, it was necessary that from the side should flow the source of salvation—a side for a side.

This popular interpretation received official church approval at the Council of Vienne in 1312. More recently, feminist writers have depicted the wound in Christ's side as a lactating breast or as a womb from which the Church is birthed. However, apart from the obvious lexical difficulty (e.g., the confusion between the terms for "pierced" and "opened"), this reading faces the additional problem of having little or no evidence that a reference to the Genesis account was indeed part of the evangelist's intentional action in this passage.

J. Ramsey Michaels contributes an interesting variation on this theme of "opening." He thinks that Mark and the Fourth Gospel give different versions of this same event. Mark's centurion and John's spear-thruster are, he argues, one and the same person. He then reasons that, since Jesus' body is the Temple (John 2:21), the rending of the temple curtain recounted in Mark is the counterpart to the "opening" in Jesus' side.[34] While such a reading does not run counter to the Rule of Faith, there is a real question as to whether it counts as an *interpretation* of the text. Raymond Brown's verdict is perhaps apt: "Such relationships [i.e., between the Temple curtain and the wound in Jesus' side] are highly speculative, and more likely the product of the interpreter's ingenuity than of the evangelist's plan."[35]

Luther. Despite its popularity among the "papists," Luther endorses Augustine's interpretation that the sacraments flow from the pierced body of Christ. "For the sacraments have their efficacy from the wounds and the blood of Christ."[36] At the same time, Luther says this interpretation is not sufficiently accurate, for it fails to affirm the connection of Jesus' blood to the gospel. So, in a kind of hermeneutical variation of the *communicatio idiomatum*, Luther says we "are washed daily through the Word."[37] Moreover, in a 1540 sermon on baptism, Luther claims that it is God—Father, Son, and Spirit—who does the bathing. This is what distinguishes baptism from other types of bathing or cleansing. And this, Luther reasons, is why John 19:34 speaks of water being mingled with the blood of Christ. Holy baptism is purchased for us precisely through Jesus' shed blood. Whenever a person receives baptism in faith, then, it is "the same as if he were visibly washed and cleaned of sin with the blood of Christ."[38]

Calvin. Calvin considers the idea that the flow of blood and water was miraculous but in the end rejects it. It is natural, he says, for congealed blood to lose its red color and become like water. No, the evangelist's intention lies elsewhere. In Calvin's view, the evangelist adapts his narrative to certain scriptural testimonies which he adds in order to make the point that Christ brought with him true atonement and true washing. The OT law prefigured this in its two sets of symbols: sacrifices and ablutions. In John 19:34 the evangelist sets before us a visible symbol of the fact that the law has been fulfilled. Now the sacraments, in their own way, do this too. So, though Calvin denies that 19:34 refers to a miracle, he too does not object to Augustine's view that the sacraments have flowed from Christ's side.

Brown and Bultmann.

Modern scholars disagree over the question of "sacramentalism" in the Fourth Gospel. On the one hand, the evangelist omits an account of the eucharistic action of Jesus at the Last Supper. On the other hand, some see symbolic references to baptism in passages that mention water and to the Eucharist in passages that mention bread (e.g., John 6). Raymond Brown nevertheless questions the hermeneutic principle that "since a passage can be understood sacramentally, it was intended sacramentally."[39] Rudolf Bultmann's commentary on this passage represents an additional twist. While he thinks the phrase "and at once there came out blood and water" is an obvious reference to the sacraments, he attributes the phrase in question to the work of an ecclesiastical redactor, not to the evangelist. In effect, Bultmann is arguing that the community's interest in spiritual formation was already making itself felt in the very redaction of the Fourth Gospel.

Thin description: the critical rule and the "physical" natural

Reading according to the catholic rule thus appears to stretch the natural sense of John 19:34 to the breaking point. Conversely, reading with modern biblical scholars according to the critical rule ("what actually happened?") tends to evacuate the text of theological significance. Such is the result when one understands the natural sense to refer to the text's ostensive, empirical reference only. There is a parallel here with approaches that describe human action in terms of bodily movements only, instead of in terms of intentional action. In both cases, the result is a reduced, if not reductionistic, or "thin" description.

By "thin" description I mean one that offers a minimal interpretation only, one that confines itself, say, to lexical issues or to issues of historical reference. What gets lost is precisely the dimension of the author's communicative action—what one is doing in using just these words in just this way. The problem with thin interpretation is that it fails to penetrate (to pierce!) the text deeply enough to reach the theological dimension. John 19:34 has prompted more than one medical doctor to try his hand at biblical interpretation, but most of these readings get no farther than blood-thinning.

Brown reminds us that "It is common knowledge that dead bodies do not bleed since the heart is no longer pumping blood through the sytem."[40] However, most physicians acknowledge that wounds inflicted very shortly after death may yield some bleeding, especially if the corpse lay in a vertical position, as was Jesus' case on the cross. What is harder to account for is the flow of water from a corpse, as well as the distinct flow of blood and water. Some maintain that the evangelist is speaking according to the medical conventions of his day. The Mishnah, for instance, asserts that "Man is evenly balanced, half of him is water, and the other half is blood." Similarly, the great Greek physician Galen believed that the right proportion of blood and water in human persons guaranteed good health. On this view, then, the evangelist would be affirming Jesus' genuine humanity. Jesus had a real physical body and underwent a real physical death—not an incidental point in a context rife with Docetic heretics who denied the reality of the incarnation. This thin or physical account, then, does yield some theological fruit. The same cannot be said for most of the others.

The title of W. Stroud's 1871 work promises much: *Treatise on the Physical Cause of the Death of Christ and Its Relation to the Principles and Practice of Christianity*.[41] He argued that Jesus' heart ruptured violently, that Jesus literally died of a "broken heart"! Blood from the ruptured heart flowed into the pericardial sac, and after clotting, it separated from the serum. The piercing by the lance opened the pericardial sac, releasing both substances. An interesting explanatory hypothesis, except that medical science today rejects the possibility of spontaneous cardiac ruptures.

Pierre Barbet in his *A Doctor At Calvary: the Passion of our Lord Jesus Christ as Described by a Surgeon* puts forward a slightly different hypothesis.[42] The watery fluid flowed from the pericardial sac, while the blood flowed from the heart itself (rather than from the pericardial sac). This interpretation received the approval of an article that appeared in the *Journal of the American Medical Association* in 1986 that was authored by consultants from the Mayo Clinic together with a pastor.[43]

A. F. Sava argues that it was the brutal scourging of Jesus hours earlier that probably produced a hemorrhage in the pleural cavity between the ribs and the lungs. This fluid could have separated into a light serous fluid and a dark red fluid. Since the pleural cavity is just inside the rib cage, even a shallow piercing could have released the two parts of blood.[44]

What is fascinating about these varied descriptions is the fact of their disagreements. Even at the most basic level of a purely physical description, we find a conflict of interpretations! The other thing to be said, of course, is that these descriptions are not really *interpretations* at all; they do not really help us to understand the evangelist's communicative intent and action.

Thick description: the canonical rule and the theological natural

The catholic rule orients us as to an important aim of theological interpretation: the building up of the church. Yet it is the natural sense that regulates this aim by providing the norm for acceptable interpretations: a *canonical* rule. Theological interpretations of Scripture that view the Bible as divine discourse will assign priority to the communicative aims of the Scriptures over the interpretive aims of the community of readers. We now turn to a "thick description" of John 19:34 that aims to describe what the author is doing in this text (e.g., the intentional action).

The evangelist is describing something that happened in which he saw considerable theological significance. Whether it was a natural or a miraculous event is a matter of secondary importance. Theological interpreters should ask not, "What actually happened?" but rather "What is the author saying/doing with these words?" I suggest that the evangelist is narrating the history of Jesus in a broader canonical and theological framework. (That the evangelist is composing history rather than fiction follows from the appeal to eyewitness testimony in 19:35). The evangelist's text is a "thick description" of the event of Jesus Christ, and our interpretations must, similarly, be thick descriptions of the evangelist's communicative act.

There are four ways of describing what the author of the Fourth Gospel is doing in this passage. Some of these only come to light when read in the canonical context of the story of Israel and the whole narrative of the Fourth Gospel. As we have seen, it is possible to offer more than one correct description of an action (e.g., moving one's index finger, pulling a trigger, etc.). Everything depends on the context in which the action, or in this case, the communicative action, is described. I list below what I think the evangelist is doing in this passage, beginning with the least obvious and proceeding to what, in context, is arguably the best "natural" sense of the text.[45]

First, *the evangelist is showing indirectly how Jesus' death gives rise to the sacraments that nourish the church.* We have already examined this interpretation. The chief difficulty with it lies in the paucity of internal textual evidence. Not only is the account of the Lord's Supper missing in the Fourth Gospel, but in those places where the evangelist might well have anticipated the sacraments, the focus is on bread rather than blood (e.g., John 6). "Blood" is never by itself used in the NT as a designation for the Lord's Supper, except in conjunction with the idea of drinking (see John 6:55).[46] There is also a minor problem in associating water from the *side* of Jesus with water baptism.

Second, *the evangelist asserts the reality of Jesus' death, and hence his genuine humanity.* According to Beasley-Murray, the evangelist "almost certainly" wanted his readers to recognize the reality of Jesus' death, and hence the reality of his humanity as a man of flesh and blood.[47] Irenaeus proposed a similar anti-doectic interpretation in his *Against Heresies*: "[if he had not been truly man] when his side was pierced, would there have come forth blood and water?"[48] Brown, however, is less certain than Beasley-Murray about the evangelist's communicative intent because first-century Docetism is not well documented. Nor does Brown believe that the intent to assert the reality of Jesus' death explains the flow of water.

Third, *the evangelist views the significance of Jesus' death as a "new Passover" and a "new Exodus."*ˇ"With this description of the evangelist's communicative action we adopt a wide-angle lens, one that encompasses OT testimony. For the stage on which the scene of Jesus' body-piercing takes place is set for Passover. It is the Day of Preparation, the day before the Sabbath and, according to v. 13, also the day before the Passover; hence a "great day" (John 7:37). Indeed, the whole scene is heavy laden with OT imagery. John 19:28 reports Jesus' saying "I thirst" to fulfill Scripture, and 19:37 notes that Scripture anticipated the piercing of Jesus' side. The episode therefore takes place in a framework of scriptural fulfillment. The evangelist describes what happens to the body of Jesus from the perspective of the broader canonical context. In order to be competent interpreters, we must do no less.

Unless one is canonically tone-deaf, it is virtually impossible not to hear a number of echoes from the Passover ritual in this passage. The evangelist has already told us that Jesus is the lamb of God (1:29). He also tells us that Jesus was handed over to Pilate at noon (19:14), the time at which the Passover lambs were slain in the temple. There are further, less explicit clues as well that provide corroborative evidence of the evangelist's intent. In the story of Israel's flight from Egypt, for example, hyssop was used to smear blood from the lamb on the doorposts of the Hebrew slaves (Exod 12:22). In the Fourth Gospel, a sponge full of vinegar is placed on hyssop and held to Jesus' mouth (John 19:29). Some might dismiss this as an incidental coincidence, but biblically literate readers will find it hard not to hear a faint echo.

The narrator explicitly tells us that these things took place so that Scripture might be fulfilled, "Not a bone of him shall be broken"; and "They shall look on him whom they have pierced"(19:36, 37). Which Scripture did the evangelist have in mind in v. 36? Two possibilities strengthen the allusion to the Passover/Exodus motif. Exodus 12:46 says that not a bone of the Passover lamb to be eaten is to be broken (as does Num 9:12). The evangelist's purpose is to strengthen the reader's faith that Jesus in his death fulfills the significance of the Passover as well as the eschatological hope for a second exodus.

Fourth, *the evangelist believes that Jesus' death" or "exodus" is the condition, now fulfilled, for a new coming of the Spirit, the giver of eternal life.* We have seen that the real interpretive difficulty lies in explaining the conjunction of the blood and water. Jesus calls his blood "true drink" in 6:55. Those who believe in him, he says, shall never thirst (6:35). Jesus says something similar in John 4: those who drink his "living water" shall never thirst, for Jesus' water "will become a spring of water welling up to eternal life" (4:14). But we find what is perhaps the most important textual clue to the evangelist's communicative intent in 7:38-39, where Jesus quotes the following passage of Scripture: "Out of his heart shall flow rivers of living water." Some interpreters also hear echoes of Num 20:11, where water flows from the rock struck (not pierced, however) by Moses.

The evangelist interrupts his own narrative flow at this point to make sure the reader is following the speech action: "Now this he said about the Spirit, which those who believe in him were to receive; for as yet the Spirit had not been given, because Jesus was not yet glorified" (7:39). Jesus is here promising that following his glorification, living water (the Spirit) would be available to those who believe in his glorification (i.e., his bloody death on behalf of sinners).

Now the evangelist has already associated Jesus' body with the temple in Jerusalem (2:19-21), and he assumes that his readers will be familiar with the passage that speaks of the flow of living water from Jerusalem and the temple at the triumphant day of the Lord (Ezek 47:1-9). We know, moreover, that for the Fourth Evangelist, Jesus is glorified in his being "lifted up" on the cross. By calling our attention to the flow of blood and water, then, the evangelist demonstrates that the promised new life—and more specifically, the gift of the Holy Spirit—has now arrived and is available. Passover, we might say, passes over into pneumatology.

What the evangelist is doing in speaking of the flow of blood and water, then, is assuring his readers that the new life of the Holy Spirit flows from the slain body of Jesus.[49]

THE NATURE OF THEOLOGICAL INTERPRETATION AND THE THEOLOGICAL INTERPRETATION OF THE NATURAL SENSE

Let us return to our two types of theological interpretation and to my suggestion that each needs the other. The aim of upbuilding the Christian community, while laudable, risks ascribing priority to the interpretive aims of the community rather than to the communicative aims of Scripture itself. To "socialize" the text so that it fits in with the community's practices may overcome one's sense of estrangement, but it also quenches the text's transformative potential. At worst, it plays into the hands of those postmoderns for whom authority is ultimately rooted in interpretive communities. Body-piercing, in the pejorative sense, would thus refer to a community's use of Scripture merely to reinforce a social identity (and agenda?) that it may have obtained from elsewhere. As I have argued, the use that must be considered normative is the authors' (and divine author's), not the readers'. The interpretive ends do not justify the means if this entails overturning or neglecting the natural sense. In sum, the interpretive aims and interests of the community should not eclipse the communicative aims and interests of God.

Theological exegesis is best construed as a "thick description" of the natural—that is, the literal, literary, authorially-intended—sense. The Rule of Faith works best when viewed as the explicit formulation of a grammar that is implicit in (and intrinsic to) Scripture. The canon is only allowed to be itself—respected as a stranger, as an other—if one follows the hermeneutical rule to read for its natural (i.e., authorially intended) sense. As we have seen from our brief hermeneutical exercise on John 19, reading for the author's natural sense need not result in thin, non-theological description. On the contrary, we saw that there were several aspects to the author's intentional action that made for a rich reading, high in theologically saturated fact.

Theological interpretation is neither merely reading with a particular community interest nor is it *merely* a matter of individuals describing, but not appropriating, authorial discourse. Each approach needs the other. To have interpretive aims without norms exposes readers to the danger of inaccurate exegesis; to have interpretive norms without aims exposes them to the danger of incomplete application. To this point, I have argued that it is not enough to have the right aims in interpretation; one must have the right norms as well in order to do justice to the integrity, the otherness, and perhaps the "wholly otherness," of the Christian Scriptures. Yet neither is it enough simply to posit the authority of the natural sense. Merely having the "right" theory of meaning is no guarantee that one will interpret rightly. Interpreters must develop interpretive virtues in order to strive for the aim of edifying reading under the norm of submitting to the intended sense.

What finally keeps the aim and the norm together, I believe, is a vision of the task of theological interpretation of Scripture in terms of giving *true witness*. Let us return to our passage once more, not to solve the problem of the meaning of the blood and water but rather to reflect on the lessons it holds for the project of theological interpretation as such.[50]

The nature of theological interpretation: reading for communicative action (19:34)

Since I have already treated the nature of theological interpretation at some length, I can here be brief. Theological interpretation of Scripture is, in large part but not wholly, a matter of describing what the biblical authors have done in using words this textual way rather than that. Fully to account for the author's communicative intent involves describing the action, as it were, against an appropriately large background so that it can be seen for what it is. The evangelist's statement in 19:34 is part of a complex testimony whose ultimate aim is to identify Jesus as the promised Christ and hence to elicit belief.

The necessity of theological interpretation: reading for true witness (19:35)

Why is it necessary to read the Bible for its communicative action, and for whom is such reading necessary? The answer to both questions, I believe, is implicit in v. 35: "He who saw it has borne witness—his testimony is true, and he knows that he tells the truth—that you also may believe." The evangelist is a paradigmatic theological interpreter of Scripture, and the passage we have been examining is not simply an illustration of an interpretive approach, but an implicit demand to embody it.

According to B. F. Westcott, v. 35 is not simply saying that the witness has given an accurate (e.g., factually true) testimony, but rather that his witness is *alethine*, "true to the idea of what a witness should be."[51] The author is not only correct, but *competent*. He has seen all that there is to be seen—the whole truth. In my terms, he is a competent and true witness because he gives a sufficiently thick description of the event. Verse 35 asks readers to believe not only what the witness reports, but also to accept its theological implications (e.g., its depth description). The prime interpretive imperative finally amounts to a familiar command: "Do not bear false witness" (Exod 20:16).[52]

If interpreters are likewise to be competent witnesses to the subject matter of the text, our testimony, like that of the narrator, must be sufficiently thick so as to discern the theological significance both of the events reported and of the report (e.g., the communicative act). After all, testimony is important because of its aim: "that you may believe." The best theological interpreter of Scripture, then, is the competent witness to what the author has said/done.

Could it be that the aim of the interpretive community ultimately coincides with that of the biblical text? Yes! For it is part and parcel of our Christian identity to be faithful witnesses. The necessity of theological interpretation is tied up with questions of Christian identity after all, and with what it means to be the church. The theological interpreter is the one who testifies truthfully to "what we have seen and heard" (1 John 1:1-3). Reading before God thus requires interpreters to be faithful—that is, true—witnesses. Here, again, we see how the "reading for communion" type of theological interpretation for Scripture is incomplete without the "reading for communication" type (and vice versa).

Jesus "effaces himself" in order to give faithful witness to the Father. Such self-effacement is similarly the vocation of the biblical interpreter. "The body of Christ keeps absenting itself from the text. Where does it go to? What the body is replaced by is the witness of the Church."[53] Our faithful witness—a "martyrdom" proper to the biblical interpreter—can itself become a source of life for those who receive it. With this thought we have arrived at the highest task of the theological interpretation of Scripture: to *interpret* "so that they may believe and have life."

The normativity of theological interpretation: reading for God's canonical action (19:36)

"For these things took place that the Scripture might be fulfilled. . . ." The competent witness to what the evangelist is doing in 19:31-37 would be remiss not to take account of the significance of the appeal to fulfilled Scripture. For what the evangelist is doing in this text is ultimately unintelligible apart from a consideration of his entire Gospel, not to mention the Scriptures of the OT as well. From Jesus' "I thirst" in 19:28 to "They shall look on him whom they have pierced" in 19:37, the evangelist has woven a thoroughly biblical framework within which to describe the piercing of Jesus' side. The divine action in word and deed only fully comes into view when seen against this broader canonical background. I believe that the concept of *canonical* action—i.e., communicative action described in canonical context—ultimately calls for an acknowledgement of divine authorship.

At this point we must pause to consider an objection. Does not the concept of divine communicative action complicate my claim that normativity in interpretation attaches to the natural sense? In particular, what about the natural sense of the OT texts cited in our passage (e.g., Ps 69:18; Exod 12:46; Zech 12:10)? Does the evangelist's use not distort their natural sense? No, but it does recontextualize it. With regard to OT prophecy, we would do well to amend Michael Polanyi's account of tacit knowledge. It is not so much that the prophets "know more than they can tell," but rather that they *tell more than they can know*. The prophets' testimony, when appropriated by the evangelist, is disambiguated. To place these OT testimonies in the larger canonical context of the story of Jesus Christ functions not to falsify their original meaning but to specify their true referents: the body of Jesus (the Messiah); the body of Christ (the Church).

Raymond Brown's distinction between literal meaning (what it meant to the [human] author), canonical meaning (what it meant to those who accepted the text as Scripture), and what it means today (to those in the church who continue to accept it as Scripture) provides a helpful template from which to distinguish the present proposal.[54] I agree with Brown about literal meaning. However, though it is legitimate to ask what it meant to those who first accepted it as Scripture, I prefer to reserve the term canonical meaning to refer to the divine intention in the text. The church has historically acknowledged the canon as divine communicative action: the Word of God. As we have seen, the theological natural refers to nature—whether celestial, human, or textual bodies—as God intends it. With regard to the biblical texts, therefore, the theological natural refers to the divine intention enacted in and by the canonical Scriptures. In short, the theological-natural sense thus refers to the way the words and texts go in their divinely appointed canonical context.

Describing the body of the text requires an expanded canonical context—thick description—as does the narrator's description of the body of Jesus. We only pierce beyond the physical to the theological (i.e., beyond the human author's intent to that of the divine author) if we describe what is done and what is said against the broader canonical context. Our role as theological interpreters is to examine the body of the text with piercing discernment. Theological interpretation of Scripture is nothing less than a kind of body-piercing, though one that does not absolve but acknowledges the theological-natural (e.g., divinely intended) sense: what *God* is saying/doing in this text. Theological interpretation of Scripture is finally less a matter of constructing our identity on the basis of the text than it is of receiving our identity as constituted by the text.

The fact that the events surrounding the piercing of Jesus' side fulfill not one but two Scriptures is itself a claim about the divine authorship of the course of *events*. In citing Scripture as he has, the narrator puts the passion events in the broader context of divine providence. God has authored both the discourse and the course of events. It should come as no surprise that theological interpretation is tied up with properly theological questions. As Christopher Seitz has recently observed, "The crisis in hermeneutics is in reality a crisis involving God's providence, a proper ecclesiology and doctrine of the Holy Spirit."[55] Providence is what has perhaps been in view throughout this essay, inasmuch as Scripture, viewed as divine communicative action, is but "providence put into writing."[56]

CONCLUSION

Body-piercing the body of Christ: how to read Scripture for a blessing

"For the word of God is living and active, sharper than any two-edged sword, piercing to the division of soul and spirit" (Heb 4:12)

The Bible is a complex, multifaceted, but ultimately unified witness to what God was doing in Jesus Christ. Yet it is not enough to equate theological interpretation with "reading for the witness," for this witness is mediated by a variety of literary forms. The contributing act of narrative, for example, is to display a world. However, it is not enough to equate theological interpretation with entering the world of the text either. Fully to describe texts as narrative witnesses or as witnessing narratives finally requires the concept of the author as communicative agent and of the text as communicative action, with their own intrinsic aims and intentions. One of these aims is to elicit the response of the reader. Theological interpretation of Scripture, therefore, involves not only describing but responding to and participating in the various forms of communicative intentions enacted in the text. For instance, it is not enough to describe a narrative world from the outside; no, in order to understand one must indwell the world of the text.

Stephen Fowl and L. Gregory Jones have brought to light the importance of the moral and interpretive virtues for the project of theological interpretation of

Scripture.[57] Scholarly exegetical skills alone are insufficient; no amount of grammatical knowledge alone can lead to holiness. It is not enough, for instance, to have the "right" theory about theological interpretation. Knowing the meaning of meaning is no guarantee for correct reading. This is why interpreting Scripture in the believing community matters. Clearly, one must approach Scripture as saint *and* scholar or one's scholarship will bear no sanctifying fruit. For it is in the church that we come to Scripture expecting to be taught, encouraged, commanded, blessed. Hence the church is the proper locus for theological interpretation of Scripture. The people of God are called together by God to embody God's Word in worship, witness, and wisdom for the sake of the world.

At the same time, however, it is not enough simply to produce edifying readings of the text. For it is one thing to use a text, even for the purposes of edification, and another to interpret it. The task of theological interpretation involves both aims and norms. At present, we are probably closer to an agreement concerning the former than the latter. What remains to be done is to secure consensus about the norm of theological interpretation, namely, the communicative intent of the human and divine authors enacted in the text at the literary and the canonical levels. Nevertheless, the prospects for a truly theological interpretation, guided by a theological hermeneutic, have never been better since the inception of *Ex Auditu*.

How, then, can the church read Scripture in order to obtain a blessing? By reading in communion (i.e., in agreement about the aims and norms of interpretation) in order to discover the divine communication therein and to be its faithful witnesses. To bear true witness to the text is both an aim and a norm. The best interpreters, to the extent that they become witnesses, participate in the event of meaning and thus become part of the action. The author of the Fourth Gospel thus becomes a paradigm for the contemporary biblical interpreter. We too are to testify to "what we have seen and heard" in Scripture. We too are to be true and competent witnesses, able to hear the music, the echoes, of previous Scripture, able to understand the event of Jesus Christ in the context of the larger story of salvation of which it is the climax and interpretive key.

The specific vocation of the interpreter of Scripture is to be a true witness: one who not only can describe, but embody, God's communicative intent. The theological interpreter describes what God, the divine author, is doing in and through the works of the human authors. The specific task of theological interpretation, then, is to read the Bible so that one encounters the Word of God. Ultimately, however, theological interpretation of Scripture is a matter not only of reading, but of being read by the text. To be a true witness involves not only describing what God is saying/doing in Scripture but embodying this message.

If the church is to be transformed by Scripture—if the body of Christ is to be "pierced" by the Word-wielding Spirit—then we must read so as to open ourselves to its communicative and transformative intent. Theological interpreters of Scripture will not only read in communion with one another, but will seek deeper communion with God by laying themselves open to the effects of God's word-acts. Reading in communion with one another is the proper corporate response to God's communication, but it does not constitute that act. On the contrary, the church, as an obedient and competent interpretive community, strives to be a faithful witness to what God has done, is doing, and will do in, with, and through Scripture. Theological interpretation of Scripture is reading for ecclesial communion (the aim) *and* for divine communication (the norm), all for the ultimate purpose of deepening our communion with the triune God.

NOTES

1. Meaning is "determinate" (i.e., it has particularity and specificity) just because of the specificity of the wording and the situation in which the words were used. It does not follow, however, that readers can "determine" with exactitude just what the author said/did. The world's weight is "determinate," but it does not follow that scientists can determine ("find out") exactly what it is. Texts may have "single determinate meanings," but they may have rough edges or, like prisms, many faces.

2. The reader may be curious as to why I prefer the terminology of "natural" as opposed to "plain" or "literal" sense. On the one hand, treatments of the literal sense (including my own) only partly succeed in distinguishing a literal from a literalistic sense. "Plain" has two disadvantages. First, it suggests that the sense of biblical texts may be obvious and non-figurative; second, it is now associated with the Yale School's belief that it is determined more by habits of reading in the believing community than by the original authors.

3. In philosophical jargon, I am describing the demise of metaphysical realism, the notion that reality, and perhaps textual meaning, is independent of the way we speak and think about it.

4. Hauerwas, *Unleashing the Scriptures: Freeing the Bible From Captivity to America* (Nashville: Abingdon, 1993), 20.

5. A. K. M. Adam, *What is Postmodern Biblical Criticism?* (Minneapolis: Fortress, 1995), 48.

6. See Kathryn Greene-McCreight, *Ad Litteram: How Augustine, Calvin, and Barth Read the "Plain Sense" of Genesis 1-3* (New York: Peter Lang, 1999), 129.

7. I treat this latter confusion in more detail in my *Is There a Meaning in this Text? the Bible, the Reader, and the Morality of Literary Knowledge* (Grand Rapids: Zondervan, 1998), 310-312.

8. For a general study of body modification practices in the non-Western world, see Arnold Rubin, ed., *Marks of Civilization: Artistic Transformation of the Human Body* (University of California Museum, 1988).

9. Ken Hewitt, *Mutilating the Body: Identity in Blood and Ink* (Bowling Green, Ohio: Bowling Green State University, 1997).

10. Anthony Giddens, *Modernity and Self-Identity* (Palo Alto, Calif.: Stanford University Press, 1991), 225.

11. Chris Shilling, *The Body and Social Theory* (London: Sage, 1993).

12. Graham Ward, "The Displaced Body of Jesus Christ," in *Radical Orthodoxy* (ed. J. Milbank, G. Ward, and C. Pickstock; London: Routledge, 1999), 169.

13. Robert Morgan, *Biblical Interpretation* (Oxford: Oxford University Press, 1988), 7.

14. Mark C. Taylor, "Text as Victim," in *Deconstruction and Theology* (ed., Thomas Altizer; New York: Crossroad, 1982), 65.

15. Stephen Fowl and L. Gregory Jones, *Reading in Communion: Scripture and Ethics in Christian Life* (Grand Rapids: Eerdmans, 1991), 20.

16. See especially Craig Bartholomew, *Reading Ecclesiastes: Old Testament Exegesis and Hermeneutical Theory* (Rome: Pontifical Bible Institute, 1998) and the recent work of Francis Watson, *Text and Truth: Redefining Biblical Theology* (Grand Rapids: Eerdmans, 1997) and Anthony Thiselton, *New Horizons in Hermeneutics* (Grand Rapids: Zondervan, 1997).

17. Hans Frei once commented that if the community had acquired the habit of reading allegorically, then that would have been the "plain sense" (Frei, "The 'Literal Reading' of Biblical Narrative in the Christian Tradition: Does it Stretch or Will it Break?," in *The Bible and the Narrative Tradition* (ed. Frank McConnell; New York: Oxford University Press, 1986), 36-77. See also Kathryn E. Tanner, "Theology and the Plain Sense," in *Scriptural Authority and Narrative Interpretation* (ed. Garrett Green; Philadelphia: Fortress, 1987).

18. Greene-McCreight, *Ad Litteram*, 244.

19. I acknowledge that all exegesis presupposes some theology or other. The question is whether interpretation provides us with an opportunity to refine, or even correct, our prior theological understanding. I maintain that it does, though it does so only if the interpreter is indeed "virtuous": both scrupulous with regard to the text and suspicious with regard to oneself.

20. Robert W. Wall, "Reading the Bible from within Our Traditions: The 'Rule of Faith' in Theological Hermeneutics," in *Between Two Horizons: Spanning New Testament Studies and Systematic Theology* (ed. Joel B. Green and Max Turner; Grand Rapids: Eerdmans, 2000), 104.

21. Hall, "Reading the Bible from within Our Traditions," 96.

22. Ibid., 103.

23. Fowl and Jones haltingly accept this point. They do want to acknowledge Scripture as some kind of standard of Christian adequacy. We do not need to believe in divine dictation of Scripture, they argue, but we do need to have a view of providence. This view, sadly, is left unspecified. All Fowl and Jones say is that "the God who has called us to be the Church would not leave us bereft of the resources we need to follow that call faithfully" (*Reading in Communion*, 38). It is not finally clear just how God is, on their view, involved with Scripture.

24. Lindbeck, "Postcritical Canonical Interpretation," in *Theological Exegesis: Essays in Honor of Brevard S. Childs* (Grand Rapids: Eerdmans, 1999), 39.

25. Ibid., 44.

26. In his response to this paper David Cunningham mistakenly ascribes to me a belief in the "container" theory of meaning. I do not believe that words, or even texts, "contain" meaning. Rather, I think that they are meaningful because they are used by authors to say and do things. Attention to the way texts are used to perform communicative acts leads to the "action" theory of communication that I here assume. For a more complete account and defense of my theory of meaning as communicative action, see *Is There a Meaning in this Text?* ch. 5.

27. We may note in passing that Irenaeus' first problem with heretics had less to do with competing interpretive interests than with their replacing the "natural" sense for some "unnatural" (his term) substitute. Such twisting of words amounts to their being wrenched away from their original authors.

28. Paul Noble, for instance, comments that Brevard Childs' canonical approach is intelligible only against the background assumption of the divine authorship of Scripture (*The Canonical Approach: A Critical Reconstruction of the Hermeneutics of Brevard S. Childs*, Leiden: Brill, 1995).

29. Note that this account of "thick description" supersedes the older notion of *sensus plenior*.

30. Lewis Ayres and Stephen E. Fowl, "(Mis)reading the Face of God: The Interpretation of the Bible in the Church," *TS* 60 (1999), 528.

31. Greene-McCreight, "The Logic of the Interpretation of Scripture and the Church's Debate Over Sexual Ethics," in *Homosexuality, Science, and the "Plain Sense of Scripture"* (Grand Rapids: Eerdmans, 2000), 249.

32. Greene-McCreight, *Ad Litteram*, 248.

33. Augustine, *Tractates on the Gospel of John 112-24* (trans. John W. Rettig; Washington, D.C.: Catholic University of America Press), 51.

34. J. Ramsey Michaels, "The Centurion's Confession and the Spear Thrust," *CBQ* 29 (1967) 102-109.

35. Raymond E. Brown, *The Gospel According to John XII-XXI* (Garden City, NY: Doubleday, 1970), 945.

36. *Luther's Works*, vol. 8 (ed., J. Pelikan; St. Louis: Concordia, 1966), 258.

37. Ibid.

38. *Luther's Works*, vol. 51 (ed., John W. Doberstein; (Philadelphia: Muhlenberg, 1959), 325.

39. Raymond E. Brown, *The Gospel According to John I-XI* (Garden City, NY: Doubleday, 1970), cxii.

40. Brown, *The Gospel According to John XII-XXI*, 946.

41. London: Hamilton & Adams, first published in 1847.

42. Garden City, NY: Doubleday, 1953.

43. "In the Physical Death of Jesus Christ," cited by George R. Beasley-Murray, *John* (Dallas: Word, 1987), 356.

44. A. F. Sava, "The Wound in the Side of Christ," *CBQ* 19 (1957) 343-346.

45. In his response to this article Cunningham worries that a belief in determinate meaning, together with the norm of author's intended meaning, results in a "totalizing" approach to biblical interpretation where one reading is elevated above all others. Cunningham is right to worry about totalizing interpretations, but wrong to associate it with my position. To say that authors enacted certain communicative intentions rather than others is not to elevate one interpretation above others but to acknowledge that *all* our interpretations—especially mine!—are ultimately accountable and answerable to something "other" than ourselves and our communities.

46. So A. E. Brooke, *Commentary on The Johannine Epistles* (Edinburgh: T. & T. Clark, 1912), 132.

47. Beasley-Murray, 356. C. K. Barrett agrees, noting that this is the force of the appeal in v. 35 to eye-witness testimony. The Docetic heresy—which claimed that Jesus only *seemed* to be a man—is addressed even more explicitly in 1 John 5:6-8 where three witnesses to Jesus' incarnation are mentioned: the water, the blood, and the Spirit. (As we saw earlier, some ancient thinkers held that the human body consisted largely of blood and water).

48. *Adv. Haer.* 3.22.2.

49. For an extended treatment of this point, see Larry Paul Jones, *The Symbol of Water in the Gospel of John*, (Sheffield: Sheffield Academic Press, 1999), 211. Stephen Moore locates the water flowing from Jesus' side as the site of deconstruction, the place where the text's carefully rendered hierarchy between physical water and living water breaks apart (*Literary Criticism and the Gospels*, New Haven, Mass.: Yale University Press, 1989, 162). The flow of water is another symbolic token of the promised living water: "That leaves us with a symbol (the flow of water) of a metaphor (living water) for the Spirit" (162). It is impossible, says Moore, to keep the literal and the figural cleanly separated in this "spiritual material." Two levels of meaning "are collapsed that should have been kept apart" (163). This, I believe, is a somewhat perverse misreading of the natural sense of the text, in which the flow of water from Jesus' side has accrued theological significance, but still manages unambiguously to refer to the release of the Spirit of life.

50. My argument is similar to Lindbeck's in calling for cooperation rather than competition between various modes of theological interpretation. How do the three approaches to Scripture that Lindbeck discusses—Childs (canonical witness), Hays (narrative world), Wolterstorff (authorial discourse)—relate to my comparison between ruled reading and canonical action? Briefly, I agree with Lindbeck that an authorial discourse approach has the potential to accommodate and clarify the concerns of these other approaches, including ruled reading. *Reading for the natural sense of Scripture is a matter of describing the narrative witness of the text in terms of what the author is doing.*

51. B. F. Westcott, *The Gospel According to St. John* (Grand Rapids: Eerdmans, 1971), liv.

52. Who is my neighbor? Can a text be a neighbor? Why not? As I indicated in my opening illustration, the text represents a voice that is not our own—the voice of a stranger, the voice of an other. The ethical task of the interpreter is to welcome and respect this voice.

53. Graham Ward, "Displaced Body," 174.

54. R. E. Brown, " 'And the Lord Said'? Biblical Reflections on Scripture as the Word of God," *TS* 42 (1981) 3-19.

55. Christopher Seitz, in *Renewing Biblical Interpretation* (ed. Craig Bartholomew; Grand Rapids: Zondervan, 2000) 63.

56. This is my counterclaim to radical postmodernity's anti-hermeneutic, with its "death of God put into writing."

57. *Reading in Communion.* (See n. 15.)

(NON-)SPEAKING TEXTS AND THE COMPLEXITY OF MEANING

DAVID S. CUNNINGHAM

Kevin Vanhoozer's is not the first name that comes to mind when the topic is body piercing. Nevertheless, he has employed the metaphor in tremendously interesting ways, offering a conceptual account of the process of interpretation as well as a practical exposition of it. There is much in the paper with which I agree completely; but as a springboard to discussion, I will focus on a couple of major disagreements.

The paper focuses on *communication:* text as communicative act, and the communicative relationship between writer and reader. Hence, the theory of communication with which it operates becomes all-important. The theory that this paper employs is one for which I have very little enthusiasm—call it the "sender-receiver" model of human communication. Under this model the writer or speaker has an idea, that idea is placed into a vehicle (the "medium" of communication), and the vehicle is sent toward the reader or hearer, who takes out the idea and possesses it. Evidence that Professor Vanhoozer employs this model can be found throughout the paper. He speaks of "the divine message *in* Scripture," regards "textual meaning" as something that can be determined independently from "community interpretation" and which is lodged "in" the text, and God is described as "doing" something "in" Scripture. Indeed, the very language of "exegesis" supposes that there is something "in" the text that must be excavated by the expert.

This sender-receiver model of human communication, which Walter Ong calls the "medium" model, is of relatively recent origin. It is a modern phenomenon, encouraged first by the development of moveable type and the widespread distribution of texts, and then re-emphasized by broadcast transmission and the even wider distribution of speech over the airwaves. As a model for the transfer of marks on a page or waves through the air, the sender-receiver model is fine. But as a model for communication, says Ong, it is wholly inadequate.[1]

Specifically, this model fails to simulate the anticipated feedback that all human communication presupposes. In order to speak or write, I have to hypothesize a particular audience. No communicative act is addressed to "everyone" or to "no one in particular." Consequently, says Ong, "Human communication is never one-way. Always, it not only calls for response but is shaped in its very form and content by anticipated response."[2] Meaning cannot be inserted into a text if its author does not know who will be trying to derive that meaning from it.

Yet Professor Vanhoozer seems to imply that the biblical authors inserted into their texts meanings for "no one in particular"—such that even a twenty-first century resident whom ancient authors could not have imagined will be able to mine a text for its meaning. This model assumes that meanings are frozen and universally retrievable across space and time. It fails to account for the differing assumptions held by authors and by varying recipients about the associations and resonances of particular words and sentences. It clearly fails to simulate what takes place in face-to-face conversation where context, body language, and interpretive questioning can help to clarify intentions and expectations.

It is therefore unhelpful to describe a text as a "container" for meaning. It is genuinely misleading to describe the text as a living body, endowed with intention and will. A text is ultimately an *artifact* and is incapable of doing anything whatsoever without human action on its behalf. To claim that the text is alive or to make it the subject of active verbs—suggesting that it "speaks" to us and "instructs" us—is not only false; it also distracts from the motives, whether benign or malignant, of the human actors who use the text to speak and to instruct. Even if God is the author of the biblical text, the text itself is an object, not a person. To endow the text with personal characteristics such as divine agency and will is to confuse the biblical word—which is made, not begotten—with the Incarnate Word, who is begotten, not made.

Professor Vanhoozer rightly claims that biblical texts should be recognized as "strange," and read "over against ourselves." We ought not to "socialize" or "totalize" these texts so as to obliterate their otherness. But the most "totalizing" approach to biblical interpretation is that which attempts to elevate one interpretation above all others—thereby seeking, however subtly, to put an end to interpretation. Such an approach is conceivable only in a culture of writing, in which the written word is artificially endowed with a single, permanent meaning. Before the modern era, multiple interpretations happily existed side by side. Think of the *Catena Aurea* of Thomas Aquinas, which moves through the text, verse by verse, assembling the differing interpretations of the Fathers, without any apparent desire to harmonize them, nor even to polemicize against them. This does not mean that "anything goes"; it does not "deregulate" interpretation. But it does mean that the purpose of biblical interpretation is emphatically *not* to settle on a single "meaning" of each verse. Today, we argue and agonize over "the" right interpretation of a text in ways that too often result in the evacuation of the text's rich significance. In such monolithic, frequently wooden interpretations, one finds, as Anne of Green Gables says, "no scope for the imagination."

Indeed, I would argue that the appeal to an imagined or reconstructed "authorial intention" is one of the most "totalizing" moves that one can make upon a text. *This* is the move that obliterates a text's otherness—including its polyvalence, its greatest source of otherness in a scientific and instrumentalist culture. The text is reduced to a mere conduit for data.

No, to insist that texts can, all by themselves, "speak over against us" is to abdicate our own responsibility. This over-againstness will not occur and certainly will have no lasting effects, until we enact it, until we commit to doing it ourselves, against ourselves. Without such a commitment, the text will never be strange to us; we will always find scholarly justifications for domesticating it. Professor Vanhoozer accepts the need for virtuous interpretation, but he wonders how this can be done without a concept of "meaning" that dwells "in" the text.

Unfortunately, he does not elaborate on this concern. I would argue that, on the contrary, the very notion that "meaning" has been inserted "into" a text tends to prevent, or at least to obstruct, virtuous interpretation. It circumvents the need for interpreters of good character. If meaning already dwells within the text, anyone with the right training in excavation can make it reappear. The only virtues to be cultivated are scholarly ones, not saintly ones. One's knowledge of ancient Near Eastern language and culture must be impeccable, but whether one believes that Jesus is Lord is irrelevant. This marks a drastic departure from the Church's tradition of reading the Scriptures, and is due, in large measure, to the modern obsession with the notion of a single meaning embedded in the text.

This brings me, finally, to Professor Vanhoozer's interpretation of John 19, which I like very much. The comparison of Christ on the cross to the Passover lamb, which is then woven into the sending of the Spirit, is insightful and appropriately intertextual. Its fluid movement between Old and New Testaments is an inspiration to theologians and preachers alike. But what makes this interpretation a good one is *not* that Professor Vanhoozer is a good *scholar* as the guild might define one; in fact, many members of that guild might well chastise him for so hegemonically appropriating the Hebrew Bible. His interpretation succeeds, not because he is a scholar, but because he is a *saint*. Which is to say he is sufficiently initiated into the biblical text and its range of theological significance that he can move around within it almost effortlessly and discover echoes of Scripture where others have found only a physician's notebook. His mistake, in my view, is not in offering this interpretation, but in acceding to the temptation to elevate it above others—indeed, above those of other saints, such as Augustine, Luther, and Calvin. He is tempted to this wholly uncharacteristic act of theological hubris not by some belief on his part that he is a better scholar or saint than Augustine, or Luther, or Calvin. Rather, he has been snared by the modern lust for determining, not "a" meaning, but "the" meaning of a text.

I doubt that Augustine or Luther lost much sleep over the question of what meaning the evangelist had inserted into the text; indeed, they were rarely willing to rest content with a single meaning. Professor Vanhoozer's catalog of their interpretations implies that they each offered only one interpretation of this text. But in fact, in a Lenten sermon on the Gospel of John—unfortunately not one of those translated in the American edition of the *Luther's Works*—Luther has other things to say about the passage.[3] He says that the description of the piercing of Jesus' side is included by the evangelist in order to remind us that even apparently trivial details about Jesus are worthy of our attention.[4] He also has a great deal to say about the relationship between Jesus and the Passover lamb—something that is assessed positively in this paper but not attributed to Luther.[5] In a lecture on Exod 12 Calvin too draws an extensive analogy between the paschal lamb and the body of Christ on the cross.[6] My point here is not to wrangle about who said it first, but to emphasize that premodern Christian interpretation was happy to move among disparate readings.

Those readings can offer just as "thick" a description of the text as can the examples that Professor Vanhoozer offers. For example, what is humanity's most common and widespread experience of water and blood flowing simultaneously from the human body? It is, of course, the experience of childbirth. This particular "thick description" of the verse in question is not mentioned in the paper, but it has been important in Christian interpretation, and particularly in Christian art in which the Church is shown being "birthed" from a vaginal opening in Jesus' side.

In the end, I would want to argue that the text of Scripture is, in general, much less like a container for meanings and much more like the script of a play.[7] It has an author whom we admire and may even venerate. But we do not have immediate and intersubjective access to that author. We do have a text; and whether or not we imagine it to contain one or more "meanings," it will only come to life when we play it. While drama critics may argue about whether one or another interpretation is more "authentic" or more "in the spirit of the author," I frankly see very little point in such conjectures; their name is Legion and are ultimately unresolvable. What matters to me is whether a particular rendition of the play builds up its audience in those moral and intellectual virtues which have most profoundly marked the Christian life over time. Judgments about the norms of such interpretive endeavors will only arise within the community and will require a much more rigorous ecclesiology than Professor Vanhoozer is willing to offer here and more, perhaps, than he would be willing to offer at all. Be that as it may, the Christian significance of an interpretation will be due *only* in part to the text having been shaped in a certain way by its author. The rest will depend, not primarily upon our scholarly exegetical training, but upon our willingness and ability to *participate* in the inner trinitarian life of that divine author.

NOTES

1. Walter J. Ong, *Orality and Literacy: The Technologizing of the Word* (London: Methuen, 1982), 176.
2. Ibid., 176.
3. Martin Luther, "Die Zwolfft Predig" (Jn. 19:25-37), *W. A.*, 52, 809-819.
4. Ibid., 811.
5. Ibid., 812f.
6. "Primum Praeceptum. Ex Exodi XII," *Ioannis Calvini opera quae supersunt omnia* 42:292.
7. See Nicholas Lash's reflections on these matters in *Believing Three Ways In One God: A Reading of the Apostles' Creed* (Notre Dame, Ind.: University of Notre Dame Press, 1992), 11-12, and "Performing the Scriptures," in *Theology on the Way to Emmaus* (London: SCM Press, 1986), 37-46.

EX AKOĒS PISTEŌS

JAMES D. G. DUNN

"The task of interpreting Scripture theologically" begins from the recognition that Scripture is *theological*: the writings which make up Scripture are oriented around the conviction that God has created all things, that God has revealed and is enacting his saving purpose for humankind, and that his human creatures should live their lives accordingly. The very term *"Scripture"* makes the same point: we are talking not simply about "writings" (*graphai*), which is the primary sense of the term in Greek; we are talking about writings regarded as *sacred*, which is always how the term *graphe/graphai* is used in the NT. The implication which follows immediately is that such writings cannot be adequately appreciated and understood unless they are treated theologically. That in turn means that the interpreter must have a sensitivity to the character of the texts being interpreted as theological, as Scripture, a capacity to appreciate the fundamental theological convictions which have shaped the whole, and an empathy with the experiences of faith from which the texts emerged and which they express. Without the theological dimension to the task of interpretation, a historical or literary approach, no matter how insightful, will never get to the heart of the text as Scripture, to the heart of its theology. In short, there needs to be a theological dynamic, an energizing or motive force in the task of interpreting Scripture, a dynamic interaction between text and interpreter without which the task of interpretation lacks energy and lasting effect.

There are many aspects of the task of interpreting Scripture so defined. But what I want to emphasize in this paper is that the dynamic, the energizing or motive force at the heart of interpreting Scripture, is not merely necessary in the interaction between present-day text and present-day interpreter. The same dynamic was also active in the very formation of Scripture, is indeed integral to its character as Scripture. To appreciate this too is important for our understanding of the task of interpretation. Without appreciation of this dynamic, within Scripture as well as in the interpretation of Scripture, Scripture cannot function as Scripture; it will function only as "theology" in the negative sense in which the term is often used today—theology as concerned with obscure or rarified subjects or with pedantic minutiae—and not as gospel.

In trying to encapsulate what I have in mind in a single phrase I have entitled the essay "*Ex akoēs pisteōs*." The phrase comes from Gal 3:2 and 5: "Was it by works of the law that you received the Spirit or by hearing with faith [*ex akoēs pisteōs*]?" "He who supplies the Spirit to you and works miracles among you—is it by works of the law or by hearing with faith [*ex akoēs pisteōs*]?" It is true that *akoē* can mean either the act of hearing or that which is heard and that most commentators and translators take the phrase in the latter sense: "as the result of preaching which demanded (only) faith,"[1] "by believing the gospel message."[2] But the whole phrase is more obviously to be taken as describing the response of the Galatians, the hearing which expressed itself in the faith through which they received the Spirit. It is thus closer than is usually appreciated to the term *hupakoē pisteōs* in Rom 1:5: through Christ "we received grace and apostleship with a view to the obedience of faith [*eis hupakoēn pisteōs*] among all the nations."Both phrases evidently reflect the sense of the Hebrew *šāmaʿ*, "to give ear to, answer, heed," thus denoting "responsive hearing"; so, in Galatians, a hearing which is characterized by faith, and in Romans, an obedience which is faith.[3]

My concern here is to highlight the interaction of faith with or within the initial hearing of the Galatians so that without the Galatians' faith the preaching of Paul and the hearing of the Galatians would not have been effective. It is for this reason that I prefer to draw on the phrase of Gal 3:2 and 5, rather than on the close and more familiar parallel of Rom 10:17: "faith comes from hearing [*ex akoēs, ex auditu*]."[4] The phrase in Romans comes in a sequence: belief from hearing, hearing from preaching, preaching from being sent (Rom 10:14-15). It tends therefore to highlight the sequential character of the process—in this case, a hearing which results in faith. But the phrase in Galatians brings out more sharply that the only hearing which is effective is the hearing of faith; or, if you like, that hearing only becomes effective when it becomes responsive hearing, hearing with faith.[5]

It is this aspect of the very beginning of the process which resulted in Scripture that I wish to focus on in what follows, the intermingling of faith from the first as integral to the character of Scripture. To illustrate the point in more detail I draw on a section of my current research into the historical Jesus and the tension about history and faith. That will be the most extensive section since it involves arguing a minority case. But then I wish to extend the argument to the whole process of reception of Scripture and to argue that, given this more dynamic concept of the emergence of the scriptural writings, in an important sense the faithful theological interpretation of Scripture is necessary for its completion, we might even say its fulfillment as Scripture.

FAITH FROM THE FIRST

My concern is the role of faith in the emergence of the scriptural writings, with reference primarily to the traditions about Jesus. As is well enough known, the tension between history and faith was a marked feature of the original quest of the historical Jesus. Indeed, "tension" is too weak a word; in nineteenth century liberal theology the relation between faith and history was seen more as an antithesis. The quest of the historical Jesus began as essentially an attempt to get behind the Christ of faith to the Jesus of history. The undergirding assumption was that the Jesus of history had been hidden under layers of subsequent doctrine and needed to be recovered. The Christ of dogma was a distortion or even a corruption of the real Jesus. Back from the Christ of faith to the Jesus of history! As the liberal quest proceeded, the beginning of the corrupting process of dogma was pushed further and further back—not simply to the later creeds and dogmas, not simply to the theologians of the second century, not simply to John and Paul, but to the Synoptic Gospels themselves. It was finally concluded that none of the NT writings had escaped the distorting effects of faith. The NT, including even the Gospel of Mark, was like an archaeological tel. To find the Jesus of history it was necessary to dig down to bedrock. The Jesus of history had to be excavated from the layers of faith and mounds of dogma.

In the reaction against liberal theology which marked the first half of the twentieth century the antithesis between faith and history was reasserted, but in favor of faith. With Bultmann the moment of faith was linked to the preaching of the gospel here and now; history was irrelevant to faith, and the character of Scripture as faith documents was detached from their character as historical documents. And although the balance was rectified to some extent in the new quest of the historical Jesus begun in the 1950s, faith still was viewed as something which hindered the critical study of the Gospels and which had to be in some degree discounted in any historical quest.[6] In the last two decades of the twentieth century, however, the old form of the antithesis has reasserted itself strongly. On the one hand, the neo-liberal quests of Dominic Crossan and Robert Funk are once again trying to dig down through the layers of tradition to "the real Jesus"[7] to save the historical Jesus from the accretions of faith, from Christianity![8] And on the other hand, postmodernism has undermined the validity of the historical-critical quest and brought into radical questioning any attempt to privilege any particular faith-response to Jesus.[9] Both undermine the task of interpreting Scripture theologically, in this case the Gospels' witness to Jesus. So their challenge cannot be ignored.

In what follows I reproduce a section of my current writing in which I draw together the threads of my critique of the various quests of the historical Jesus, past and present, and attempt to sketch out a more realistic approach which takes what I regard as a more appropriate account of the faith dimension of the writings in question. I pose the question thus: When did a faith perspective first influence the Jesus tradition? Several aspects call for comment.

First, *what is the historical Jesus*? The Enlightenment ideal of historical objectivity projected a false goal onto the quest of the historical Jesus. For from its inception, questers have made the assumption that behind the text of the Gospels, behind the traditions which they incorporate, there is a "historical Jesus," an objective historical datum, who will be different from the dogmatic Christ, or from the Jesus of the Gospels, and who will enable us to criticize the dogmatic Christ and the Jesus of the Gospels.

An important factor in all this has been the confusion injected into the quest by the key phrase itself—"historical Jesus." It is true that whenever a definition is offered for the phrase, the person offering the definition is clear that the "historical Jesus" is *the Jesus constructed by historical research.*[10] Despite that, however, the phrase is used again and again in a casual way to refer to the Jesus of Nazareth who walked the hills of Galilee, and it is that sense which predominates overall. Or to be more precise, the phrase "the historical Jesus" as typically used is something of an amalgam of the two senses. The quest has generally assumed its capacity to construct (from the available data) a Jesus who will be the real Jesus: the historical Jesus (reconstructed) will be the historical Jesus (actual);

again and again the one sense elides indistinguishably into the other.[11] It is this confusion which largely lies behind the surprising confidence of the late nineteenth and late twentieth century questers that a Jesus reconstructed from the sources available would be a sound base (the actual Jesus) for a critique of the Jesus of these sources.[12] It needs to be said once again, then, that the "historical Jesus" is properly speaking a nineteenth/twentieth century construction using the data provided by the Synoptic tradition, not Jesus back then, and not a figure in history whom we can realistically use to critique the portrayal of Jesus in the Synoptic tradition.

Second, *Kähler's point*. It is here that the key observation made by Martin Kähler in his famously entitled *Der sogennante historische Jesus und der geschichtliche biblische Christus* (1896)[13] needs to be reasserted. For Kähler the idea that the Jesus reconstructed from the Gospel traditions (the so-called "historical Jesus," significantly different from the Jesus of the Gospels) is actually the Jesus who taught in Galilee (the historical Jesus!) is nothing more than an illusion. The idea that we can see through the faith perspective of the NT writings to a Jesus who did not inspire faith or who inspired faith in a different way is a figment of the imagination. There is no such Jesus. It is true that we do have some echoes of an outsider's perspective in Josephus, Roman, and rabbinic sources.[14] But we simply do not have portrayals of Jesus as seen through the eyes of the high priests or the Roman authorities or the *'ammê hā-'ēreṣ* (people of the land). All we have in the NT Gospels is Jesus *seen with the eye of faith*. We do not have a "historical Jesus," only the "historic Christ." The proof of the pudding is in the diverse Jesuses constructed by the questers, particularly the liberal and now neo-liberal Jesuses. In each case, the distinctiveness of the "objective Jesus" is largely the creation of the historical critic. The irony indeed is that the typical "historical Jesus" is as much a theological Jesus as any Gospel portrayal, since the constructed Jesus has been almost always an amalgam of the historian's own ideals (the fifth Gospel according to Kähler) and critically (selectively) worked data.[15]

The move of the neo-liberals to provide new sources and to point to major differences between sources might seem to meet Kähler's point. The more differentiated the data, the greater the possibility of reconstructing a historical Jesus different from all the later representations. It is very doubtful, however, whether these new sources make a significant difference. For example, the confidence of James Robinson that in the stratification of Q into Q^1, Q^2 and Q^3, Q^1 gives direct access to the Jesus of history[16] goes well beyond the argument of John Kloppenborg,[17] on whose thesis Robinson depends. Helmut Koester's attempt to topple the primacy of the Synoptic tradition in Jesus research and to replace it with the primacy of the Gospel of Thomas is vulnerable to the charge of *petitio principii*, question-begging.[18] And outside Crossan's own circle no one has been persuaded by his reconstruction of a "Cross Gospel" as the basis for the Synoptic passion narrative.[19]

Kähler's point therefore continues to be applicable. There are effectively no other historical sources for Jesus tradition outside the Synoptic Gospels. Even if there may be a number of individual sayings which have been retained in other sources outside the Synoptics, the reality is that recognition of them as original Jesus tradition depends on being able to demonstrate their compatibility with the

Synoptic tradition. Funk's reconstructed Jesus simply illustrates Kähler's point once again: that the only other real source for the so-called historical Jesus (apart from the canonical Gospels) is the convictions and aspirations of the quester himself.[20]

Third, *form criticism's missed opportunity*. Form-criticism opened up a new possibility of penetrating behind the earliest written sources. It also recognized that faith had shaped these earlier forms. But its practitioners were distracted from the implications of this recognition for "life of Jesus" research by focusing on the way faith had shaped the forms toward their final form in the Gospels. They neglected to inquire very far about the faith stimulus which *started* the traditioning process. Or else they took Easter faith as the starting point for the tradition, assuming that the portrayal of Jesus is entirely post-Easter in creation and the product of developed faith.[21] In a sense we have suffered from the false idea that "form-criticism" is the translation of *Formgeschichte* (literally "form-history") in that study of the history of transmission of the tradition (from the first) has been too often subverted into a study of the forms themselves. So too the recognition that forms have a *Sitz-im-Leben* (life-setting) diverted attention too much from the process of transmission to the communities which gave the forms their shape.

The point here is that insofar as form-criticism has been used in service of "life of Jesus" research, it has succumbed to the same illusion that Kähler identified. For there has been a *de facto* assumption that the forms also had a vital life outside the communities of faith, as though the forms were to be found in storytelling round the campfires of travellers or in the casual conversations of the marketplace,[22] as though the Evangelists hunted out tales about Jesus in the way that European composers in the first half of the twentieth century hunted out the folk songs and folk tunes of their people for their own compositions. But again we have to ask whether we have in the Synoptic tradition *any* data which is untouched by faith from the outset.

Fourth, *disciple-response*. It is at this point that we can draw upon the insights of postmodern literary criticism that the meaning of a text is in some sense the product of a creative encounter between text and reader. For though the point being made is usually with regard to the present day reader's reception of literary texts, it actually applies also to the tradition process itself which lies behind the Synoptic Gospels. Here Hans-Georg Gadamer's concept of the *Wirkungsgeschichte* of a text (the history of its effect)[23] is also to the point, since it applies also to the moment in which the tradition was itself created. There is in fact *no* gap to be bridged between a Jesus historically conceived and the subsequent tradition which has "effected consciousness"; all we have is disciples "effected" (as we might say) by Jesus and the disciples thus effected expressing their "effection" (as we might say) by formulating the tradition which effects.[24] The traditions which lie behind the Gospels began from the various encounters between Jesus and those who by virtue of these encounters became disciples. The earliest traditions are the product of disciple-response. There is not an objectified meaning to be uncovered by stripping away the accretions of disciple faith. The tradition itself, in its earliest form is in a crucially important sense the creation of faith; or to be more precise, it is the product of the encounters between Jesus and the ones who became his disciples. The hearing and witnessing of the first disciples was already a hermeneutical act, already caught in the hermeneutical circle. The exegetes and interpreters of the twenty-first century do not begin the hermeneutical dialogue; they continue a dialogue which began in the initial formation of the tradition.[25]

The point for us now, therefore, is that the saying, the account attests the impact made by Jesus.[26] But that does not enable us to get behind that impact to a Jesus who might have been heard otherwise. For the original impulse behind these records was, to put the point more accurately, *sayings of Jesus as heard and received*, and *actions of Jesus as witnessed and retained in the memory* (both parts of each phrase being important). We have to add in both cases, *and as reflected on thereafter*, of course. However, what we have in these traditions is not just the end-product of that reflection. It is rather the faith creating word/event, as itself a force shaping faith and as retained and rehearsed by the faith thus created and being created. In other words, the Jesus tradition gives immediate access not to a dispassionately recorded word or deed, nor only to the end product (the faith of the 50s, 60s, 70s, or 80s), but also to the process between the two, to the tradition which began with the initial impact of Jesus' word or deed and which continued to influence intermediate retellers of the tradition until crystallized in Mark's or Matthew's or Luke's account. In short, we must take seriously the character of the tradition as disciple-response, and the depth of the tradition as well as its final form.

Fifth, *the remembered Jesus*. We can therefore press Kähler's point still further to one of fundamental principle. The Synoptic tradition provides evidence not so much for what Jesus did or said in itself, but for what Jesus was *remembered* as doing or saying by his first disciples, or as we might say, for the *impact* of what he did and said on his first disciples. Bearing in mind the point just made, we may say that it is precisely the process of "remembering" which fuses the horizons of past and present (Gadamer), by making the past present again (*Vergegenwärtigung*).[27] What we actually have in the earliest retellings of what is now the Synoptic tradition, then, are the memories of the first disciples—not Jesus himself, but the remembered Jesus.[28] The idea that we can get back to an objective historical reality, which we can wholly separate and disentangle from the disciples' memories, and which we can then use as a check and control over the way the tradition was developed during the oral and earliest written transmission, is simply unrealistic. This observation would have been more obvious had more attention been given to the narrative tradition, as distinct from the sayings tradition, over the past 150 years. For narratives about Jesus never began with Jesus; at best they began with eyewitnesses. From the first we are confronted not so much with Jesus, but with how he was perceived. And the same is actually true of the sayings tradition: at best what we have are the teachings of Jesus as they impacted the individuals who stored them in their memories and began the process of oral transmission.[29]

In one sense, of course, we are simply recognizing the nature of the evidence which any biographer has to weigh who has no access to any writings of the biography's subject. That is to say, a portrayal of Jesus as seen through the eyes and heard through the ears of his first disciples is neither an illegitimate nor an impossible task, and such a portrayal, carefully drawn in terms of the evidence available, should not be dismissed or disparaged as inadmissible. After all, it is precisely the impact which Jesus made and which resulted in the emergence of

Christianity which historians (not just Christians) want to recover. Of course it would be wonderful and intriguing if we could portray Jesus as seen by Pilate or Herod, by Caiaphas or the house of Shammai. But we simply do not have sufficient evidence for that, and even if we had, what would it tell us about the beginnings of Christianity, about the character and impact of a mission which transformed fishermen and toll collectors into disciples and apostles? In terms of pivotal individuals on whom the history of the world has turned, it is the latter in whom we are most interested. And the Synoptic tradition is precisely what we need for the task.

Sixth, *when then did faith begin?* The significance of the step being advocated here, therefore, should not be missed. For it is tantamount to asserting that faith goes back to the very origins of the Jesus tradition, that the Jesus tradition emerged from the very first as the expression of faith. Initially not faith as it developed in the light of all that happened, and particularly of Good Friday and Easter day. But the teaching and events of Jesus' ministry did not suddenly become significant in the light of Easter—more significant, no doubt, as various markers in the Gospels indicate,[30] but not significant for the first time. The suggestion that the remembered Jesus was wholly insignificant, unfascinating and unintriguing, having no impact prior to his death and resurrection is simply incredible. Peter and the others did not first become disciples on Easter day. There was already a response of faith, already a bond of trust, inspired by what they first and subsequently heard and saw Jesus say and do. Only so can we explain how the Jesus tradition is so rich and full as it is—hardly the deposit of casual and vague memories first jerked into faith by Easter. In short, the tension between faith and history has too often been seen as destructive of good history. On the contrary, however, it is the recognition that Jesus can *only* be perceived through the impact he made on his first disciples (that is, their faith) which is the key to a historical recognition (and assessment) of that impact.

It should not go unobserved that if this insight is justified it provides some sort of solution to the seemingly unbridgeable gulf between history and faith. For in the historical moment(s) of creation of the Jesus tradition we have historical faith. The problem of history and faith, we might say, has been occasioned by the fact that further down the stream of faith and history the two have seemed so difficult to reconcile. But if it is in fact possible to trace the two streams, history and faith, back to the origins of the Jesus tradition, we find that we can step back and forth across the rivulets (pressing the analogy of a river's sources) with much less difficulty. Of course we are only at the *beginning* of faith at this point; but it is the beginning of *faith*. And nothing that has been so far said is intended to deny or discount the fact that the tradition developed: that there were accretions of faith, that post-Easter retellings conveyed post-Easter faith, that the tradition was elaborated in the passing on. All I am saying at this point is that the actual Synoptic tradition, with its record of things Jesus did and said, bears witness to a continuity between pre-Easter memory and post-Easter proclamation, a continuity of faith. However great the shock of Good Friday and Easter for the first disciples, it would be unjustified to assume that these events marked a discontinuity with their initial disciple-response, that they brought about complete disruption of their earlier disciple faith, and that the traditioning process only began from that point on.

Seventh, *the diversity of faith.* One other aspect of postmodern criticism should not be ignored, namely the pluralism endemic to the recognition that readers respond differently to texts and so produce multiple meanings. Applied to the beginnings of the Jesus tradition, that insight reminds us that Jesus would have impacted variously on different individuals. Or in terms of the present discussion, there would have been diversity of faith from the very first. That is not, or should not be a problem. For the evidence of the Synoptic tradition is of a homogeneity of impression made by Jesus on those who first created and then transmitted that tradition. The overall homogeneity of the Synoptic tradition points to the consistency of the impact made by Jesus as attested by that tradition. To put it another way, it is the consistency of disciple-response which gives the tradition its consistency.

At the same time it is important to remember, given the diversity (and fissiparity) of subsequent Christianity, that the circle of discipleship was not uniform from the beginning, and that a diversity of responses could be and was contained within the homogeneity of the overall response, within the discipleship which gave rise in due course to the earliest churches. If Jesus was always the unifying factor, along with disciple-faith in him, it was a unity embracing and holding together the diversity of the faith responses from the first.[31]

HEARING WITH FAITH

My first point, then, is that faith was bound up with the formation of the central writings which now constitute the Christian Scriptures from the very first; there is no pre-faith or non-faith tradition within the Gospels. Interpreters must orient their understanding of the task of interpretation accordingly. That may seem uncontroversial—at least for a symposium working from the concept of "Scripture." So let me press my second point, albeit briefly, with a view to provoking some discussion.

If my point about the dynamic of the first phase of emerging Scripture is sound, then it can also apply to the process of "hearing" Scripture today—that "hearing with faith" is also integral to Scripture's on-going function as Scripture. There is always a "becoming" of Scripture, Scripture conceived as itself a process incomplete without "faith-hearing."

This second point can be illustrated from the phenomenon of prophecy. I have always been struck by the fact that Paul sees two sides to the prophecy he experienced and encouraged in the churches which he established. When he speaks of such prophecy he regularly envisages a process whereby the congregation "tests" the prophecy, "evaluates" what has been said. The clearest summary statement appears in what was probably his earliest letter: "Do not quench the Spirit; do not despise prophecy; but test everything, hold to what is good and keep away from every form of evil" (1 Thess 5:19-22). But the concern is clear in 1 Corinthians also, especially 1 Cor 12:10 ("to another prophecy, to another discerning of spirits") and 14:29 ("let two or three prophets speak and let the others evaluate"). An inspired utterance which said "Accursed be Jesus" was not to be recognized as prophecy (12:3).[32] The point is that in an important sense a prophecy is not given until it is received. The speaking may be inspired, but if the sense of the prophecy is not perceived, then it is no more useful or effective in the assembly than glossolalia. Inspiration of speaker alone is not what makes an utterance into "prophecy"; it only functions as prophecy when it is received by the community within which the inspired utterance is given.

This, we might say, is the other end of Gadamer's "history of effect/history of reception." It is as true of the beginning of the process as of contemporary reception. The community's reception of an inspired utterance is integral not simply to its ongoing effect but to its initial effect. The form in which the prophecy is received and preserved not only attests the effect of the prophecy, but is itself the effect which constitutes the utterance as prophecy. In the famous case of Jer 28, for example, who was to say in the first instance whether Hananiah was the true prophet or Jeremiah? It was the community recognizing, whether then or subsequently, that Jeremiah spoke from God which ensured that it was Jeremiah's words which were treasured as prophecy and Hananiah's which were discounted.

A further example are the letters of the NT. Why are they in the NT in the first place? Not simply because a Paul wrote what he did under inspiration. We know that he wrote at least several other letters which have long since been lost. Why were some preserved and others disregarded? Presumably the answer is that the ones preserved made an impact analogous to the impact which Jesus made on his first followers. They were heard with faith, as faith-shaping, and were preserved as such and for that reason. Only as written with faith and received with faith, or as we might say, "from faith to faith," were they treasured, preserved, and further circulated to become in due course part of the NT Scripture.

This further example can be pressed to include the process of canonization itself. In terms of so-called "canonical criticism" I confess to siding with James Sanders rather than Brevard Childs. This is because it seems to me unwise to focus too much attention on the canonical moment of the final canonical text (Childs). What we have to appreciate, rather, is a process in which, first, utterances and formulations and traditions were recognized as authoritative by a faith-community; they were then incorporated into written texts, which in turn were recognized and treasured as authoritative by a widening circle of faith-communities; these writings in turn were finally recognized as more widely authoritative by respected church leaders and formally categorized as canonical.[33] In short, the Scriptures were not first given a canonical status by Athanasius or some church council, a status which they had not previously enjoyed. Rather, the formal statement of canonization was a recognition and affirmation of the authority which these documents had exercised from the first.

The same line of argument extends, *à la* Gadamer, to the present day and helps illuminate the task of interpretation. For too long the understanding of the NT as Scripture focused almost exclusively on the inspiration which gave birth to these writings. "Scripture" could be defined simply and sufficiently (it would appear) as writings inspired by the Holy Spirit. Surprisingly little attention was given to the other side of the process, to the reception and interpretation of these writings. "Interpretation" was evidently not very much of a problem for the fathers of evangelicalism. Over against the Catholic insistence that Scripture could only be heard aright through the tradition of the church, Protestantism replied that Scripture was self-interpreting, its meaning perspicacious. But even without the postmodern challenge to such overconfidence, the history of Protestant fragmentation into denominations and sects should be reminder enough that interpretation is more problematic than such theoretical confidence allowed.

My point here, in contrast, is that interpretation needs to be seen as far more integral to the function of Scripture as Scripture than Protestantism has traditionally allowed. We must overcome Protestant "antithesizing" of Scripture and tradition and see Scripture more as a process of living tradition. By that I mean a tradition which has to be received ever afresh and reactualized as Scripture in our present (*Vergegenwärtigung*). Interpretation of Scripture, therefore, is not to be conceived solely by the effort to express and define historical distance between historical text and hearer/reader—important as that is. But to interpret Scripture theologically means to engage with it in a way that allows the text to be heard again as Scripture, the theology of its message not explained away or reduced to sociological or literary observations, but heard with faith (*ex akoēs pisteōs*), responded to as theology. At the individual level it means that the living experience of faith is necessary if the interpreter is to interpret the text theologically. At the communal level it means that the text must be assisted to come alive in the assembly of faith, so that it might function again as Scripture and speak again with the power which first set it on the road to canonization.

CONCLUDING REMARKS

In short, the task of interpreting Scripture theologically cannot, in my view, be undertaken with any hope of success unless the dynamic of faith recognizing and responding to faith is appreciated. We will not do justice to Scripture as Scripture unless we acknowledge that it is itself faith response and faith expression through and through. Not faith as a later perspective, or faith as some kind of secondary layer on a historical, non-faith substratum, but faith formulated from the first and by means of the first verbal account of what Jesus did and said. That same faith, the experience of believing, is necessary in the modern interpreter. The expression of such faith will be very different from the expressions of the first century—more refined and matured, we hope—but we can be sure that Scripture only functions as Scripture when it speaks and is heard in a faith-creating, faith-shaping way.

NOTES

1. BAGD, *akoē*, sec. 2.

2. NEB/REB; so NIV, NJB, NRSV.

3. See also S. K. Williams, "The Hearing of Faith: AKOĒ PISTEŌS in Galatians 3," *NTS* 35 (1989) 82-93. The popular reading of *pistis* in Gal 3 as referring to "the faith of Christ" can hardly apply here (Gal 3:2, 5), since Paul immediately continues: "Just as Abraham believed God ..." (3:6).

4. See further my *Romans* (WBC 38; Dallas: Word, 1988) 623.

5. 1 Thess 1:5 provides a further alternative way of expressing the nexus between preaching, hearing, and faith: "our gospel came to you not in word only but in power and in the Holy Spirit and with full conviction [*plērophoria pollē*]."

6. Cf. not least J. P. Meier, "The Present State of the 'Third Quest' for the Historical Jesus: Loss and Gains," *Biblica* 80 (1999) 459-487 (here 463-464).

7. Note the archaeological imagery used by Funk when he describes the first of "two pillars of modern biblical criticism" as "the distinction between the historical Jesus, to be uncovered by historical excavation, and the Christ of faith encapsulated in the first creeds" (R. W. Funk, et al., *The Five Gospels: The Search for the Authentic Words of Jesus*, New York: Macmillan: Polebridge, 1993, 3). Similarly Burton Mack's description of his own and earlier "archaeological efforts" (*A Myth of Innocence: Mark and Christian Origins,* Philadelphia: Fortress, 1988, xi-xiii, 5). John Kloppenborg's new book, *Excavating Q* (Edinburgh: T. & T. Clark, 2000) uses the same imagery. Fundamental to Crossan's method is the "stratification" of his sources, an imagery again drawn from archaeology; see J. D. Crossan, *The Historical Jesus: The Life of a Mediterranean Jewish Peasant* (San Francisco: Harper, 1991).

8. Funk in particular has made no secret of his intention to mount "a frontal assault on a pervasive religious illiteracy that blinds and intimidates, even those, or perhaps especially those, in positions of authority in the church and in our society" (*Honest To Jesus*, HarperSanFrancisco: Polebridge, 1996, 6-7).

9. See e.g., G. Aichele, et al., *The Postmodern Bible* (New Haven: Yale University, 1995).

10. E.g., J. M. Robinson, *A New Quest of the Historical Jesus* (London: SCM, 1959) 26; L. E. Keck, *A Future for the Historical Jesus* (Nashville: Abingdon, 1971) 20, 35 ("the historical Jesus is the historian's Jesus, not a Kantian *Ding an sich*"); J. P. Meier, *The Marginal Jew: Rethinking the Historical Jesus,* Vol. One (New York: Doubleday, 1991) 21-26.

11. A similar confusion between real reader, ideal reader, and implied reader often vitiates much reader response criticism, as also confusion with regard to what Q refers to in criticism of the Synoptic Gospels, whether to the actual material common to Matthew and Luke or to the document on which Matthew and Luke probably drew.

12. This is why the move of the neo-liberals to provide new sources and to point to major differences between sources is so important; particularly Crossan, who claims to have identified three major sources which can be dated confidently to the period 30-60 C.E.—the Gospel of Thomas, the earliest stratum of Q, and the *Cross Gospel*, a linked narrative of Jesus' crucifixion and resurrection, which Crossan himself has constructed out of the Gospel of Peter, itself to be dated to the mid second century C.E., and postulated by Crossan as the source for the canonical passion narratives (*Historical Jesus*, 427-429); and H. Koester, *Ancient Christian Gospels: Their History and Development* (London: SCM/Philadelphia: TPI, 1990), who argues similarly with regard to Thomas and Q (75-171).

13. English translation: *The So-called Historical Jesus and the Historic Biblical Christ*, ed. C. E. Braaten (Philadelphia: Fortress, 1964).

14. See e.g., Meier, *Marginal Jew*, 56-111.

15. The resemblances between Crossan's Galilean peasant and those shaped by the oppression suffered by the Irish peasantry in the nineteenth century should hardly surprise us then. Funk himself notes that "the use of 'itinerant' or 'transient' [in relation to Jesus] may merely echo academic empathy for our own rootless age" (*Honest to Jesus*, 87).

16. J. M. Robinson, "The Critical Edition of Q and the Study of Jesus," a paper delivered at the Colloquium Biblicum Lovaniense XLIX (July 2000) on *The Sayings Source Q and the Historical Jesus.*

17. J. S. Kloppenborg, *The Formation of Q* (Philadelphia: Fortress, 1987).

18. *Ancient Christian Gospels* 92-99. He assumes that the lack of apocalyptic in the Gospel of Thomas indicates that the earliest layer in the Jesus tradition was also non-apocalyptic, when the more plausible hypothesis is that Thomas has omitted Q's apocalyptic material, with which Thomas' gnosticizing theology was unhappy, including Q's Baptist traditions, despite the fact that the Baptist in all the NT sources is always regarded as the beginning of the gospel.

19. Even Koester is unpersuaded (*Ancient Christian Gospels*, 218-220, 220 n.2, and 231 n.3).

20. See also L. T. Johnson, *The Real Jesus* (HarperSanFrancisco, 1996) who attempts to "do a Kähler" with regard to the neo-liberal quest, though not quite so effectively as Kähler.

21. Too much neglected has been the demonstration by H. Schürmann of sayings on kingdom, repentance, judgment, love of enemy, eschatological preparedness, etc., in the Synoptic tra-

dition which show no trace of post-Easter influence ("Die vorösterlichen Anfänge der Logientradition: Versuch eines formgeschichtlichen Zugangs zum Leben Jesu,") in H. Ristow & K. Matthiae, eds., *Der historische Jesus und der kerygmatische Christus*, Berlin: Evangelische, 1962, 342-370).

22. Cf. particularly E. Trocmé, *Jesus and his Contemporaries* (London: SCM, 1973), 104: "the setting in which the miracle stories originated and were handed down for a time is not a Christian one, but must be sought in . . . the village society of north-eastern Galilee or the area immediately surrounding Lake Tiberias. Story-tellers at markets and during winter evenings found a ready audience for narratives with no literary pretensions, but too sensational to leave a popular audience unmoved. . . . We owe to him (Mark) the introduction of these narratives into a Christian setting"; and the stimulating novelistic treatment of G. Theissen, *The Shadow of the Galilean: the Quest of the Historical Jesus in Narrative Form* (London: SCM, 1987).

23. H.-G. Gadamer, *Truth and Method* (New York: Continuum, 1989), 300-307. The more significant term is actually the more elaborate phrase, *wirkungsgeschichtliches Bewusstsein*, "historically effected consciousness" (301).

24. Cf. Paul Ricoeur's observation that the phenomenon of distance and difference refers not simply to the modern reading of an ancient text: "The distance is given at the beginning. It is the very first distance between the hearer and the witness of the event." See "Preface to Bultmann"(i.e., to the French edition of *Jesus and the Word* and *Jesus Christ and Mythology*, 1968), *Essays on Biblical Interpretation* (Philadelphia: Fortress, 1980), 56.

25. Francis Watson also seems to think only in terms of a significance seen retrospectively; see his *Text and Truth: Redefining Biblical Theology* (Edinburgh: T. & T. Clark, 1997), 52-53.

26. For want of a better way of describing it, I speak of the "impact" of Jesus. Similarly P. Barnett, *Jesus and the Rise of Early Christianity: A History of New Testament Times* (Downers Grove, Ill.: InterVarsity, 1999) ch. 2; as earlier of "the percussive impact of Jesus the Teacher" (*Jesus and the Logic of History*, Grand Rapids: Eerdmans, 1997, pp. 56, 102, 127). But it should also be recalled that form-critical analysis of the Jesus tradition was predicated on the assumption that the tradition was retained as live tradition, precisely in that the tradition continued to influence and shape the lives of the earliest disciples and communities. It is more or less self-evident that teaching like Matt 7:24-27/Luke 6:47-49 and Mark 8:34-38 pars. must have made a faith-creating impact on those who passed it on.

27. Cf. particularly J. Schröter, *Erinnerung an Jesu Worte: Studien zur Rezeption der Logien Überlieferung in Markus, Q und Thomas* (WMANT 76; Neukirchen-Vluyn: Neukirchener, 1997) 3-4; "Recall of the Jesus tradition can be understood accordingly as a selective process by which the actual present becomes meaningful by reference to the person of Jesus" (463-464).

28. Ben Meyer also emphasises "the overarching fact . . . that Palestinian Christianity was nourished on the memory of Jesus." See B. F. Meyer, *The Aims of Jesus* (London: SCM, 1979), 69, 72-73).

29. Another important aspect of my present research is on the oral character of the Synoptic tradition; I present a preliminary account of it in "Jesus in Oral Memory," *SBL 2000 Seminar Papers* (Atlanta: Scholars, 2000) 287-326.

30. E.g., Mark 9:9; John 2:22.

31. See further my *Unity and Diversity in the New Testament* (London: SCM, 1977, 1990). It is true that there were initially other responses which fell short of discipleship, or which understood discipleship differently, or which stopped short of Good Friday and Easter (as Mark 9:38-41 and Acts 19:1-7 may well imply). They were presumably either absorbed into the mainstream of Christianity represented by the NT, or diverged further into forms of Christianity regarded subsequently as "heretical." The important fact for us remains that Q was not retained within mainstream Christianity except as integrated with the Gospel format initiated by Mark, and Thomas was rejected by the emerging great Church. The very concern of the neo-liberals to justify use of the Gospel of Thomas by seeking to demonstrate its consistency with a stripped down Synoptic tradition is actually a back-handed recognition of the normativeness of the Synoptic tradition.

32. See further my *Jesus and the Spirit* (London: SCM, 1975) 233-236, 293-297. The fresh emphasis on the importance of religious experience in L. T. Johnson, *Religious Experience in Earliest Christianity* (Minneapolis: Fortress, 1998) is to be warmly welcomed.

33. See further my "Levels of Canonical Authority," *Horizons in Biblical Theology* 4 (1982) 13-60 (particularly 15 and n.14), reprinted in *The Living Word* (London: SCM, 1987) 141-174, 186-192 (particularly 142-143 and n.14).

RESPONSE TO DUNN

DAVID P. MOESSNER

Before sketching points of agreement and then proceeding to certain major disagreements, I would like to express my sincere thanks to Professor Dunn for the sheer delight in reading this paper with its no holds-barred expression of thought and infectious quality of faith which shines through every page. I almost found myself from the very outset reading "from faith to faith"!

I agree wholeheartedly with the general thesis that Scripture is through and through theological and that this theological character defines the very core of Scripture qua Scripture. Exegesis today and every day *anno Domini* which does not wrestle with the theos-logic of the Christian Bible does not do justice to the very nature of these texts—texts which the church has revered as Scripture for the better part of two millennia—and thus cannot be termed genuine Scripture exegesis.[1]

I particularly enjoyed the summary of the "historical Jesus/Christ of faith" debate of the Enlightenment/post-Enlightenment period, and agree fundamentally with the way he has formulated the essential issues and summarized the problematic: "The idea that we can get back to an objective historical reality, which we can wholly separate and disentangle from the disciples' memories, and which we can then use as a check and control over the way the tradition was developed during the oral and earliest written transmission, is simply unrealistic." The discussion summarizes fairly and accurately Kähler's insights and adds depth and precision to the entire debate, before arguing in more detail the specific thesis regarding the Jesus tradition as heuristic for the whole of Scripture interpretation.

However, I find myself in essential disagreement (as well as in not a little wonderment) with the insistence that the first memories of Jesus which constitute the beginning of the Synoptic tradition must somehow be identified with faith or that the earliest disciple-responses to Jesus must spring *from faith.* I concede the specific thesis, if by "faith" is meant some form of devotion which began with the earliest calls of the disciples and continued on after the passion and resurrection into the discipleship of the church. But this definition does not seem very helpful, let alone Christian, in clarifying the phenomenon that we call the "Synoptic tradition." If the case were built upon the description of "disciple-response" and the impact of the "remembered Jesus," rather than upon "faith" as a religious experience at the core of those memories, then I would have nothing but affirmation for the overall approach. But this is clearly not what is argued. Three questions will expand my critique.

One, can we so easily identify the impact of Jesus on the disciples during his public ministry with the "faith" of the disciples, however weak and beggarly that faith might have been in these alleged initial responses? I could not agree more with the statement concerning the significance of Good Friday and Easter for the disciples, that "it would be unjustified to assume that these events . . . brought about complete disruption of their earlier disciple faith, and that the traditioning process only began from that point on." Certainly the Synoptic Gospel material stems from the disciples' memories "of all that Jesus began to do and teach" (Acts 1:1). To try to make the tradition begin only from Easter onward would be to void Jesus' death and resurrection of the very significance that the Easter faith claims it to be, to sever the climax of the plot from the plot itself, to place the passion and events of Easter into a vacuum of meaningless ghost players and surreal actions.

But unfortunately, that is not all that is being said. Rather, Dunn insists on equating these earliest remembrances of the impact of Jesus upon the disciples with *responses of faith.* The experiences of Jesus' miracles and radical demands and premonitions (if not predictions of his coming passion, etc.) are etched only in the memories of the disciples as *responses with faith.* To be sure, Dunn allows that these responses would become enriched and expanded by the disciples' experience of Good Friday and Easter. Yet the disciples' pre-passion responses to Jesus, Dunn argues, are of a kind with the apostolic faith of the church, subsumed under the same category as the post-Pentecost variety of "faith" which eventually will enable the likes of a Peter or a James to expound from the Scriptures the whole "plan of God" (Acts 2:14-36, esp. v. 23; 15:13-21) or to say to a dead corpse, "little girl (*talitha*/Tabitha) arise" (Acts 9:40; Mark 5:41; cf. Luke 8:54). How do we explain that in all of the ancient accounts from the Greco-Roman period of famous teachers, holy men, miracle workers, and the like, the Synoptic Gospels are the only narratives which portray the followers/successors of a famous person in an incredibly negative light, in short, in the unmistakable hues and tones of "un-faith"? And more than that, how is it that these disparaging accounts are authored or authorized by these followers themselves? I am not thinking only or even primarily of the triplex Synoptic (not to mention Johannine) traditions of Peter's denial.[2] Rather, how do we account for traditions in which the disciples act contrary to faith, or, at best, without the smallest "increment" of a trust requisite for the Kingdom of God.[3] Are we to suggest that, for instance, in Luke 9:52-56, when James and John entreat Jesus to call down fire upon an inhospitable Samaritan village that this experience is remembered and appreciated and cultivated because their experience with Jesus can be characterized from the first as "faith"? Perhaps here a "bond of trust" is in evidence, but hardly the right kind of bond or of trust, for that matter. Similarly after the Transfiguration in all three of the Synoptists *the disciples* provoke Jesus' cry and lament of a "faithless and twisted generation" (Mark 9:2-29 pars.), because of the disciples' "poverty of faith" (Matt 17:20) or pride "as the greatest" (Luke 9:46-48, 49-50). Are these accounts explainable because of the disciples' harking back to their faith experiences? Or might it not be more the opposite "continuity," the contrast of their "unfaith" to the "wondrous acts of God" (cf. Luke 9:43)?

Other traditions could be included.[4] But who in their right mind produces propaganda literature with themselves playing the lead roles which will climax as the co-conspirators and co-complicitors and even the dupes of those determined to put the famous leader to death? And conversely, how do we account for such denunciations of the followers by the master as "Get behind me, Satan," precisely at the moment when the disciples are acclaiming Jesus' stature as God's specially anointed (Mark 8:33)?[5] My point is not that the disciples sometimes were not faithful or occasionally let Jesus down at crucial moments. Nor am I suggesting that the disciples cannot or should not be singled out from the rest of the crowds because of their heeding the call of Jesus with its sacrifices of home and occupation, or even to receive special promises for their unique roles in an unparalleled drama.[6] Rather, my point is more fundamentally theological as will be seen in my second question.

But first, let me throw out this caveat. When Dunn answers the questions "When did a faith perspective first influence the Jesus tradition?" or, "Do we have in the Synoptic tradition *any* data which is untouched by faith from the outset?" is he not succumbing to the older liberal "idea" or "concept" fallacy, the assumption that the farther we can go back to the origins of a particular historical phenomenon, the closer we approach the purer essence or essential nature of this phenomenon?[7] Is he not searching for the earliest *source expression* of an idea or *topos* because allegedly it is the purest form and thus closest and most reliable expression of that idea itself, while later expressions are inescapably distortions, whether accretions or disfigurations?[8]

Two, when treating the Jesus tradition as heuristic for the theological character of Scripture as a whole, is not the merit of the specific thesis far too dependent upon only one and, rather extreme, "position" for relating "the historical Jesus" to the "Christ of faith," and, at the same time, severed from a far more reliable traditioning process, namely, the church's re-interpretation of their Scriptures? Is not the solution "from faith to faith" tied too closely to a misleading, if not dubious, dichotomy for the larger problematic, namely, the starting point of Easter faith, *on the one side*, and the wholly insignificant memories of Jesus, *on the other*? When Dunn says Jesus can *only* be perceived through the "impact he made on his first disciples, i.e., their faith, which is the key to a historical recognition (and assessment) of that impact," is he not rendering unintended legitimacy to liberal theology's "straw antithesis" between faith and history by arguing wholesale only on the "side" of faith, such that religious experience, namely "faith," can be the only reliable point of contact between the pre-Easter and post-Easter periods? Why is it so critical that from the *very first* encounters and pristine memories, "faith" be the telling template which must emblazon the Synoptic Jesus tradition throughout its traditioning process in becoming Scripture, the "energizing or motive force" *within the Scriptures themselves*? Can it not be equally the case that the first responses were significant for reasons other than the "intermingling of faith" and remembered as encounters with the Jesus of their "historical" experience?

Further, might it not be the case with the Gospel narratives that the plot itself holds a more fundamental key to the significance of the individual events *as Scripture*, rather than some imaginatively created scenario of inner faith experiences of the disciples which are no longer, if ever, accessible? In short, is Dunn not asking faith *to do too much*, while at the same time inadvertently devaluing the epistemological role of Scripture and of Scripture's fulfillment through the death and resurrection of Messiah in connecting the pre- and post-Easter periods?[9]

Luke alone of the Synoptists reveals what Jesus was about during the period of his resurrection appearances. Jesus' Bible studies transform a group of well-intending, zealous, but severely misguided disciples into the authentic witnesses of the whole of Scriptures' plan of salvation for the world.[10] "You foolish folk, sluggish of heart to believe all that the prophets have spoken! Was it not necessary that the Messiah had to suffer so as to enter into his glory?" And beginning with Moses and *all of the prophets, he opened up to them in all of the Scriptures the things concerning himself!* (Luke 24:25-27). Without the events of Messiah's ministry consummated by rejection by his own people *of Israel* upon the world stage of Roman rule, there would be no Jesus tradition to analyze! At the heart of this tradition in both its Synoptic and Johannine forms is the incredible story that even the best of intentions, the bonds of trust, the responses of "faith" to Jesus could only in the end yield to disassociation, scattering abandonment, denial, and even betrayal (cf. Mark 14:50 par.; Luke 22:38; Matt 27:46 par.). None of these statements of betrayal makes any sense at all unless they are construed in the light of the whole narrative story which *itself* constitutes the "Gospel according to." None of the Gospels as a whole makes sense apart from its plotted sequence of a Messiah who fulfills, however ironically, *all of Israel's Scriptures*. In other words, the events of passion and Easter in climaxing the public ministry of Jesus *and* their interpretation from the light of the whole of the Scriptures are not only "significant, no doubt, as various markers in the Gospels indicate," but rather are themselves, passion and Easter, the all transforming, earthshaking epistemological keys to the very *raison d'être* of the Gospels.

But how could it be that the trusty companionship of such well-meaning supporters of Jesus seemed to disintegrate precipitously, that the memories of these devoted followers suddenly could not recall knowing Jesus, or that one of the disciples led the arresting party and had Jesus delivered over to the ultimate criminal's death? Yet, these same folk were transformed into those who themselves became marginalized as "ignorant," "uneducated" low brows who were embarrassed publicly, thrown into prisons, and stoned in rituals which were thought to honor God—all because of their allegiance to Jesus of Nazareth. How could such drastic turnabouts have taken place? Are they conceivable historically? Does this transformation not constitute the core of the vital task Dunn envisages for historians of Christianity?

At the end of Luke's Gospel, it is Jesus himself who provides the decisive clue to such sensational "about-faces" when *a shift of comprehension of cosmic proportions takes place, a floodlight of understanding that illumines the minds of the bewildered disciples:* "he opened their mind (*nous*)to comprehend the Scriptures" (24:45). The hermeneutical circle is broken and given a new center, a new point of focus! We notice that Jesus goes on to commission the eleven apostles to "proclaim in his name to all the nations, beginning from Jerusalem, *a change of mind* (*meta-noia*) leading to the release/forgiveness of sins" (v. 47). What is the primary referent for this "transformed, radically altered mind"? The minds of the disciples were changed in no other way than in the new understanding, the new eyes, yes, *of faith* which read the Scriptures in a new way and led to the new mind set of a transformed life. And, what is often missed in this passage, Luke 24:44-

49, is that this new comprehension of the Scriptures is itself to be announced to all the world! This new hermeneutic is to be proclaimed as the heart of Christian mission because it is at the heart of the disciples' memories of the impact of Jesus *as the experience of the unfathomable grace of God in forgiving them for their radical un-faith.* Or in quintessential Lukan terms, only as they understand their own role and bear in their own witness the *"plan of God" for the rejection of Messiah by his own people*, can the first disciples understand the Scriptures and begin to formulate the apostolic tradition, indeed, begin the radical revisioning of their own public experiences with Jesus into what we now know as the Synoptic Gospel tradition.[11]

Three, did a particular Gospel attain canonical status primarily because the traditions contained therein were faith traditions and the Gospel thereby affirmed as authoritative "from the first"; or was it more the case that the apostolic tradition embraced a particular Gospel (and distanced itself from others) primarily because the plotted narrative sequence was affirmed as true to the apostles' comprehension of the Scriptures with Jesus Christ himself their fulfillment and authoritative hermeneut?

Our earliest external data concerning the origins of the Jesus tradition and its formation into narrative Gospels is, of course, the Papias tradition, cited by Eusebius (*Hist. eccl.* III.39.3-4, 15-16), where the Gospels of Mark and Matthew are mentioned explicitly:[12] Papias is one of a few "of the ancients" whose "recorded reminiscences [*hypomnemata*] of the apostolic teachings" have survived as "the tradition" down to Eusebius' own day.[13]

Papias insists that he was not interested in learning about the teachings of the church as they had developed through these "followers" of the apostles but rather only those traditions which had been given to the apostles "from the Lord" himself. Since Eusebius regards Papias generally as one of "very little intelligence," his citation of Papias' characterization of the Gospels appears relatively reliable, especially as it buttresses Eusebius' unfolding presentation of the authoritative tradition down to his own day. Central to this authority is the "living and continuing voice" of the disciples and elders of the first generation which, according to Papias, represents the voice of the Lord himself, *regardless of whether individual tradition units were thought to stem from the pre- or from the post-resurrection periods.* Despite his low esteem of Papias' intellect, there is no doubt in Eusebius' mind that the "living and continuing voice" of the Lord resounding through the overall configuration of each Gospel, in both part and whole, is the voice of the Lord—not that of Peter or of Mark or of any other apostle or "follower of an apostle."

More decisive, however, in discerning the rationale of the scriptural dynamic which resulted in the acceptance of only four "canonical" Gospels are the criticisms that were being leveled at Mark's Gospel around the turn of the first and second centuries and Papias' corresponding defense of Mark which Eusebius considers illuminating of the authentic marks of tradition.[15] We have, in fact, toward the end of the trajectory of Synoptic Gospel formation precisely the kind of historical evidence which points to those forces which toward the beginning had motivated and combined to steer the process of "accreditation" along its entire course. Against the charges that, 1) Mark's order did not meet the conventions acceptable for a formal narrative account (*syntaxis*) such that, 2) Mark thereby distorted the picture of Jesus created by this confusing and misleading narrative sequence (*Hist. eccl.* III.39.15), Papias cites John the Elder's response that Mark was only imitating Peter's own way of stringing together sayings and deeds (*ta logia*) of Jesus as the various teaching occasions of mission would dictate (III.39.15). Since Peter did not present the words and deeds of Jesus in any coherent, acceptable literary fashion, Mark likewise "did not do anything wrong" in following the same procedure! Indeed, because of Peter's own depiction and correlation of individual scenes that are faithfully remembered by Mark, Mark's readers can be assured of a "reliable" enough understanding in and through the individual units of his Gospel. Mark is simply following Peter in an apostolic configuration of the whole, that is to say, a sequence of the sayings and events of Jesus—notwithstanding its narrative limitations—that has been affirmed as authoritative! Moreover, Eusebius summons Papias' words on Matthew's Gospel to clinch this defense of Mark. Matthew, himself an apostle, provides a paragon of diegetic reliability (*syntaxis*), an authoritative plotted sequence of what Jesus said and did (*ta logia*) whose "family resemblance" to Mark is obvious. Matthew's only "fault" is that many cannot make sense of its Aramaic/Hebrew language! (*Hist. eccl.* III.39.16).

What is telling then in Eusebius' argumentation is the insistence on the apostolic arrangement or story. However faint Peter's voice may reverberate through Mark's turbid "order," the fact that Mark represents Peter's own apostolic configuration qualifies his Gospel, similar to Matthew, as authoritative and therefore as Scripture. But this authoritative way of telling the story now gives every motivation for the disciples to "re-remember" their pre-passion encounters with Jesus. Not cherished "faith traditions" of the disciples' pre-passion encounters with Jesus, but rather the "new faith remembrances" of those encounters is now cherished. Now their first remembrances of Jesus are brought into the service of the whole as seen from the "goal" of Jesus' public ministry. Coupled with Jesus' explanation and enactment of the Scriptures, their many encounters of misunderstanding and mis-faith are now valued and handed down and proclaimed as part of a larger intention of God for their own (and the world's) salvation. Now a true "Christian faith" redeems those first remembrances to become part and parcel of God's "good news" in the dawning of his Kingdom through the broken but raised Messiah Jesus. Both failure and faith, disobedience and trust, and much misunderstanding and devotion in between, are valued because of "all that stands written" and is now believed to be decisively fulfilled. The primary homogeneity of the Synoptics, then, is the apostolically shaped story of the words and deeds of Jesus which changed the world forever—not the more genuine or greater number of faith-generated traditions of one Gospel compared with another.

NOTES

1. Cf. Calvin's remark on the internal testimony or illumination of the Spirit required for all biblical exegesis: "a man on his own with all his wits is as incapable of understanding the mysteries of God as an ass is unsuited for music" (*Commentary on 1 Corinthians*).

2. Matt 26:69-75; Mark 14:66-72; Luke 22:54-62; John 18:15-18, 25-27.

3. E.g., Matt 9:13-15 pars.; Mark 10:35-40 par.; Luke 17:1-10 pars.; et al.

4. For example, the negative response to the parables described with language from Isa 6 of hardened hearts (Matt 13:1-15, 18-30 pars.); or passages speaking of "favorable but delinquent response" (such as Luke 11:33-36 par.; 8:18b par.; and 11:27-28).

5. This Markan example is particularly poignant since the earliest tradition about Mark's Gospel (the Papias fragment, cited by Eusebius, *Hist. eccl.* III.39.1-4; 15-16; cf.II.15.1-2) characterizes its whole form and content as corresponding to the "living voice" of the "written remembrance of the tradition delivered orally" by Peter.

6. E.g., Matt 19:28 par.

7. Notice Dunn's frequent use of expressions such as "from the first," "from the beginning," "initially," etc.

8. Dunn himself speaks of the disciples' "accretions of faith." Cf. the Tübingen School's purer essence of the gospel in the preaching (*logos*) of Paul over against the later dilutions and distortions of the "narrative" Gospels with the "historization" by Luke of the earlier, purer kergyma of the Gospel of Mark of the Bultmann school.

9. The significance of the Jewish Scriptures, or eventually the church's OT, seem to be entirely absent from Dunn's formulations.

10. See especially Luke 24:21a.

11. Dunn's evaluation of "prophetic utterance" in the Pauline churches which can become genuine prophecy only once both utterance and interpretation are received and confirmed is an illuminating analogy of the critical role that the Jewish Scriptures played in reconstituting the Jesus tradition. Cf., e.g., Jesus' opening of "all that stands written" concerning him "in the law of Moses and the prophets and the Psalms" and the "openings" of Pss 68 and 108 in Acts 1:15-26 and 15 and 109 in Acts 2:14-36.

12. The fact that for Q there are no narrative contextual parallels between Matthew and Luke, except for the baptism of Jesus by John at the chronological beginning of the public ministry of Jesus, argues strongly against a Q Gospel. Hence Q cannot function as an analogue, let alone precedent or *Vorlage*, for the Gospel of Thomas. Paleographical evidence indicates that the latter is a later configuration (*syntaxis*) than the Synoptic Gospels, though, to be sure, it contains a number of *logia* commensurate with the Synoptic tradition.

13. *Hist. Eccl.* III.37.4; III.39.1; and see esp. III.24.16; cf. Acts 21:16 of Mnason.

14. "Those who had followed the elders" (See III.39.1-4; cf. 39.7, 12-13, and 15).

15. 1) "Mark did nothing wrong (*hemarten*) in thus writing down single points as he remembered them. 2) For to one thing he gave attention, to leave out nothing of what he had heard and to make no false statements in or through them (en autois)" *(Hist. Eccl.* III.39.15).

ON THE INTERPRETATION OF THE OLD TESTAMENT BY THE CHURCH

ROLF P. KNIERIM

The focus of this symposium on the *theological* interpretation of Scripture, or on how to interpret Scripture *theologically,* indicates that the planners and conveners of the symposium presuppose:

> that some methods of interpreting the Bible do not focus on or include theological interpretation,
>
> that—assuming the subsidiary function of all other methods—interpreting the Bible theologically should be the focal task in scholarly interpretation because the Bible is before everything else theological literature, and
>
> that this kind of interpretation has to be the inescapable priority in the use of the Bible by the church, as long as it is church and its Bible is Scripture, and especially inasmuch as particular churches identify themselves as grounded above all else in Scripture.

Strictly speaking, the expression "theological interpretation of Scripture" amounts to a pleonasm. Scripture is to be interpreted theologically as such.

The conveners' emphasis that this symposium on the theological interpretation of the Bible is to serve the church deserves special attention. It means that the setting of the church in which Scripture is interpreted is different from research about it in the settings of the scholarly societies. It means that the use of Scripture for its preaching, teaching, and counseling in the church is different from its use for the sake of scholarship. It also means that the people involved in the two different settings have different tasks and competence and are, by and large, not the same. We are to address the theological interpretation of Scripture for the church, as actually to be done in and by the church itself.

This means that the participants in this colloquium are not just asked to discuss how to interpret the Bible theologically among ourselves in the setting of a biblical society. We are asked to step over into the setting of the church and to discuss how the theological interpretation of the Bible can, may, and should be done in and through the church itself, in and through the church's preaching, teaching, and counseling, and by the church's practitioners. In addition to and beyond the tasks in our scholarly settings, we need to attend to the tasks in the practitioners' settings, including our own tasks when we work in those settings. In short, whatever we professors do by teaching and publication, we are to offer guidelines which help the practitioners to do interpretation of the Scripture themselves rather than to do such interpretation for them.

For many reasons I find it preposterous to describe, let alone prescribe, a program for practitioners in the ministry which is both comprehensive and detailed. In the following I prefer to highlight aspects concerning the interpretation of Scripture that seem to me to be relevant and desirable for all practitioners in ministry.

I want first to say a few things about what should and should not be expected of practitioners. Then I wish to highlight a particular issue which normally does not receive its due consideration: the practitioners' experience with Scripture as a part of their biography, often from childhood on. This kind of experience includes much more than what is formally studied. It includes the church's, often life long, influence on them, an influence that brought most into the ministry in the first place. Before having become interpreters of Scripture for the church, many of us have been influenced by the interpretation which we have received from the church. We carry this interpretation alongside what we constantly add, and it contributes to the chance for us to learn more and more how to discern between the better and our less, or not at all, helpful experiences in interpretation.

It is important that each of us not forget her/his own experience. As an example for the development of the awareness of the issue of theological interpretation, I would like to describe a few cases from my own biography. I will conclude this paper by pointing to some aspects which in my opinion are indispensable for carrying out the (theological) interpretation of Scripture by everyone.

WHAT SHOULD AND SHOULD NOT BE EXPECTED OF PRACTITIONERS IN MINISTRY

Church practitioners must not be expected to have the competence in biblical interpretation which is expected of professors for teaching and research in this field. Professors who educate students preparing for the practical ministry will have to know that they educate for that goal, not for a Ph.D. program in Old or New Testament. It certainly will not hurt if professors have some experience of the practical ministry themselves.

The task of the practitioners, most of whom are in parishes, is vastly different from the task of professors. While the scholars are essentially focused on their scholarly subjects, the practitioners are essentially involved with human beings and communities. Compared to the full range of the practitioners' varied and constantly changing obligations and the full range of all fields of study and information from which they must draw, the life of scholars who are paid for their specialization looks like the fulfillment of a dream of a lifelong personal hobby.

The respectable competence for biblical interpretation realistically to be expected from Church practitioners is conditioned by what they can regularly do from week to week. Earned degrees and personal potential make a difference, but they pale in light of all regular obligations in the trenches of full time ministry. Under those conditions a level of acquired competence should be expected which is irreducible and which should be maintained and improved through regular, weekly, practice.

From their formal education practitioners should have become aware of the general framework within which their interpretation of Scripture always takes place. This framework includes the interplay of the theologies in Scripture and the doctrines of the churches, the interplay of the worldviews in Scripture and our own worldview(s)—including the awareness of the vast historical distance between the biblical time and our own, and the interplay of the approach to texts through acquired methods and the learning of methods emerging from the study of the texts. The more a practitioner is working in this framework, the better her/his interpretation of the theologies in Scripture for our own times will be.

Interpretation of Scripture's theologies is never separate from the kinds of interplay just mentioned. Yet it is distinct from them, and to discern and hold this distinctiveness is essential if the theological voice of Scripture is to be recognized in its own right. While acknowledging the total framework, I want to refer to those aspects which I consider irreducible in the practitioners' interpretation of Scripture as Scripture itself. I am thereby emphasizing those work habits that encourage and improve the interpreter's own individual constructive contribution in interpretation. From what is usually taught in seminaries I want to highlight suggestions that are particularly important.

For "theological" interpretation of Scripture the search for the theologies of and in the texts has to be the basic focus. To practice this maxim is not self-evident. It is easier said than done and requires growing experience.

In practice, the interpreter has to deal with two main approaches: the interpretation of texts and the interpretation of issues or topics. A third approach is perhaps practiced less: the study of words and word fields.

Texts should be studied for what they are before us: written documents about whatever they say. They are units in and for which parts, verses, sentences, and words are composed and function. The study of their structures leads to the discovery of their—structured!—meaning, i.e., of what is at issue in the whole unit, of the message, the purpose, the topic, and the conceptual presupposition.[1]

The practitioner may not have the time to do even the exegesis of a text itself each week, let alone the work on what it means for us and on how to organize the communication of it to the congregation. But he/she should afford to set time and effort aside to focus on what a given text means as a whole and how this whole is supported by its parts. Thus, the understanding of its theology emerges.

This effort is most profitable when it is the practitioner's own initiative. When that is done, good commentaries ought to be consulted. They will show shortfalls and errors in one's own result and help to upgrade or change it. And a wonder: sometimes one recognizes that one's own findings are more on target and better verifiable than those of the scholarly commentator!

I believe that this pattern can be pursued from week to week. To use Hebrew or Greek is thereby very helpful, if someone is able and can afford it. Otherwise, a good English translation is a legitimate basis for pursuing the mentioned goal as approximately as possible.

Every preacher knows that when preaching about a text one must eventually define what it is all about, and therefore what the topic for it should be. In this case, the formulation of the topic evolves from, and is confined by, the text—

sometimes to one's dismay when the studied text resists certain ideas initially more projected into it than legitimately derived from it.

The situation is different when the preacher, concerned with certain issues, needs to speak about a formulated topic for which he/she has to find the proper text or set of texts. Despite the frequency of this approach, it is more difficult than the approach from text to topic. It requires finding the right texts and avoiding inappropriate ones and also requires especially a good deal of experience with the topical and conceptual aspects in Scripture, aspects which are at issue and operative in the texts while not defined there topically. It requires conscious attention to, familiarity with, and growing experience of the relationship between the cases and their ideas in the texts. (Examples from my own experience follow in the next section.)

For the topical approach the interpreter needs to consult equivalent publications such as Old and New Testament Theologies, at best more than one of each, or monographs. Development of a personal core library is inevitable, and as much as possible the careful study of at least one twenty-page chapter per week from such a publication, preferably a study directly related to the interpreter's own work. Interpretation of Scripture's theologies does not happen without these fundamental and regular activities of the interpreter. More may always be done, but these belong to the basics.

There are the words, especially the great words, in the Bible that serve as entries to the interpretation of Scripture's theologies, words such as justice, righteousness, peace, love, freedom, forgiveness, atonement, injustice, sin, judgment, punishment, hate, war, violence, and so on. Despite difficulties, their study opens revealing perspectives at the outset as any look into an English concordance shows. At least the interpreter should know the Hebrew and Greek alphabet in order to use her/his Hebrew and Greek lexica and concordances. One should also know the fundamentals of types of words and of grammar and syntax.

There is no end to the possible growth, but it is important that the practitioner not be prevented from interpreting Scripture "theologically" by her/his limits.

MY OWN HISTORY OF EXPERIENCE IN THEOLOGICAL INTERPRETATION OF SCRIPTURE

At points my experience is similar to that of others and in other respects is unique. It reflects various types of encounter with Scripture. Above all, long before I could contribute to interpreting Scripture for the church, I was the recipient of the Church's interpretation for me.

A few examples selected from an endless line of experiences might illustrate the road signs alongside which my "reading the Bible theologically" developed. Rather than being forgotten, many of these experiences remained present throughout this development. They kept driving me to understand what was not clear to me, which certainly had to do with the integration into my Christian rootage of what I was told and told myself.

Before I started going to school in 1935, I encountered in the church's Sunday school two things that stand out in my memory: The name "Jesus" and the

German version of the song "Jesus Loves Me . . .": "Jesus liebt mich ganz gewiss, denn die Bibel sagt mir dies." I believe I remember from that earliest time some of the stories about Jesus from the Gospels, which we were told in childlike fashion. These stories functioned to impress the name "Jesus" on me. Although I did not understand what I was singing, I sang the three things that the song made me sing: I know; because the Bible tells me; that Jesus loves me. Of course, I "knew" it via singing the song, not via my reading of the Bible, which did not happen for years at any rate. Not a bad beginning for any one, at any age, of the reading of the Bible theologically—certainly controlled by a method of interpretation. One must recognize the erudite systemic theological order which is the matrix for generating this simple text for a childlike song.

We also sang and heard that Jesus loves the sinners. Experience of this was not more than intuitive. He also loves the sinners, not only me, but the sinners were the others because they behaved immorally. The reach of this notion from Scripture's theology into my life kept me increasingly searching why something like this could be said. Much later, actually not before the lectures of my NT university professors, I began to understand the rationale, especially in Paul's theology of justification. The impact on me of this sudden clarity after years of feeling that I did not know what I was believing and talking about amounted to an experience of personal conversion—in the lecture hall of the university—unlike any of the conversions I had experienced before. It put my future ministry onto a very new ground. I do not believe that I would have been impacted the way I was if the need for this clarity had not for many years been internalized in me.

Of course, in Rom 8:31-38 it is *God* who loves us, in John 3:16 it is God who loved the world so that he gave his son, and in Luke 15:11-32 Jesus speaks not about his love but about the love of "that father."

By the time I was fifteen I became aware that the rhetoric of the church emphasized Jesus Christ so one-sidedly that the difference between Christ and God, which I clearly found in my own reading of the Bible, was practically reduced to a sort of christomonistic theology of Scripture. The awareness of the problem of that rhetoric and of the findings in Scripture which were always known to systematic theologians—became the beginning of a long learning process in the understanding and interpretation of the theologies of Scripture in both testaments. Indeed, the distinctions in Scripture between its theology of God and its Christology appear to me to be even more important for the biblical theology of the future than they have ever been.

The next memory of "theological interpretation of the Bible" happened in 1935-1936 during my first grade in school, which in Germany has always included religion and still does. The teacher told us stories from Genesis. The girl with me in that class, who twenty years later became my wife, remembers with me the stories about the creation of the world, Adam and Eve, Cain and Abel, the tower of Babel, and Lot and Sodom and Gomorrah. Without knowing and being told, and certainly without reading the texts ourselves, we were in the OT.

We especially remember vividly the teacher's dramatic performance of the story of Noah and the flood, especially of Noah before the beginning of the flood. God, dissatisfied with all people, commanded Noah, a good man, to go to the people and admonish them to quit being bad, or God would bring a big flood and wipe them all out. He also ordered Noah to build a big ark so that he and his family would be saved if the people would not listen. One reason this story stands out in our memories is that the teacher narrated with great passion how Noah appeared in the inn, or pub, of his town—really in one of the inns of our own small home town, where many men were regularly getting drunk from the wine produced by the town's farmers and had no more money for feeding their wives and children. The teacher stepped high on a table and silenced the noise by shouting, "God has sent me to tell you that a great flood will wipe you all out if you don't stop getting drunk but return and be good to your families." But the men laughed at him and threw him out, and he went into his ark and the flood came and drowned them all.

Of many aspects regarding this theological reading of the Bible, I can mention only a few. Specific for my wife's and my recollection of this story was not only the passion of the teacher's performance, but the impression on us that this story was not, as the other stories, taking place in a far away, unknown land and in a long gone past, but in our own time and in our own home town known by us all. It was the story of our own experience. Today, we call this an example of hermeneutical biblical actualization.

In his theological interpretation of the story directly into our homes the teacher made it appear that a story from the OT was just as important as any from the New, that to talk about God from the Bible without talking about Jesus was just as unquestionable as it was customary to talk about Jesus or Jesus Christ, and that it also meant talking about kinds of experience with God other than merely, or only, whether or not to be personally saved.

It is important for us to know that in Germany in those days the OT was taught in the churches and public schools according the religio-historical hermeneutic of the nineteenth century, and neither according to the Barthian theology nor through the lenses of any part of the NT, especially not for children. We were on the way to asking ever more clearly whether things said in the OT are true because they are genuinely and originally Christian, or whether Jesus and the Christians have adopted things because they recognized them as true.

We also experienced our teacher's use of powerful, awe inspiring rhetoric. It was not only his localization of Noah's public appearance in the inns of our vineyard farmers' town, but also his forcefully performed rhetoric which impressed the persuasiveness of what he said on our minds. The genre of rhetoric and its public oratory have played a great role throughout the history of all societies and in their various institutions, including the history of preaching as any church historian will tell us. Rhetorical art and passion are important in preaching today. Particularly, their study takes a significant place in modern biblical scholarship. What are the criteria for the validity of the evidence for, or reference to, rhetoric in Scripture in the interpretation of its theologies?

On account of his persuasive rhetoric, our teacher's theological interpretation of Scripture did very well. He certainly influenced us to internalize the importance of the Bible. Against the background of this influence the awareness grew more and more over the years—later irresistibly reinforced by the memory of the rhetoric of Hitler and Goebbels that more, and something different, had to be recognized as the ground of truth in the interpretation of scriptural theology.

Our teacher's pedagogical intuition did not prevent him from overlooking a few things in his tale of Noah. These things became important later when as a student exegeting Genesis and learning how to read texts correctly I discovered discrepancies between what I was studying and what I remembered.

First of all, the narrative of the text says nothing at all of Noah's public appearance and call on the people to repent—be that at the LORD's order (as in the case of Jonah) or at Noah's own initiative. Second, the introduction to the flood story, Gen 6:5-8, does not say that all life had lost its right to continue to exist and would therefore be wiped out because of the universal capital sin of alcoholism—bad as alcoholism is, but because of the universal corruption of—not only the humans but—the whole earth by violence! One thing must be very clear at the outset; reading the Bible theologicaly has to start with, and must be accountable to, the texts.

As is well known by exegetes from the Book of Genesis on and from the Old Testament's terminology for sin, the word "violence" is used as the decisive label at this juncture in Genesis' primeval history. It is inclusive of all other "sins," for the irreparably corrupted condition of the whole earth, and thus as the compelling reason for the flood.

Compared to this massive reason for the flood, our teacher's hermeneutical application to the pervasive breadth of alcoholism in our town —bad as it was and as bad as alcoholism is—amounted to a trivialization of the theology of the flood story. It was not a recontextualization of the plot and concept of the story, but a reconceptualization. It changed the concept of the irreducible reason for the ruin of the whole earth to a concept of the damage to the fabric of families by uncontrolled social attitudes in a wine region—and that in 1935-1936, a time increasingly terrorizing Germany by violence, a development which in the end brought the whole earth, only for the second time after the first "flood," to the brink of another annihilation. Today and from now on, the earth can be ruined by violence, not by alcoholism.

How tragically we can misread the signs of our own times when our theological interpretation of Scripture is more influenced by our immediate concerns than by a close reading and exegesis, yes, exegesis of the texts. One thing must be very clear: reading the Bible theologicaly has to start with, and must be accountable to, the texts. As one remains committed to exegesis, one has again and again to update, upgrade, and correct previous interpretations and theological interpretations.

The picture of narrative art and of rhetoric alluded to is just one example for the basic discussion of the criteria for the validity of the categories of narrative and rhetorical interpretation in interpreting the Bible theologically. There is no theological interpretation of the Bible that does not also take place by, in, and through narrative and rhetoric; but the fact of narrative and/or rhetoric—the Bible's as well as ours—is, as such, no evidence for a sufficient reading of the Bible theologically, not even as it refers to God or Jesus. Neither the fact of it being narrative, as compared to other types of language, nor its more or less forceful performance, nor its persuasive or unpersuasive effects in communication, nor even a particular content prove as such theological validity.

The beginning of my awareness of what it means to speak of "Scripture"—in the singular—dates back to the time of my confirmation in the spring of 1943. At the public examination before the congregation the minister asked me to recount the names, or titles, of all the books of the Bible, beginning with the Books of "Moses" and ending with the Book of Revelation. At that time I was unfamiliar with most of the contents of that whole Bible. But I began to realize that Scripture is a written book which consists of many Books. I was beginning to realize that I was living with more than a few words, passages, stories, Psalms, and with more than some of the Books in the Bible. I was living with the whole Bible with all its books literally in my hand. Over the years this knowledge of the names of all the books, and even more their contents, has meant that I must distinguish between the interpretation of the theology of a particular text (or book, or topic or concept) and the interpretation of the theology of the whole Bible.

The two foci in interpretation are not the same. Since any part of Scripture may mean the same as that of another part, be similar to, be more or less important, or agree with some and disagree with other parts, I cannot accept that the theological interpretation of Scripture is understood sufficiently as long as it interprets a part of Scripture in isolation without considering the question of the relationship of this theology to the theology, and theologies, of all other parts. As long as interpretation of the theology of any part in Scripture is left standing alone, it should be called interpretation of the theology of a text or topic or concept, but not interpretation of Scripture. Interpretation of Scripture means more. While presupposing the indispensable interpretation of the theology of any part, it has to interpret the theology of each in the light of its relationship to all—or its interpretation is not interpretation of that part as Scripture.

If this demand seems to be too lofty for practitioners—even theoreticians have difficulty seeing the rationale for it, I should like to ask what happens in the mind and rhetoric of a preacher who from Sunday to Sunday preaches on a different text, subject, or aspect. Is he or she not aware that he/she must in one way or another avoid saying something in one sermon which contradicts what he/she has said before? Or must he/she wait until an attentive parishioner points the contradictions out to her/him when shaking hands at the exit? Of course, in order to approach this demand, it is necessary that one has read the whole Bible and keeps reading it—which was in my case a precondition for being admitted to theological studies.

By the time I was seventeen (1946) I decided to solve the disparity between the picture of creation in Gen 1 and of the Natural Sciences by writing for my own benefit a seventy page paper. Some palaeontological literature, already then outdated, told me that the human race was five million years old, the animals older, the earth still older, and the universe even more so.

That information triggered my curiosity because it did not seem to agree with what I had heard my minister either say or imply: that the world was created in six days 5761 years ago. Since the Bible could not be wrong and those sciences would have to be at least halfway wrong, at any rate not more than speculative, I set out to solve the problem by establishing a synthesis between the natural sciences and the Bible on the basis that the "days" in Gen 1 should be read in light of Ps 90:4: "For a thousand years in thy sight are but as yesterday when it is past, or as a watch in the night." As a result, if one is a bit flexible, one thousand may be expanded to ten thousand or one hundred thousand (to a million would be ideal but seemed too daring), while one should assume that those "scientists" guess too much and their number of some five million might amount to half or a tenth as much. I concluded that sometime in the future, both the natural scientific and the biblical counting would coincide.

My minister read, approved, and complimented me for my theory; one of my professors looked at it, did not touch it, smiled, said nothing, and walked away. I do not know what happened to the script, but I do know what happened to me. The issue would be, and for many is, laughable at best if it would not play a highly visible role in many churches and also in the politics of education in no less than an enlightened country such as the United States. Since then I have learned that I knew nothing about reading the Bible on its own terms, its texts and their contexts, and their variations and individual presuppositions. I have learned that all the while I was trying to defend the Bible against the ever advancing modern sciences of all fields I knew nothing about the broad evidence in the Bible itself about its own knowledge of the state of sciences at its times. Apart from the fact that Gen 1 explicitly reflected the meaning of the Jewish Sabbath, one of the two main signals for Jewish identity (the other being circumcision), I had not even recognized that the text was not interested at all in how many years ago the world was created. Genesis 1 was above all interested in depicting the creation of the world as a cosmos structured out of chaos with a depiction of its spatial formation, which with its wrong geocentric view is very different from our knowledge today (cf. e.g., Ps 19:1-6), and also with a depiction of time focusing on a pattern of a never-ending cycle of seven days, regardless of the seasonal cycles otherwise attested in the Bible and even those indicated in Gen 1 itself.

In trying to defend the Bible I had to realize that I was actually undermining its validity and influence, simply because I did not know anything about the terms for proper exegesis, including the exegesis of its theological interest. Such exegesis would show that the Bible is in principle not in a running contest with the empirical data established by the sciences, but accompanies all of them at all times as to the meaning of and the question for truth in these developments for our understanding of the world, of life, human life, and our own lives.

Ten years later, 1957, I had to teach religion in a senior class of a German high school in economics. The agenda prescribed OT. My reading assignment for the start was Gen 1. Before the discussion started, one student asked, "Do you believe this nonsense?" We started analyzing the structure of that text, and for the rest of the entire year all structures until the Books of Samuel. I never had a problem with these economists.

If in our churches we consider the Bible as a textbook for the natural sciences in competition with or even instead of the relentlessly ongoing scientific discoveries, or even if we treat this issue as a mute one in our churches, the Bible is by our own influence bound to lose its role as a compass for the future of the human race. Whether the biblical depictions of the world are derived from the state of sciences at the time or are mythopoeic or derived from patterns of real experiences (as in the Wisdom literature), they represent, perfectly legitimately, the knowledge of their time, which in some respects reflects our own experiences and in many others does not.

Moreover, we are confronted for the first time in all of human history with developments that were never imagined or believed possible by the biblical generations. We can destroy all life on earth ourselves, and I must leave it to the ethicists as to what to say about our dealings with the genetic code and a few more minor problems. What, then, may the role be of the theological reading of the Bible in the light of today's scientific development for the life of humanity?

In the fall of 1949, the year before the beginning of my theological studies, I was in my second year as a full time apprentice for the ministry in the German Methodist Church. In a smaller town there was a week of tent-evangelism, with an extra daily hour for young teenagers in the afternoon. Assigned to conduct such an hour, I proposed to the more than forty boys and girls present to tell them the biblical story about David and Goliath (from 1 Sam 17). Whereupon I met with their collective roar, "We know that story." I had to catch my breath, but immediately shifted saying, "O.K., then let's enact the story, and you design the enactment following the story step by step." That was new for them, and it became quickly clear that their knowledge of the story was very superficial. This afforded me the opportunity to set the story up by telling them each part specifically. Of course, the lot had to determine who would belong to the army of the Philistines! I myself picked the smallest boy for David and the biggest one against his resistance for Goliath.

After all was set and each of the prime contestants in front of his army made his proper speech to the other, I finally turned the two loose against each other. Contrary to the narrative, my Goliath was not prepared to let himself be beaten by the little boy. Instead, he lifted him up, threw him on the floor, sat over him, triumphantly raised his hand and shouted, supported by the roar of his "Philistine" army, "Victory," while little David and his "Israelite army" roared "Foul."

I had my second major problem in this hour, this time in terms of substance rather than merely of didactics. My Goliath's victory was against the narrative, but it was not against common human experience, according to which the powerful and heavily armed defeat the little people and more poorly armed. David is called, among other things, "a man of valor, a man of war" (1 Sam 16:18), and he was obviously expert in using his shepherd's sling with five smooth stones instead of the king's heavy armor (1 Sam 17:38-40). Yet when he responds to Goliath he does not say: "You come to me with a sword and with a spear and with a javelin; but I come to you with my shepherd's sling, five smooth stones and my military training of this weapon, and I will demonstrate to you the superiority of a light weapon over heavy armament." He says: "I come to you in the name of the LORD of hosts, the God of the armies of Israel, whom you have defied. This day the LORD will deliver you into my hand" . . . so that "all this assembly may know that the LORD saves not with sword and spear." The narrative does not continue "but with a sling"; it continues "for the battle is the Lord's, and he will give you into our hand," (1 Sam 17:45-47). David answers Goliath with a theological, not with a military argument or with a theological focus on the weapon he is using.

Thus, I had to explain to my teenagers what in this very moment I had to find out myself, something no one had taught me, namely, why in their enactment the big boy's victory is quite normal, and also why in the narrative David was victorious because he was the anointed one, the messiah. I had to tell them a bit from the context which is presupposed for 1 Sam 17, without which David's victory cannot be understood. This context, and the entire complex of 1 Sam 9-31, is based on the concept of messiah and of the first two messiahs in the history of Israel's election.

Of course, the theology of this story stands in the context of an endless number of texts in the OT about Yahweh's role in war and peace, about the difference between the validity of military might and justice and righteousness in the earth (cf. Jer 9:23-24) or the fear of Yahweh and the hope in his steadfast love (cf. Ps 33:13-19), and many other aspects. One has to be careful. As desirable as it may be to say that, e.g., on the basis of the Old Testament's theology of creation or of its eschatology, war is sin, this would mean that God himself is the greatest sinner, at least as long as he is involved in the arena of human history. Also, the prohibition "you shall not kill" or "murder" obviously extends neither to killing in warfare nor to the prescriptions for the death penalty for a host of typical violations. NATO parlance now emphasizes the need in the armaments of its soldiers for their heightened "lethality" effects on the enemy.

It is very clear that when reading the Bible theologically, we are not suddenly on a ground where all problems of Bible reading are behind us. On the contrary, the theological aspects of the texts create the question before us precisely because of our need for their interpretation as Scripture. And if anyone has a final recipe for the application of foregone conclusions on this or any other issue, I have not seen it.

Whatever my experiences in Bible reading had been up to the years of my theological studies, and have been since then, was decisively streamlined through the lectures and seminars in OT and NT. One basic result of that education was that it indelibly impressed on my mind that in any responsible reading of the Bible I had first of all to be accountable to what a text says and, as far as can be determined, means, with particular attention to the aspect of its original places and times. In other words, historical-critical exegesis and its tools became a steady companion of my work with the Bible. It taught me to focus on texts, individually, on their flow, the parts within them, and on their sentences and words. I think that this kind of education proved to be the most effective for my preparation of Bible lessons and sermons throughout my ministry and career until today.

Surely, I continue to experience what many others also experience. Knowing that I have to preach a sermon, I imagine my subject and also a text—which I presume to have known for a long time—and begin to draft or even write my sermon until, needing to check at least a quote, I recognize that the text says and means something different and aims at a direction which is very different from the direction for which I want to use it for my own message.

The other big experience in biblical studies was my growing awareness of the genre of NT and OT theology through the encounter with the great designs of NT Theology by Rudolf Bultmann and of OT Theology by Gerhard von Rad, who was to become my mentor. In the trenches of my ministry, i.e., in my weekly work for my sermons and Bible studies, I was certainly influenced by the grand designs of these and other theologies. However, I became more immediately impacted by my regular involvement with the exegesis of the texts and the stressful need to come to grips with the question, What is the text's point? Despite growing exegetical experience, that need has never ceased to be intellectually challenging and laborious.

Interpretation via exegesis of texts is thereby only one approach to theological interpretation. What about the treatment of a biblical topic, which requires attention to texts but focuses on perspectives sought across many texts? Theological interpretation of Scripture does not happen through exegesis of texts alone. How often does a preacher speak about a text, how often about a biblical topic, and how often about a topic for which references to Scripture are at best a parenthetical matter?

Bultmann's work may be an example. In his commentaries he follows the order of a biblical book at a time. By contrast, his theology is systematically built across literary corpora, e.g., the entire Pauline corpus, according to the major ideas or concepts of each corpus. Not to be overlooked is the great number of his specific studies about particular subjects. Such specific studies on particular topics deserve primary attention. Rather than having to contend with big volumes on the entire theology, the minister can afford to study a particular subject, and even learn from it how to study a subject on her/his own.

It is that ongoing weekly task in the minister's life for which he/she needs no prefabricated solutions but guidelines which are helpful for doing interpretation her/himself. Such guidelines should be helpful, not oppressively and discouragingly demanding. They ought to point to what can be done, even as always more can be done. A preacher who knows that he/she has not come to grips with all is better off than one who is very sure of her/his opinion.

ESSENTIAL GUIDELINES FOR THEOLOGICAL INTERPRETATION OF SCRIPTURE—WITH PARTICULAR CONSIDERATION OF THE OLD TESTAMENT

The following suggestions do not cover all that can be done, but they focus on the essentials for interpreting Scripture theologically which can be practiced by all practitioners. The approach to interpretation needs to distinguish between two steps: 1) the exegesis of the theology of an individual text or texts; and 2) the interpretation of its/their meaning in the horizon of Scripture as a whole.

For working out the message of a text or a biblical theological topic, the practitioner does her/his own work applying all learning achieved. He/she will make sure to compare results with those of others published in commentaries and lexica. In this respect, I am saying what seminary education has always said.

However, I wish to emphasize a particular aspect in exegetical work, the decisive importance of which as a distinct methodological step in exegesis is either not taught at all, or highlighted insufficiently. It is at least not clearly observed in interpretation and even in scholarly commentaries not clearly recognized. It concerns the interpreter's specific attention to the role of concepts in the texts. Any exegesis that fails to recognize the concept on which a text rests and by which a text, each text, is controlled, will fall short of a sufficient interpretation.

By concept is meant a maxim, or ideological principle, on which the plot or message of a text rests. It may or may not be directly stated in the text. For example, one may have a text that is based on a concept saying or meaning that

"Justice is what God does," in contrast to a text based on a concept saying or meaning that "God does what is just," or "Justice for all is what serves God's relationship to his chosen people Israel or the Christian believers," in contrast to "Justice for Israel or the Christian believers is what serves God's relationship to all of God's creatures."

The theological interpretation of the Scriptures cannot avoid realizing the theological concepts which are operative in and control the texts. The concepts are at work in the stories of texts, within biblical books, and across all biblical books. They can be discerned from the study of the texts and are often directly signaled in them. Their identification has nothing to do with the abuse of the texts for the sake of abstracting ideas from them; it has everything to do with the conceptual side of the texts themselves.

Critics have objected that the focus on concepts would amount to a retrogression from exegetical advancements into medieval methods, into a world of abstract ideas, that it would mean to subject the biblical texts to philosophical ideas imposed upon them from outside, that the search for concepts and their systemic nature would be totally foreign to the Bible. All these objections are indefensible. They reflect what I consider outdated positions regarding the nature of the biblical literature itself, of any literature for that matter.

I know of no text within which a concept is not operative, which could be renarrated or recited verbatim but not understood or misunderstood without its concept. Its understanding belongs inevitably to the interpretation of the reality of a text, not to an abstraction from it. A text does not only speak, it also thinks, just as God is depicted not only as speaking and acting, but also as a thinking God. Compare, for the start, texts about "the plan of Yahweh" or the thoughts of Yahweh.

To interpret the texts' theological concepts means more than to retell their story, their topic or theme, and plot. At least in its narrated text, each story is unique, whereas many stories can belong to the same concept. When retold on its own terms, the story of a text is retold best, not only alongside its plot, but in transparency to its concept. While the story represents the side of a concept actualized, the concept represents the side of the story in its basic perspective.

Concepts are by and large undergirding texts without being explicitly named in them. They are often also explicitly pointed out in the texts by the Bible's own or our big interpreting words: creation, history, existence, purity, impurity, sin, injustice, violence, oppression, law, justice, liberation, love, mercy, peace, an eschatologically based worldview, a view of an indefinitely ongoing world (as a basis for ethical orientation), the election of Israel, the nations, faith, wisdom, fear of Yahweh, knowledge of God, and so on.

I would like to remind ministers of the fact that with their sermons they virtually always have a topic which is conceptualized even when it is kept in close contact with the exposition of a text. Whether they default on meeting the text and its concept or not, they are certainly correct in assuming that when speaking in terms of both the story of a text and its concept, they keep together what belongs together.

Whoever asks for the conceptual maxims/principles for the sake of the theological interpretation of Scripture will be sent on to a way of studying and finding results that lead beyond much that one has been taught or is found in various publications.

Examples of concepts by which texts are controlled. In 1 Sam 11 is the story of how King Saul liberated Israel from the Ammonite invasion. Inspired by the Spirit he united the tribes, defeated the Ammonites, and granted pardon to those in Israel who had rejected him as king. The charisma unites the Israelite tribes, gives victory over the foreign aggressors, and gives pardon domestically for those under death sentence by the judgment of the people!

One has to understand the concept on which the entire story of Saul rests. Saul had just been anointed (1 Sam 9:1-10:16) and elected as king (10:17-27). He was Israel's first Messiah—as king. This is the threefold way his messianic role functions. Compare the total loss of this empowerment after his rejection for one act of disobedience. The one who had pardoned the criminals mercilessly persecutes the innocent David. The spirit of the medium at Endor can only reveal his defeat to him who originally was empowered by the Spirit. He who was victorious ends in defeat and suicide. The story is part of the concept of Messiah and its variations throughout Old and New Testament times.

Another example from Saul: after his victory he was "magnanimous" against those who had despised him (1 Sam 10:27), those of whom his followers now demanded—not revenge but, legitimately!—the death penalty, he exercised what we call the prerogative of heads of state to grant the legal act of pardon to convicted criminals. Saul pardoned these criminals, not by saying "I feel great today" but by referring to a higher legal maxim: "Not a man shall be put to death this day, for today the LORD has wrought deliverance in Israel" (1 Sam 11:13). The granting of pardon is a forensic act to celebrate an event of liberation (from danger or injustice) or a state of liberty in which societal divisions are overcome and the ground is laid for societal peace. Whatever any society's stance is on the death penalty issue, it should be clear for biblically experienced people that a system of justice in which there is no room for pardon or clemency is trapped in a dead-end street in which there is no alternative for those deserving death, but only the final solution—to be wiped off the face of the earth and out of the community of the living. We can see here reflected the awareness of the tension between punishment and pardon in the system of justice and the notion that pardon is, not an alternative to, but the better kind of justice, ethically to be implemented wherever possible in consonant with the existing or special well-being of the society.

Of course, to refuse pardon or mercy on the grounds that a sentence, when reviewed, is confirmed to have been correct, that no fault has been found in the proceedings leading to it, means that whoever takes such a stance has not yet understood the principle in the first place on which pardon rests. Pardon is not granted when a condemnation is proved wrong. Nobody wrongly condemned needs to be pardoned. He/she deserves to be restored, and a wrong judgment must be confessed by those who had rendered it. When pardon is granted, it is granted in the light of a correct, and even confirmed, condemnation. Lastly, pardon represents the forensic matrix for the theology of the forgiveness of sinners!

It should be obvious that the issue of justice and righteousness, above all the aspect of the justice of God, is at stake in and assumed by all OT books. This issue is not confined only to those texts in which the terminology for it occurs or where its subject is the issue under discussion. The issue of God's justice is biblically indivisible, and at any rate much more prevalent as is commonly seen. Indeed, it is difficult to assume that the Old Testament's "knowledge of God" is anywhere unrelated to its concept of God's justice. How could God be anything but the God of justice above all else? The subject of theodicy is an all-encompassing, central biblical issue, not an invention by philosophical theologians.

A third example is in Hos 11:1-9, a text which reflects the conflict between the justice of punishment and the justice of pardon in God's own heart. God's decision is to pardon Israel, not because of his feelings but because "I am God and not man, the Holy one in your midst, and I will not come to destroy" (v. 9). Pardon is known as the better justice. Not to exercise it would mean Israel's end in destruction. That the concept of justice is not seen simplistically in Scripture can be extensively studied. To be sure, the prophets' condemnation of injustice, above all social injustice, and their call for the establishment or restoration of justice towers forever in all human history as a signal for what it means to speak about God among the humans.

As a fourth example, Ps 82 depicts a trial proceeding in heaven, the moment in which the transition happens from polytheism to monotheism, on the ground that the God of Israel (the one who is meant in the Psalm) condemns the gods to death because they have judged unjustly, shown partiality to the wicked, and failed to protect the weak, fatherless, afflicted, destitute, and needy. Thus, he is to rise and judge all the nations. The protection of the underprivileged is the decisive criterion for the justification, the legitimization of the universal Lordship of God—monotheistically! What we have here is not a concept that monotheism is a proof of truth as such, but that it depends itself on a proof of truth: the truth of universally inclusive justice for which the specific criterion is the deity's protection of the lowly.

Similarly Abraham engages God in a theological argument, persuading God to admit that it is a better kind of justice to try to save a sinful community on account of a few righteous people, than to destroy all—including a few righteous ones on account of the overwhelming mass of sinners (Gen 18:22-33). Compare God's better justice toward Nineveh in the Book of Jonah, in contrast to the prophets' understanding of justice. Of course, one does not yet speak about the separation of the righteous and the sinners into separate communities, and heaven and hell, nor about the salvation of all by the righteousness of the One.

I would also like to point out that the concept of liberation is never unrelated to the concept of justice in the texts. It is subordinate to the concept of justice, a part in the process of justice. Liberation is liberation from injustice and oppressing realities and aims beyond itself at justice. Justice is the criterion for the truth of liberation.

Scripture's total range. Any interpretation of Scripture, and the interpretation of any part of it via texts or topics, requires that one is aware of Scripture's total range, and as far as possible familiar with its contents. For the NT this means not only knowledge of the Gospels and Acts but knowledge of all other writings. The matter is much more complicated for the OT. Not only is it more than three times as long (more than five times when one includes the Apocrypha and Pseudepigrapha as the Roman Catholic Church does), it is also much less known and in

Christian communities has been considered as less important than the NT.

It is for many reasons unrealistic and unfair to discuss the issue of theological interpretation of the OT without facing the vast perspectives that are open before us in the contents of the OT Scriptures. In the Pentateuch come the themes of creation, fall, primordial history of humanity, the election of the patriarchs, the life of Moses from his birth to his death from Exodus through Deuteronomy, the rise and oppression of Israel in and its liberation from Egypt, the Deity's covenant with Israel at Sinai, the preparation for and execution of the cultic-military campaign toward the Promised Land. Then, from Joshua on we are told of the conquest of and settlement in the land, the times of the judges and the centuries of the monarchies in the north and the south with its capital Jerusalem and their end, much of it complemented by the Books of Chronicles. This is to say nothing of the books of the prophets, the Psalms—a Bible all by itself—and the books called the Writings, or Wisdom Literature. Practitioners should and can be familiar with these contents.

In view of the vast panorama of endlessly changing divers issues and perspectives, any quest for theological interpretation of Scripture is confronted with the question of how any individual text or topic appears in light of all others—precisely because all coexist within the same whole. Of course, one must allow that nobody knows all, let alone at all times, that everybody grows gradually into dealing with these materials, from case (study) to case (study), and that all about them cannot be said at any one time.

What is needed is a focus on such guidelines that enable every interpreter to pursue a line of searching that is always applicable, guidelines that alert her/him as to what to look for when trying to compare an individual theology with what Scripture teaches as a whole. In the following, I want to point to those guidelines which in my experience are basic, can be pursued by everyone, and lead to better understanding without being restrictive.

The relative importance of the so-called "unifiers." In the field of biblical theology one frequently finds reference to notions which point to the unity of the Bible. Such unifiers, which in one sense or another are common to the biblical books, must not be ignored. However, whatever their importance, they cannot solve the problem of the theological diversity in these books, not even the conceptual diversity within a unifier itself.

The Bible is monotheistically based, but its monotheism is within itself theologically pluralistic. The same is true for concepts such as inspiration or revelation. The entire Bible is inspired or revealed by God or the Holy Spirit. But then, it was God or the Holy Spirit himself who dictated divers, sometimes complementary and sometimes contradictory messages, contents, and concepts, all of which can be "harmonized" only at the expense of the gross violation of what they say and mean. None of the unifiers lends itself to answering the phenomenon of diversity in the Bible.

Also, the remark that the Bible speaks about God is supposed to be such a unifier. It too does not help, quite apart from the fact that it does not reflect correctly the horizon of all Scripture when it speaks of God. Apart from the Book of Esther, the Bible speaks from its first page in the OT to its last in the NT about the relationship of God to the—God's—world and the relationship of the world to

God—and in this order! It speaks specifically about the presence of God in God's world and the ways of this presence. It speaks neither about God without God's world, nor about a world without God.

In order to distinguish between the view of the world vis à vis God and the view of both God and world, I use the word "reality" for the latter. For the biblical view of reality, the aspect of both God and world is fundamental, whereas the biblical view of world signifies the view of creation vis à vis God—the created, sustained and to be consummated. Even this unifier, the view of the relationship of God and world in a view of total reality, cannot solve the problem of the great diversity of the kinds and degrees within that framework. Nevertheless, it does represent, as far as I see, the one aspect by which theological interpretation of Scripture can be defined, recognized, and pursued. It is the aspect of the totality of reality as perceived in the relationship of God and the totality of the world.

God's relation to the whole world. The biblical vision that God is related to the whole world is fundamental. It means that God is in principle understood as the God of the whole world and that any understanding of God's particular relationship to a particular part of the world needs to consider that kind of relationship in light of God's relationship to the whole world. The part itself must be considered as part of the whole world, not as a separate entity in isolation from "the rest" of the world, and that God himself is indivisible. In the biblical understanding the God who would not everywhere and always be the God of all would be no god at all.

That God is always understood as the God of all does not require that this notion is always explicitly at issue. But it is at issue implicitly in everything the Bible says about God's relationship to anything in the world. Practically, that means that when dealing with any particular biblical subject, the minister—indeed we all—should be aware that this subject should be seen in light of its meaning in the whole.

References to biblical evidence regarding this perspective abound. The created world does not end when human history begins, and human history does not end when the history of the election of the patriarchs and of Israel begins. As much as the largest portions of the OT focus on Israel, nowhere is Israel understood as the only nation on earth or in isolation from the other nations, even where it sets itself apart by its own kind of Yahweh based monotheism. The same must be said for the Old Testament's attention to individuals, especially in many Psalms and the Wisdom literature. Of course, the inclusion of the particular, e.g., individual persons, under the universal does not mean at all that the deity's attention to individuals would be irrelevant.

In biblical theological interpretation attention to the specific or particular and to the whole or universal should go hand in hand. Whether any particular aspect is thereby particularistically separate or exemplifies the presence of God universally has to be asked and determined.

The election of Israel. The OT is for its most part overwhelmingly preoccupied with the theological focus on Israel's election by the universal God Yahweh as his one special nation among all nations, indeed, in the entire cosmos. This basic concept consists of a variety of aspects which are especially expressed in some covenants (most prominently in the covenants of Abraham, Sinai, Moses-

Deuteronomy, and David-Zion/Jerusalem). It is explicit in or undergirds the entire Pentateuch, all historical and prophetic books, the Psalms, and can scarcely be excluded from the Wisdom Books with their Yahwehistic orientation. That Israel is considered as especially elected, chosen by God, must not be ignored let alone questioned or disputed. This theological notion is a basic fact of Israel's historical identity. It must be accepted and respected by all. Inasmuch as Israel has been persecuted and oppressed for it as such, such oppression has always been wrong, and Israel's election must forever be defended by all.

Under discussion has to be how the theology of this election depicts Israel's relationship to the nations, and the nations', i.e., the Gentiles', relationship to Israel, and how it depicts the relationship between the God of Israel and the God of all nations. For Israel's election means everywhere its special place among the nations, and nowhere the replacement of the nations on earth by the one nation Israel. Through having elected Israel, God is considered as the deity of both the nations and Israel and not as the deity of either alone.

The interpretation of these perspectives has to focus on whether the texts depict Israel as the paradigm for the life on earth of all humanity with God, as the light to the nations for their own way following Israel's example, or whether they depict the election of Israel—and, e.g., its Messiah-king—as the satrap or viceroy or governor entitled and empowered to rule the world. In other words, is Israel's election not only claimed but explicated to function in the service of God's presence among and for all nations equally, or is it explicated in the sense that the nations are considered to be witness to and in the service of Yahweh's special, preferred, or even exclusive, covenant relationship with Israel. Is Israel elected for the salvation of humanity, or is humanity's salvation—to whatever extent at all—seen through its submission to the election of Israel?

As far as the deity is concerned, who is always the universal God and never only a national God of Israel, does God as the universal Lord use his election of Israel as the example on earth for his like, equal, equitable relationship to all his nations, or does the same universal Lord use the nations for the sake and benefit of his especially elect and separate Israel? In other words, is justice determined by what God says and does, i.e., by the authority of God, or does God say and do what is just. Is the divinity of God justified by God's commitment to justice?

One may say that whatever Scripture says has to be accepted by us. Then, however, one should be prepared to admit that God is understood as the God of all because he is the God of his people Israel, rather than that God is understood as the God of his people Israel because he is the God of all. The difference affects the basic understanding of any God theology.

The relationship between Israel and the Gentiles and the relationship of God to both the nations and Israel is not a Christian issue. It is an issue between Israel and the nations which is broadly present in the OT, regardless of the NT or any of the other religions or ideologies in the history of humanity. But it affects any and all of these Gentile nations and their own reaction to the persuasiveness or unpersuasiveness of the Old Testament's picture of Israel's and God's relationship to them.

It is doubtful that the nations would at any time be persuaded to heed a warning such as given in Ps 2 to submit to Yahweh and his king installed on

Mount Zion to become the king's heritage, or else the king shall break them with a rod of iron and dash them in pieces like a potter's vessel, lest the Lord be angry and they perish in the way. It is even more than doubtful that this ideology and its rhetoric should represent a believable rationale of the true relationship of the universal God to all his nations.

In a seminar for Jewish teachers of the Jewish Bible, I gave an exegesis of Gen 32:22-32. The last verse relates the custom of the Israelites not to eat from the sinew of the hip because he, Jacob's attacker, had "touched" the hollow of Jacob's thigh so that he was limping. I said that here the Israelites identify with that experience of Jacob, as people struck, perhaps even crippled by God. That is the destiny of the people who have been blessed by being encountered by God: they are God's cripples. One of the rabbis present, knowing that I was not Jewish, asked, "Who do you think these people are?" I said, "Whoever is met this way by God." He said, "No, these are only Jewish people." Whereupon I had to say, "Then your God has nothing to do with the Gentiles, and the Gentiles nothing with your god. We will respect you and your claim, but will go our own way." What I did not want to say to avoid being provocative was what I know as a Christian—that I too am crucified with Christ.

Values. No interpretation that takes the theological nature of the Scriptures seriously can ignore the fundamental fact that they are in everything they address preoccupied with the focus on value, that they are value-based and value-oriented. They do not consider anything as value-neutral or, for that matter, as equi-valent.

To look for values seems today for some to be an obsolete mode in a (post)modern philosophy of pluralism—while even at the same time the whole word cries out over the loss of values, for the need for a quality of life (whatever is meant by this), and for priorities globally, in our society, our families, and individual lives.

Our attention to the Bible's fundamental preoccupation with value—or anti-value—has to be very different from phenomenologically based, value-neutral descriptions of its statements of facts or more or less raw data. Whatever the merits are of such usages of the Bible in auxiliary disciplines, they do not meet its own *raison d'être*.

The Old Testament's recognition of value has nothing to do with a transcendentalist God ontology through which a code of moral values would be "revealed." It reflects the reality of values in Israel's—and not only Israel's—experience of the world, the reality of the world as it is. In this experience, values are marked by different extents and weights, and by opposite qualities for which the two words "good" and "bad" or "evil" are the most general and by no means lightweight expressions.

The values, and the anti-values as well, are experienced as of higher and lower degrees. Things are "better" or "worse"; they are experienced systemically and are in certain types of texts presented systematically. They are in such texts themselves critically prioritized, which is the result of their comparison. And their systemic nature can be studied by us. It is thereby relative whether we point to evidence for the systematization of value-relations in the Bible itself, generated by its writers, or whether we do such systematizing of biblical aspects ourselves even where the Bible has not left us with extra treatises on all possible subjects. At any rate, no theological interpretation of the OT at least can claim validity which fails to face the issue of values and, yes, their systemic relationship in and across the texts.

It becomes inevitable that the value systems intrinsic to the theologies of the different biblical corpora—and those theologies themselves—are compared. They appear to be either complementary or in graded—or to be graded—relation, or in opposition to each other.

According to Deut 26:1-11 the Israelites are expected to bring their tithes from the blessing received in their harvest—thanksgiving for experienced material harvest. In 520 B.C.E. the people had not yet started rebuilding the temple. Their excuse was that they were without any means, too poor, with nothing to give, and that the Lord had not blessed them. Haggai told them they must build the temple first, then the blessing of the Lord will come to you. The difference is that between giving as thanksgiving for received blessing versus giving as condition for the promise of blessing. Of course, the first temple building theology under Solomon was not concerned with the question of the blessing for the people at all. It had to be built by recruited forced labor.

Whether the OT has in any of its corpora presented an all-inclusive doctrine of sin, a totally systematized hamartiology—which it has not—is insignificant compared to the fact that all its references to sin function systemically, i.e., first of all in a framework for an understanding of sin, of anti-value, as opposed to a framework for an understanding of wholeness or justice and/or righteousness, of value. Within this framework for sin, there occur almost one hundred different words for sin which, of course, represent a bewildering variety and diversity of aspects. When studied, regardless of how they appear in the texts, one can see that not every "sin" is equally grave or as light as all others, that their co-existence is not chaotic or value neutral, and that criteria must be recognized for the prioritization of the levels of the gravity of sins, for their systemic understanding, whether it is actualized in some texts or available potentially for actualization.

A theft of someone's property is less grave than the physical damage to that person, and again much less than the murder of a free man(!), compared to the killing of a slave or a woman. While all may be called "violence," the violence done to one or a few is much less grave than violence having corrupted the whole earth. The latter case is but one of many examples that the value orientation of the OT texts is based on both qualifying and quantifying criteria expressed in words, sentences, and texts.

The same systemic nature must also be recognized as underlying the Old Testament's references to punishment for crimes and sins. There are stipulations for compensations, graded according to the degree and/or kind of damage done, for various degrees of fines, for remedial punishment, and for nothing but punishment for the sake of punishment, that also graded, with the ultimate being capital punishment for a very broad list of crimes.

RETROSPECT AND PROSPECT

I have tried to focus especially on the problem of the theological interpretation of the OT and to give the OT the right to its own opinion, without interference from the perspectives of the NT. I have left on the sideline the hermeneutical question, the question of the Old Testament's significance, validity, and truth for today.

It should be clear that the word "interpretation" points to a task that includes more than merely Bible reading in a pre-interpretative way. It points to our responsibility for conscious accounting of what we read. Such interpretation is demanded of us precisely because the Bible does not do it for us.

We must neither forget nor overlook that the Bible, including the OT, has been read by millions of individuals throughout many generations for their daily edification or guidance, and that without the knowledge of a more or less elaborate interpretative framework, and it continues to be read that way today. Also, it has had its place in our hymns, which is especially true for the Psalms and some prophetic voices. These kinds of experience are very much part of the biography of many of us, with their beneficial sides without which many of us would not be where we are, but also with their deficient and often quite faulty sides. My life time experience with the Bible teaches me that I am not automatically on the right track, following God's footsteps simply because and as long as I read the Bible. Interpretation is therefore more than reading it at face value.

Now, we may imply that we are on the right track when we interpret the Bible "theologically," in distinction from archeological, sociological, or historical interpretation, interpretation as literature, descriptive interpretation, and so on. Are we assuming, then, that interpreting "theologically," or even by "theologizing," is fail safe interpretation, especially when we develop it with the support of our exegetical and interpretative methods?

Is not the opposite true? Is it not true that the more we exegete especially the theologies of the texts and the more we discern their concepts, the more the pluralism of these theologies, their diversity and even divisions appear? Does interpretation "theologically" not confront us with the problem more than any other interpretation, namely, with the fact that "theology" does not solve but radicalizes the problem? Which theology? What kind of "theology"? What are the theological criteria, not for interpreting the Bible theologically, but for interpreting the true theologies in it, or their network, in the face of their own higher or lower grades of validity or even their invalid theologies? Unless we face these questions, our talk about interpreting Scripture theologically may reveal us as nothing more than apologists, a priori defenders of the Bible, regardless of what it says, simply on the ground that everything it says is canonized, canonic, the canon, and beyond questioning.

It is for these reasons that I have tried to demarcate a set of guidelines which can be of help to every serious student of Scripture to pursue the search—the search!—for the better theological perspective in her or his theological reading of the Bible:

1) keeping the total Bible in mind, not only parts of it
2) realizing that the "unifiers" do not answer the aspects of theological diversity
3) realizing that the relationship between God and the world is from beginning to the end of the world the most universal and founda-

tional perspective, or God is not God and the world is not God's, and that God is known and experienced through the experience of the world which is the script and the handwriting of God
4) looking for the concepts of and in the texts, not only for their stories, but looking for both concept and story
5) realizing the importance of values in the texts and their concepts and of anti-values, because nothing is value-neutral or equivalent
6) finally and always following the Bible's own heuristic mechanism for comparing the theologies and their values, for recognizing their systemic order, and for finding the better ones.

For interpreting the OT theologically what, then, is the perspective in it that is foundational to all other ones? It appears to me that the one theological criterion by which the OT determines its own theological relevance, without which it could not stand up in its own right, without which everything else it says would become theologically meaningless and irrelevant, is its conviction about God's relationship to and presence in his world, especially among the humans—all humans—and in the history of the nations—all nations, and therefore the world's relationship to God.

This criterion does not ignore the importance of the election of Israel. But a theology of the OT in which God is not first of all perceived as the God of all, in whose service for all also the elect have their place, would amount to its fundamental contradiction of what is also affirmed in it, i.e., the universality of God. It knows that the God who is not first of all the God of all, is a no-god. As the relationship of God and the world and humans is fundamental, so are the values in that relationship, the positive values, not the destructive ones, the values that are signaled by the concepts of goodness, blessing, justice, peace.

In the texts, these values are mostly discussed within the framework of Israel's society. Yet it is the question of whether they are only relevant for Israel, or whether they are relevant for Israel because they are the values for the life of all humans and nations. If the latter aspect is denied, God's relationship to the nations through these values would be irrelevant, unless the nations claim these values for themselves anyway, which is indeed what many of us have been doing when we apply prophetic messages about justice in Israel to all of us. We can do this because they belong to all, or God is not first of all the God of all. The decisive criterion for the theological truth of the OT and for the validity of its own theologies lies in the possibility to interpret it for the benefit of the coexistence of the nations in human history, their coexistence in mutual pursuit of justice, peace, and blessing equally for all.

NOTE

1. On the analysis of the structures of the Old Testament's texts, cf. *The Forms of the Old Testament Literature* (Grand Rapids: Eerdmans). It is technical, but the only biblical commentary series which is based on the presentation of the structure of all texts. Cf. also the collection of essays *Reading the Bible for a New Millennium: Form, Concept, and Theological Perspective*; vol. 1: *Theological and Hermeneutical Studies*; vol. 2: *Exegetical and Theological Studies*; (ed. W. Kim et al.; Harrisburg, Penn.: Trinity Press International, 2000).

RESPONSE TO KNIERIM

Stephen Chapman

I thank Prof. Knierim for his reflections on the theological interpretation of Scripture, for his effort to formulate principles or guidelines according to which such interpretation is best done and, above all perhaps, for his extended reminder of the importance of personal experience in the formulation of biblical theology and the formation of biblical theologians.

Of course, that personal experience plays an important role in interpretation is a "given," but the character of personal experience varies, as Knierim himself notes. I would still emphasize that we should caution ourselves not to presume that the category of "personal experience" possesses a uniform profile or that it is in any way autonomous. As Knierim shows, his own personal experience was formed in interactions with other individuals and communities, most notably for him (because it seems to have been largely negative) the church.

This aspect of experience poses a question that Knierim does not address: namely, whether any discussion of the theological interpretation of Scripture must not also reflect on which ecclesial practices best model a vital and fruitful interaction with the Bible, especially for young people in the church (e.g., pre-seminary!). In Knierim's case these practices seem to have been misleading in various ways—at least from his perspective—which thus appears to frame the larger issue for him as one in which the critical scholar must work autonomously, free from what "they" do in the church.

Today the most pressing need for biblical studies is not greater "critical distance" from the church and its traditions, but for joint discussion and common endeavor, such as we are about here at this conference. Knierim strongly implies the contrary, that "real" theological interpretation is better left to the experts who reside in the ivy-covered walls of academe.

Let me mention those points about which Knierim and I seem to be in substantial agreement. First, I agree whole-heartedly that theological interpretation has to "start with" and "be accountable to" the biblical text, that it is not enough simply to use religious rhetoric in a loud voice. I also agree that the interpreter cannot only view individual texts in isolation (although procedurally it may be important at times), but in theological interpretation must move beyond a single text to the rest of Scripture, seeking a consistent view of the whole Bible in its "total range." In other words, one cannot finally preach Paul's view of faith without mentioning James' teaching on good works and vice versa—not necessarily in the same sermon, but certainly within a single term of ministry in a particular congregation! I also agree that theological features are integral to the biblical text, that these features are conceptual (or at least can be described conceptually), and that the explication of such concepts involves more than renarration.

I think I also agree that theological interpretation must be "critical," although here I question exactly how Knierim understands this term. He glosses this aspect as a matter of "original places in biblical times," but for me this formulation does not describe the "critical" dimension of theological interpretation fully or even fairly enough. If I understand Knierim correctly when he rejects "phenomenologically-based, value-neutral descriptions" as incommensurate with the Bible's own preoccupation with "value," then I also agree with him on this point (although I have difficulty reconciling this phrase with his earlier talk of the need for an "objective" unifier!). Finally, I agree with Knierim that theological interpretation does not represent a "failsafe option" in and of itself, that it cannot be conducted in isolation from other approaches to the biblical text, that theological interpretation cannot consist of "special pleading" or "pious harmonizing" and that the learning of interpretation cannot be restricted to seminary, but must be pursued as part of a life-long engagement with the Bible.

Perhaps at this point I have not gotten some of this exactly right, but if I have, then my basic criticism of Knierim's essay is that I do not quite see how his rhetoric and his suggested guidelines are compatible with his exegesis, especially the negative examples ("paradigms") he relates. Let me briefly describe a few instances of what I mean.

Knierim levels the charge of "christomonism" against the Sunday School song "Jesus Loves Me" alleging that although it provided an early sense of the Bible that was for him not a "bad beginning," in this song the critical NT distinction between God and Christ is effaced through a "thoughtless rendering."

There is, I would admit, a potential theological problem inherent in such an effacement. G. E. Wright certainly milked this same problem for all it was worth in the heyday of the biblical theology movement by criticizing just about any hymn directed to Jesus rather than to God.[1] On the other hand, I have extreme difficulty in agreeing that the theological consequences of little children singing "Jesus Loves Me" can possibly be so dire! Moreover, and more to the point, what about those NT texts in which the "distance" between the first and second persons of the Trinity is so shockingly overcome (e.g., Jn 10:30; 17:22), or in which Jesus himself is addressed as Savior and Lord (e.g., Acts 2:36)? Is Knierim suggesting that from the perspective of the NT "faith in God" and "faith in Christ" constitute rival claims? What happened all of a sudden to Knierim's point about the wider context of "whole Bible" interpretation?

A similar phenomenon occurs when Knierim asserts that "violence" is the reason given in the text as a warrant for the flood in Genesis 6-9. Here Knierim appears to make a judgment about the passage based on his prior hamartiological study of the OT as a whole.[2] In the course of this work he has concluded that no sin is "more grave than that of violence." Yet the narrative itself also mentions that the earth was "corrupt" (Gen 6:11-12) and that humankind was "wicked" and its imagination "evil" (Gen 6:5, thus forming an envelope structure with Gen 8:21 that now brackets the entire flood account!). I do not see any exegetical indication that one of these terms functions more importantly than the others. Here Knierim seems to read into the narrative an earlier conceptual judgment.

Other aspects of Knierim's treatment of the flood account are also instructive. In his discussion he issues two exegetically-based judgments against an interpretation he remembers by his one-time elementary school teacher. (As he notes, religious instruction was also in a sense "church-related" in Germany at this time, as it is today.) He commends the teacher for his forceful rhetoric and a powerful "actualization" of the biblical account, but eventually terms the interpretation erroneous and not "accountable to the text." Knierim's two criticisms? First, that contrary to his teacher's interpretation the sin which provoked the flood was not drunkenness, but violence; and second, that Noah nowhere in the Genesis narrative warns his contemporaries of their impending doom, as his teacher had instructed the class in their re-enactment of the story.

As Knierim himself notes, there actually is an indication in the later narrative that drunkenness is not completely foreign to the story (Gen 9:20-27), although here the drinking is post- rather than ante-diluvian. To play devil's advocate for a moment, I must say that I found myself wondering to what extent Knierim's teacher perhaps might simply have approached the flood narrative from the standpoint of the NT (even if unconsciously). According to Matt 24:37-39, "in the days before the flood" people were "drinking, marrying and giving in marriage." Moreover, in 2 Pet 2:5 Noah is remembered explicitly as a "herald of righteousness," which might well explain how Knierim's teacher had retold the story as he did (cf. 1 Pet 3:18-20 on the building of the ark as a public witness). This aspect of the Noah tradition also appears in Josephus (*Antiq*. III.2.1), Theophilus of Antioch, and Clement of Rome (e.g., *1 Clement* 7:6: "Noah preached repentance and those who listened to him were saved").[3] I agree completely that this feature is missing from Gen 6-9, but I would also suggest that Knierim's teacher may well have been neither arbitrary nor irresponsibly opportunistic in his interpretation. Rather, he may have been observing certain interpretive contours from the wider biblical context and/or from an ecclesial interpretive tradition. Whether or not this possibility is actually correct, I believe the question such a possibility poses is the following: would this kind of traditional or "canonical" interpretation be acceptable to Knierim as "responsible" theological interpretation of Scripture? Or would he rule it simply "out of bounds"?

In each of the three preceding examples, I remain unconvinced that the interpretations of these passages has: 1) in fact been as theologically deficient as Knierim suggests; and 2) really violated the guidelines Knierim himself proposes. Actually, it often seems to me that the interpretations he criticizes accord better with his guidelines than his criticism of them does!

At this point I would like to make a few final remarks regarding Knierim's positive proposal of "God and the world" as a "conceptual unifier" for OT Scripture. While I agree with Knierim that the purpose and goal of Israel's role within the OT is to bring blessing "to the world" (e.g., Gen 12:1-3), I am highly skeptical of the advisability of any "unifier" for the OT in which the place of Israel is merely implied. I know that Knierim feels keenly the burden of Christian anti-Jewish biblical scholarship. I imagine that at this point he may feel that it should be Jews instead of Christians who evaluate the role of Israel, hoping to avoid the all-too-familiar prejudices of the past, but Knierim's "unifier" is far too broad to be useful. How many religious literatures are not about "God and the world"? Have we really described anything particular to the OT with such a formulation? Or have we abstracted a lowest common denominator that no longer contains much content?[4] Even "God with Israel for the world" would be much better! Or, perhaps, "God's choosing, judging and renewing of Israel for the world" (Knierim himself points to "election" and "covenant" as central). Or, for the Christian Bible as a whole, "God's way for the world with Israel and in Jesus Christ." Without expressing sufficient distinguishing characteristics any unifier will lack adequate interpretive power.

Furthermore, I must admit that finally I am also skeptical of the ability of any single conceptual unifier to do justice to the whole of the OT. Here is the point at which I think we would do well to continue to ponder the theological significance of canonization, even with all of its historical ambiguities and uncertainties. The unity of the entire OT is not to be located in a "concept" or a logical "center," or even within a reconstructed history of Israel, but in the recognition by Israel and the church of a literature that was considered by them reliably to express the fullness of revelation. The formal "unity of the Bible" is thus to be found in the outer boundaries that the canon provides, rather than in some kind of inner canon-within-a-canon. In this way, the operation of a "canon" does not remove a text from questioning, but provides its proper interpretive context (contra Knierim). Thus, the canon actually allows for various "centers" to emerge within the ongoing activity of interpretation, even requiring this kind of multivalency as a reflection of Israel's multiplex witness.

NOTES

1. G. E. Wright, "Theology and Christomonism," in his *The Old Testament and Theology* (New York: Harper & Row, 1969) 13-38; esp. 21-22.

2. R. P. Knierim, *Die Hauptbegriffe für Sünde im Alten Testamen*t (Gütersloh: G. Mohn, 1965); cf. his "Zur Gestalt alttestamentlicher Hamartiologie," in *Sünde: Ein unverständlich gewordenes Thema* (ed. S. Brandt, M. H. Suchocki and M. Welker; Neukirchen-Vluyn: Neukirchener, 1997), 71-114.

3. On later Noah traditions, see J. Daniélou, *Holy Pagans of the Old Testament* (trans. F. Faber; London/New York: Longmans, Green, 1957), esp. 73-74.

4. On this typical liberal Protestant move and the way it actually disrespects difference, see K. Tanner, "Respect for Other Religions: A Christian Antidote to Colonialist Discourse," *Modern Theology* 9 (1993) 1-18.

GOD IN HUMAN FORM

ULRICH MAUSER

One of the reformed confessions of faith, the Confessio Belgica of 1561, provides in Article IV a list of canonical writings which provide the foundation on which reformed faith rests. The canon of Scripture, so article V continues, is not only confirmed to be of divine origin by the witness of the Holy Spirit in our hearts, but the prophecies contained in Scripture have been fulfilled so manifestly that even the blind can grasp it.[1] The Belgica does not spell out what it means by biblical prophecies, nor does it elaborate what it considers to be their fulfillment. But there can be no doubt in the context of the definition of Scripture as a canon of Old and New Testaments, the Confessio Belgica thinks of a correlation of Old and New Testaments along the lines of promise and fulfillment and that it considers the correlation so self-evident that even the blind can comprehend it.

More than four hundred years after the Belgica one is sorely tempted to reverse the confession's claim. At the beginning of the third millennium C.E. does one not have to be blind to the mass of evidence accumulated by historical investigation of biblical books and the materials provided by comparative studies of ancient religions and cultures, if one persists in claiming a clearly discernible thread running from the Old to the New Testament that would enable us today to speak of a theology common to the two parts of the Christian canon of Scripture? We are all aware that, sometimes with a tinge of sadness and sometimes with a note of malicious joy, biblical theology has been declared dead, and hand in hand with this declaration a practice of interpretation of biblical texts is offered that replaces a theological quest for understanding with alternate models of investigation.

Yet, in my contribution to this symposium I put before you the thesis that the essence of the NT message is the culmination, although in astoundingly novel and unexpected shape, of a relationship between Israel's God and some of this God's most outstanding servants. It remains central to the proclamation of the NT that a specific, historically identifiable, human being is acknowledged as the Word, the Son, the Image, the Glory and Imprint of God, with such power that in him one of human form and likeness is invested with the name of God (Phil 2:7 and 10-11), and hence with divine identity. In the OT no claim of that kind is made for a human being. The identification of the nature and deed of a human life with the nature and deed of God remains a characteristic of the NT that has no true antecedents in the Hebrew Scriptures. In fact, the prohibition of images, the second commandment of the Decalogue, is extended in the OT to the representation of YHWH in human form (Deut 4:16), a prohibition, we must not forget, which is not superseded but emphatically reaffirmed in the NT (Rom 1:23). But in spite of the awareness of the absolute qualitative difference between God and humans in the OT there is also the realization that certain special individuals are so decisively seized by God that their lives become a simile, a reflection, of God. In limited, imperfect, and partial form, the lives of these extraordinary servants of God are molded into veritable parables of YHWH so that, on rare but significant occasions, they can even be called "gods" who are singled out to stand for the divine in the midst of the mundane.

MOSES THE MEDIATOR.

In the Hebrew canon of Scripture the Torah occupies the place of honor. Torah is the first and foundational part of the canon. In this preeminent section of Scripture Moses is by far the most dominating human actor. He is the leading figure in the entire corpus of texts from the beginning of Exodus to the end of Deuteronomy. While the large complex of literary production is the result of centuries of growth whose historical stages we can still trace with a fair amount of certainty, it remains remarkable that, in the texts as we now have them, Moses is connected with all major themes in this far flung literature. He is the human activist who accomplishes Israel's liberation from slavery in Egypt, he is the commanding figure during the sojourn in the wilderness, he is the cardinal recipient of the revelation on Mount Sinai, the entire collection of laws is attributed to his mediation, and he is even associated with some conquest stories in Transjordan before his death outside the borders of the promised land. There can be no doubt: among all the humans that populate the Pentateuch Moses is the man of gigantic proportions whose stature exceeds even the Patriarchs.

Yet the hero Moses is participant in a story that is by no means the product of his own historic will or of his religious genius. This "giant of history" is, viewed from a metahistorical angle of vision, the messenger, the servant, the utterly dependent subject who is guided, step by step, by the vastly superior force of his one mighty God YHWH. In some sources of the Pentateuch the decidedly passive nature of Moses is emphasized so much that Moses' initiative in the events is severely curtailed. For the Priestly Code YHWH is the only true actor in the narrative while Moses is reduced to the role of an instrument in God's hands.[2] But in the other sources also the dependency of Moses on his God is never forgotten. The man Moses has a face with two distinct features. He is, on the one side, the humble executor of a superior whose will and power he represents, and, on the other side, an activist imbued with a unique authority that shapes his life into a form brimming with divine energy.[3]

Already in the story of Moses' call (Exod 3:1-4:31) these two features are evident. Moses answers God's commission by a whole series of objections that are invalidated by YHWH's replies. In the course of this dialogue in Exod 4 the word "to believe" becomes a crucial term. No less than six times the word appears in this chapter (4:1, 5, 8 twice, 9, 31), more than in any other chapter in the Hebrew Scriptures, and it is used with both God and Moses as the object of belief.[4] Moses objects to God's call by raising the possibility that the Israelites will not believe him when he encounters them with God's commission (4:1). YHWH answers the objection by promising two authenticating signs which must have the effect to make Israel "believe" in the authenticity of Moses' commission (4:5, 8). Should they still refuse to "believe," a third sign will be ready to convince them (4:9). In these verses Moses is unambiguously the object of faith. God's commission has invested him with an authority that binds the enactment of God's act of liberation to this one person. The passage on Moses' commission ends with the note that Moses' and Aaron's joining the people resulted in a faith response: "The people believed; and when they heard that YHWH had given heed to the Israelites and that he had seen their misery, they bowed down and worshipped" (4:31). The phrase "they bowed down and worshipped" has in mind the veneration due to YHWH alone, and consequently the belief of the people in 4:31 is an expression of faith in the liberator God. But in line with the other statements in Exod 4 about faith in Moses, it must be concluded that faith in God's saving activity includes faith in the man whose words and signs are part and parcel of Israel's salvation from Egypt. It sounds like a repeated echo of Exod 4 when, in later chapters of the book, faith in YHWH and faith in Moses are pointedly placed together. The summation of the narrative about Israel's deliverance from the Egyptians at the sea concludes with the words: "So the people feared YHWH and believed in YHWH and in his servant Moses" (Exod 14:31). Shortly thereafter, at a moment of highest solemnity after the disclosure of YHWH's election of Israel, Moses is addressed by God in confirmation of his unique authority with the words: "I am going to come to you in a dense cloud, in order that the people may hear when I speak with you and so have faith in you forever" (Exod 19:9). Faith in YHWH and faith in Moses are inseparable.

But the narrative goes further. One of Moses' objections against God's call is his recognition that he is slow of speech and slow of tongue (Exod 4:10). God's answer to the objection places Aaron as speaker at Moses' side. Aaron is to be Moses' mouth but Moses will be Aaron's "ʾĕlōhîm" (4:16). A few chapters later, in a passage similar to 4:16, Moses is told by God that he will be "ʾĕlōhîm" to Pharaoh as his brother Aaron will be his prophet (7:1). In these astonishing sentences Moses is attributed the stature of divinity. In neither declaration is Moses identified with YHWH. The term used in the declarations is "ʾĕlōhîm," a word general enough to connote divinity.[5] In both instances it is YHWH, the speaker, who confers a new status on Moses, and Moses remains entirely subordinate to the will and word of YHWH in carrying out his commission. But that cannot diminish the fact that in relation to his brother and to the king of Egypt—who in Egyptian eyes is himself of divine origin—Moses is invested with divine authority and insight. As the executor of God's act of liberation, Moses shares the dignity of heavenly beings who he represents in his dealings with his brother and with the Pharaoh of Egypt.

To Aaron, the future originator of the priesthood in Israel, and to Pharaoh, the child of a god according to Egyptian concepts, Moses incorporates the presence of the divine. He can do this because he is bound to his God YHWH in a singular relation of intimacy. In exceptional moments some of Moses' closest associates are reported to be with him when he is on the mountain to meet God (Exod 24:1, 9-11). But the narrative does not tire in emphasizing that Moses was a lone figure encountering his God on Sinai. The dread of the epiphany of God keeps people at a distance (Exod 19:12, 21, 24; 20:21; 24:2). Only Moses can bear to stand the presence of the Holy One (Exod 19:3, 20). There is more than a prophet in Moses because of his singular intimacy with God. Numbers 12:6-8 states it this way: "When there are prophets among you, I YHWH make myself known to them in visions; I speak to them in dreams. Not so with my servant Moses; he is entrusted with all my house. With him I speak face to face—clearly, not in riddles; and he beholds the form of YHWH."

Another passage broaches the mystery of Moses' intimacy with his God more cautiously. After the incident of the golden calf Moses asks to be granted a vision of YHWH's glory. YHWH answers by putting him in the cleft of a rock and letting his glory pass by, covering Moses' face with the hand till he has passed by so that Moses can see his back but not his face (Exod 33:17-23). In one of the most daring anthropomorphisms in the OT this magnificent tale reaffirms the unique stature of Moses who is permitted to experience the sight of God's glory albeit in the broken fashion of glancing at its movement as it were from behind. Yet another text puts Moses into the full presence of God's glory. After the establishment of the covenant we read:

> The glory of YHWH settled on Mount Sinai, and the cloud covered it for six days; on the seventh day he called to Moses out of the cloud. Now the appearance of the glory of YHWH was like a devouring fire on the top of the mountain in the sight of the people of Israel. Moses entered the cloud, and went up on the mountain. Moses was on the mountain for forty days and forty nights (Exod 24:15-18).

And again, following the renewal of the covenant, Moses descends from the mountain with his face shining "because he had been talking with God" (Exod 34:29). It is the radiance of the glory of God's presence that has transfigured Moses' face. The Israelites cannot bear the sight so that Moses has to cover his face, because he has become bodily transfused with the radiant glory of God, and nobody can see God's glory and live (Exod 34:30; cf. 33:20).

The glorious sweep of the Moses traditions from Exodus to Deuteronomy speaks of a life of immense consequence that cannot be adequately subsumed under normal categories of human existence. The composite portrait of Moses in the Pentateuch has prophetic, military, judicial, magical, and thaumaturgical features that have been produced by centuries of growth.[6] Yet behind these different features lies the secret of a commission by the God of Israel who caused one special human life to be drawn into unparalleled closeness. Moses becomes participant in the glory of God in a manner that has no comparable antecedents. The glory of God enters into him and makes him the heroic figure who sets God's work of liberation in motion. God's delivery of Israel from captivity is Moses' act (Exod 3:8-9), rebellion against Moses is rebellion against YHWH (Exod 16:8), and the huge complex of laws collected in the books of Exodus to Deuteronomy are founded on the authority of Moses who is the original paradigm of the hearing and communicating of YHWH's instruction to the community. In Moses God is represented and displayed, he is truly God's mediator. Yet in spite of its gigantic proportions, the Pentateuch's picture of Moses does not identify him with YHWH. He remains the servant of God (Exod 4:10) and a shadow is spread over his story by the memory of some wrongdoing with which he offended his God (Num 20:12; 27:13-14;

Deut 32:51).

SYMBOLIC ACTS OF THE PROPHETS

The figure of Moses is associated with events in which Israel saw the foundation of its life with God. The liberation from the Egyptian bondage, the wanderings under YHWH's care through the wilderness, and the giving of the law on Sinai provided the sacred memory that informed Israel's worship and conduct and grounded the confidence in its special status as God's people. In these foundational traditions Moses stood at the core of Israel's treasured inheritance, the mediator of God's gracious acts and God's ultimate friend, privy to the splendor of divine glory who thus became the human representative of the divine in the world.

In a very different way and under vastly changed conditions the writing prophets of the northern and southern kingdoms of Israel/Judah in the seventh and sixth centuries B.C.E. become once more human mediators of their God YHWH. The circumstances, viewed against the backdrop of the Moses narratives, are drastically altered. From Amos down to the destruction of Samaria and Jerusalem, the prophets initiated a new chapter in the relationship of YHWH to his people. The two nations are accused of abandoning faith in their God, turning the rock of their security into a hostile aggressor who will execute his fierce displeasure by enabling foreign conquerors to turn Israel and Judah into has-beens. The prophets from Amos to Jeremiah and Ezekiel are heralds of this catastrophic reversal. Their way of representing God among their contemporaries can therefore not have the heroic traits of the Moses saga. But their way of imaging God is no less compelling.

The medium by which the prophets disclosed the truth of their God to their people is quite predominantly the spoken, and quite early also, the written word. But there is, alongside the prophetic oracles, a not so small number of symbolic actions that involve the prophets' personal lives.[7] In some cases they are physical illustrations of the prophets' message designed to underscore the spoken word. But at least some of the symbolic actions of the prophets' are more than pedagogical devices. They show the very life of the prophet being shaped into a form that makes the prophet a double of God. In some prophetic symbolic acts, YHWH, who is beyond all pictures fashioned by human hands or imagination, forges a prophetic life into an analogue that serves as his image.

In what follows we will concentrate on the prophet Hosea[8] and add only a few short comments on symbolic actions by other OT prophets.

HOSEA

The book of Hosea is composed of two main sections. Part one consists of the first three chapters whose central section tells of the divorce proceedings of the husband YHWH against his wife Israel (2:1-21) which is framed by the account of Hosea's marriage and the names of three children (1:2-11) and by Hosea's purchase of an unnamed woman (3:1-5). The topic of marital relations provides the thematic link in these chapters. Part two (chapters 4-14) is almost entirely a collection of words of YHWH. In many of them God speaks in the first person singular. The book offers a striking number of oracles in form of direct divine speech. The collection of sayings is again and again a self-communication of YHWH. In unrestrained anthropomorphisms and anthropopathisms YHWH opens his heart as a person moved by love whose original affection was returned by the partner of his love, only to be quickly and cruelly disappointed later. The pain of rejected love is the pain of God who speaks in the oracles of Hosea.

YHWH reminisces about the first discovery of Israel in the wilderness as a surprising, precious find:

> Like grapes in the wilderness, I found Israel. Like the first fruit on the fig tree, in its first season, I saw your ancestor. But they came to Baal-Peor, and consecrated themselves to a thing of shame, and became detestable like the thing they loved (9:10).

YHWH grieves over the destroyed relationship to a son who was greatly loved in his youth:

> When Israel was a child, I loved him, and out of Egypt I called my son. The more I called them, the more they went from me; they kept sacrificing to the Baals, and offering incense to idols (11:1-2).

Israel is confronted directly by a forsaken God:

> I have been YHWH your God ever since the land of Egypt; you know no God but me, and besides me there is no savior. It was I who fed you in the wilderness, in the land of drought. When I fed them they were satisfied; they were satisfied, and their heart was proud; therefore they forgot me (13:4-6).

YHWH is bound so much to the partner of his love that the abiding affection causes a conflict within him between outbursts of pity and the rage of a spurned lover. On the one hand God can no longer restrain his wrath:

> Shall I ransom them from the power of Sheol? Shall I redeem them from the power of Death? O Death where are your plagues? O Sheol, where is your destruction? Compassion is hidden from my eyes (13:14).

On the other hand, God cannot give up the people he loves so dearly:

> How can I give you up, Ephraim? How can I hand you over, O Israel? How can I make you like Admah? How can I treat you like Zeboim? My heart recoils within me; my compassion grows warm and tender. I will not execute my fierce anger; I will not again destroy Ephraim; for I am God and no human, the Holy One in your midst, and I will not come in wrath (11:8-9).

Similar expressions of extreme anger and continued care and love occur repeatedly in God's oracles to Hosea (cf. 9:15 with 14:5 and 5:10 with 11:9).

The anthropopathisms of Hosea's language of God are extremely daring. They present a God who is torn by a struggle within himself. The infidelity of his people erects a barrier against the outpouring of YHWH's care so that he is struggling between letting disaffection run its course and allowing renewed love to triumph. The God who speaks to and through Hosea is a God whose relationship to his human partners includes consequences for the divine being. Not only Israel as partner in God's covenant is ineluctably affected through its common life with this God for blessing or for curse, but God also has bound himself to his human partner. YHWH does not occupy a place of abstract transcendence far above, and unaffected by, the vicissitudes of Israel's history. He is, rather, most seriously affected by Israel's response to him. If Israel returns his love, it causes him delight; Israel's ingratitude causes him pain. He participates fully in the tensions brought about by Israel's changing attitudes toward him, and he is thus carried in the stream of Israel's change from fidelity to infidelity. YHWH is not exempt from the mutations of history, but takes part in history's course. He can, therefore, rejoice now, and then be angry, he can even be involved in a struggle within himself in which his disaffection stands in conflict with his love. The God of Hosea is wedded to the history of his people.

YHWH speaks as a married man who accuses his wife Israel of infidelity that is leading to a divorce. It is entirely clear that the use of sexual and marital imagery cannot aim at picturing YHWH as a God of sexuality. Hosea is engaged in an uncompromising polemic against a Baal cult whose point is the veneration of sexual potency as a divine power. Israel has become a whore precisely because of its deification of sexuality, and it must not be forgotten that Israel's males are included in the verdict of whoredom over Israel (4:13-14). The impact of the husband-wife imagery in Hos 2 is, therefore, not at all the image of God as a male who has a female partner and engenders children in this union. In bold partial adoption and transformation of Canaanite language the husband-wife image expresses for Hosea that YHWH has committed himself to being bound to a human partner. It is his decision to take Israel forever "in righteousness and in justice, in steadfast love and in mercy" (2:19).

But in Hosea's time, the relationship of YHWH to Israel is poisoned through and through. It cannot be likened to a sound marriage, rather it has the characteristics of rampant promiscuity on the part of the wife. Israel's infidelity is manifest in a religious perversion. The natural bounty of the land is no longer understood as YHWH's gift, but as the yield of the worship of Baal (2:5, 8). It is in Israel's cultic practices that this perversion takes place. Israel's festivals, new moons, and sabbaths are infected by the baalistic virus (2:11), and YHWH is about to punish her precisely for her religious celebrations: "I will punish her for the festival days of the Baals, when she offered incense to them and decked herself with her ring and jewelry, and went after her lovers, and forgot me, says YHWH" (2:13). The wife Israel has become a prostitute, and the charge of whoredom includes the incorporation of overtly sexual acts as part of the Baal cult that sponsored male and female prostitution (4:14).

Facing this corrupt relationship the husband YHWH is going to discipline Israel by the total deprivation of all natural blessings that the wife Israel expected from the Baals. She will become reduced to being like parched land (2:3), forced back into the wilderness (2:14). Husband YHWH will withdraw all his support, taking back his grain, his wine, and his flax (2:9). Israel will be forced to living at point zero, in the desert where the election began, and only in this reduction to the initial circumstances will there be hope for her (2:15).

This grim picture of the faithless wife Israel is flanked by two accounts of incidents from Hosea's life. In chapter 1 a third person tells of Hosea's marriage to Gomer and the birth of three children. Chapter 3 recounts in Hosea's own words the episode of the prophet's purchase of an adulteress and the strange living arrangements which he imposes on her. Both narratives provide fragments of a biography of the prophet, but they are not designed to satisfy the readers' curiosity about Hosea's marital history. The point of both stories is an analogy between Hosea and YHWH. We direct our attention only to this point.

According to Hos 1:2 the prophet is not free to marry whom he pleases, he is told by God to take "a wife of whoredom and have children of whoredom because the land commits great whoredom by forsaking YHWH." The bizarre incident of chapter 3 begins "Go love a woman who has a lover and is an adulteress, just as YHWH loved the people of Israel, though they turn to other gods and love raisin cakes" (3:1). The two snapshots of Hosea's marriage to Gomer and his relationship to the adulteress emphasize the same point: the prophet is placed into a position in which he is to share YHWH's situation.

The description of Gomer as a wife of whoredom is probably not meant to degrade Hosea's wife in a moral sense. It is at least very possible that the phrase connotes a girl who had participated in baalistic fertility rites, had in this way, in Hosea's eyes, mixed herself up with idolatrous cultic practices, and thus broken faith with YHWH. Her children, then, are called children of whoredom, not because their mother was untrue to her husband, but because they owe their existence to a foreign god.[9] These children are branded with names that shout out in perpetuity the corruption of Israel in forsaking YHWH. The first son's name, Jezreel, placards the habitual practice of murdering kings in the northern kingdom epitomized by Jehu's wholesale massacre of an entire royal house (2 Kgs 9-10). The girl's name, Lo-ruhamah, negates Israel's faith that YHWH is gracious and merciful. And, worst of all, the youngest son's name, Lo-ammi, cuts the root of Israel's basic reliance, the fact of being YHWH's people. It is hard to squelch the thought that Hosea has done his level best to provide himself with a dysfunctional family. But that is exactly what Hos 1, in dead seriousness, is meant to convey: in his family life the prophet is a human duplicate of YHWH living in a non-functioning marriage.

Chapter 3 presents another glimpse into Hosea's troubled marital life. On YHWH's word he has to take a woman into his house who is called an adulteress. Hosea obeys, buys the woman for 50 shekels of silver, and tells her that she will have to remain in seclusion in the house for many days, precluding her from having sexual relations with a man from the outside, but that the prophet also will not be her partner. The woman is unnamed, and a connection to the Gomer of chapter 1 can only be made by filling in a presumed history of Gomer of which chapter 1 says nothing. It is preferable, therefore, to take Hosea's own account of his relations with the adulteress in chapter 3 as a narrative independent of the Gomer story, a unit that is meaningful entirely on its own terms.

Taken as that, the episode exhibits some traits that are quite bizarre. Hosea purchases a woman whose sexual behavior is scandalous. She was once married, but has now become a prostitute, perhaps a temple prostitute. The intention of the purchase is not doubtful. Through it the prophet acquires the legal right to have the woman as his partner to the exclusion of all other men. But the obvious aim of the purchase is negated by Hosea's decision not to consummate the relationship. Twice in the short chapter the analogy between YHWH's love for Israel and Hosea's love for the nameless woman is stated as the reason for the prophet's astonishing behavior. He is to love a person whose life is marked by infidelity, as YHWH's love is directed toward a people who forsake their own true God and turn their devotion to other gods (3:1). In addition there is another analogy between YHWH's love and Hosea's odd arrangement. The prophet and his God share the situation that the expected fruit of their love will not grow. Life with YHWH is meant to signify for Israel the blessing of a secure national life, healthy worship, and divine guidance in its decisions. But instead, the pillars of public life and of the cult will be removed from the nation. The benefits of life under YHWH will be totally taken away. By the same token, Hosea takes into his house a female partner who must have expected from this shared life full support and the unabridged benefit of conjugal rights. But exactly the expectation of fully married communion is frustrated through Hosea's ordering of the relation.

Like God, Hosea has to live in a relationship whose natural consequences are the enjoyment of the fruit of this common life with all its blessings. But the relationship is not allowed to bear fruit. The situation is grotesque. Hosea has a woman in his home day in and day out, but she is not his; he has paid for her as one pays for a concubine, but he does not reap the pay-off for his purchase; everything in the relationship demands full union, but the union is not established. Hosea has placed himself into a situation that is a manifest contradiction. Yet this he has done at YHWH's prompting; in this way he loves as God loves. For, YHWH's devotion to fickle Israel is also a grotesque and unnatural affair. It has involved God in a history in which the God who seeks and desires full communion cannot achieve what his heart is longing to have.

The God of the prophet Hosea is unashamedly anthropomorph. He has so poured himself into the human history of a particular people that he is, in a manner completely superior to human possibilities (Hos 11:9), revealed in his love and in his pain in his will to participate in the earthly life of his people. But the prophet of this God is also daringly theomorph. Essential manifestations of his life are cast into conformity with his God YHWH, the lover of Israel. There is no identification of the ever superior God with his earthly messenger. But there is, at certain points of the prophet's life a parabolic character of his existence which, partially and within limits, displays the image of God.

SYMBOLIC ACTIONS OF OTHER PROPHETS

Hosea was not the only one of the prophets whose life was so captivated by YHWH that it was molded into an image of God. In the southern kingdom of Judah, Hosea's virtual contemporary Isaiah gives exceedingly strange and offensive names to two sons, reminiscent of the naming of Hosea's children. Isaiah is commanded by his God to inscribe a tablet with the message Maher-shalal-hash-baz ("the spoil speeds, the prey hastens"), a message presaging the impending disaster of the Assyrian invasion which is to become flesh and blood in Isaiah's son who is, at the time of the inscription, not even conceived (8:1-4). There is another son of Isaiah named Shear-jashub ("a remnant shall return") who in his name carries around the divine verdict that Israel's trust in being YHWH's people is void because only a remnant will be sustained through the coming catastrophe (7:3).

Isaiah's family bears the imprint of the power of God's word that has seized the most intimate, personal space expressed in the sons' names. No less shocking is God's command that the prophet move about barefoot and naked for three years to become a sign for all those of his people who trust in Egypt and Ethiopia as defenders against Sargon of Assyria. Isaiah must walk in public like a prisoner of war exhibiting in his physical appearance the state of utter humiliation and ridicule (20:1-6).

About a century later, Jeremiah receives instruction from his God that isolates him from the rest of his contemporaries just as YHWH is isolated from his people. He is not to marry but be barred from the joy of having a family, he is not to participate in the mourning customs designed to comfort the bereaved because there is no consolation for a nation under God's judgment, and he is not to participate in feasts and merry-making because God is banishing from Judah mirth and gladness and the joys of wedding celebrations (16:1-9). At another time Jeremiah is told to walk the streets of Jerusalem with a wooden yoke strapped to his shoulders, carrying the burden of the coming enslavement by Nebuchadnezzar of Babylonia in his body as a present incarnation of the future reality. When the confident opposition against Jeremiah, personified in the counter-prophet Hananiah, breaks the wooden yoke, Jeremiah replaces, at God's commend, the wooden yoke with an iron one (27-28).

In the book of Ezekiel we find the greatest accumulation of reports about symbolic acts. A dozen accounts of Ezekiel becoming a sign to his contemporaries are collected, some of them actions that the prophet carries out, and sometimes conditions that are imposed on him, often reducing the prophet to extremely restricting and painful experiences. Ezekiel is portrayed in these events as the living picture of the God who disciplines a wayward Israel.

THE IMAGE OF GOD

In the towering figure of Moses we saw the human mediator of God to God's people, but also the mediator of the people to God. In this mediating role Moses represents the divine world both to the super-power Egypt and its Pharaoh and to the community of YHWH. Moses is God's intimate friend to such a degree that his acts and words have the authority of God and that his very life becomes a reflection of YHWH's glory.

Some of the symbolic acts of the OT prophets opened up ways of living human lives in a manner that human history becomes an image, a parable, a sign of God. Certain aspects of the lives of these prophets are not only living representations of their message, but a participation in God's passionate involvement with his people. If anywhere in the OT, the prophets act as historical manifestations of the crowning sentence of the creation story of Genesis: "God created the human being [ʾādām] in his image, in the image of God he created them" (Gen 1:27).

The question must be raised, however, if the designation of the human being as God's image in the creation story has anything to do with the accounts of prophetic actions as signs of God's actions with his people. Genesis 1 is, in the form in which we have received it, a very late part of the OT tradition. It belongs to the priestly account of Israel's early history that is dated well after the Babylonian captivity. Interests in the prophetic movement are to the priestly author(s), in contrast to the Deuteronomistic historians, no characteristic feature. The origin and meaning of the concept of the human as God's image cannot be sought in the prophetic movement.

The pronouncement of Gen 1:27 has produced a huge amount of literature that has yielded a great number of different interpretations. To these interpretations I want to add two suggestions which, to the best of my knowledge, have not received sufficient attention or have been omitted from consideration. The suggestions state two theses: 1) the sentence of ʾādām being created as the image of God is part of an Israelite polemic against polytheistic cultures and their veneration of idols as images of the divine; 2) the notion of the image of God in Gen 1 is related to the priestly laws and practices as they are described in the succeeding chapters of the priestly code. The meaning of the idea of God's image in ʾādām must be sought in analogies that are suggested by the set of notions that can be shown to have ruled the priestly writer(s).

With regard to the first thesis, at the 1998 meeting of North Park's Symposium, Professor Iain Provan observed that the Hebrew word *ṣelem*, translated in the NRSV of Gen 1:27 with "image," is used repeatedly in reference to idols.[10] One example may be cited: "You shall drive out all the inhabitants of the land from before you, destroy all their figured stones, destroy all their cast images (ṣalmê massēkōtām), and demolish all their high places" (Num 33:52). One of the words used in Gen 1:27 to denote the "image" of God is employed in anti-idolatrous passages of the OT to castigate pagan worship that is carried out through the veneration of material pictures of the divine (2 Kgs 11:18; Ezek 7:20; 23:14; Amos 5:26). It is generally acknowledged that the priestly account of creation in Gen 1 has the tendency to engage in an unspoken, but definite, polemic against polytheistic notions of the beginnings of the cosmos. Heavenly forces like the sun and stars are no longer gods, banned is the battle among the gods for supremacy which explains in some polytheistic cultures the movement from original chaos to the ordered world, and the dominion over different domains of life attributed to distinct divinities is completely eliminated. Genesis 1 knows only a single divine being whose word and work creates the entire universe. Gods beside this one God deserve no mention except that some have preserved their names in the reduction to designations of natural phenomena that have their origin solely in the creative will of the one God. In this twilight of the idols pronounced in Gen 1, the creation of the human as the culmination of the work of creation takes on a stark, polemical significance. In polytheistic cults images of the gods abound in temples and in shrines. But the one God of Israelite faith also has an image. It is not found in statues of metal, stone, or wood. In fact, it is no product of human ingenuity and industry at all. The real image of the one, true God is the living human being itself. This person is the one true form of God in the world. To be human means to be created "theomorph."

In turning to the second thesis, an awareness of the anti-idolatrous element in the affirmation of Gen 1:27, however, cannot suffice to explain the idea of God's creation of ʾādām as God's image. Israelite priests could not possibly engage in idealistic notions about the essence of human existence without regard to the forces of disobedience to God, of the impurity of human conduct, and of the need for constant cleansing of the human condition. Many interpreters of the priestly creation account in recent years have drawn attention to a teleological element that pervades the narrative of Gen 1 if it is placed within the context of the whole priestly narration with its cultic ordinances. The creation story extends itself into the later establishment of Israel's worship as it is enacted by the ministration of the Aaronite priesthood. Creation drives forward towards its actualization in Israel's cult.

The story of God's rest on the seventh day of creation (Gen 2:1-3) finds its historical realization in the institution of the Sabbath in Israel (Exod 31:12-17). The careful distinctions between forms of vegetation and animal life which are ordered each in its own kind in Gen 1 have their counterpart in the Mosaic laws governing dietary practices in which distinctions are to be observed. Detailed observations of language and narrative structure in the priestly story of creation and in the description of the erection of the sanctuary at Sinai (Exod 24:12-31:18) suggest the conclusion that the creation account and the establishment of the wilderness sanctuary are purposefully coordinated. Creation speaks of a destiny that is reached in the establishment of Israel's worship and conduct. The mystery of creation stretches forward towards its manifestation in a definite space and a definite time that is the origin of Israel's cult in which the dwelling of God amidst his people assumes concrete form.[11]

The question raises itself whether the creation of the human being in the image of God might not also be related to later elements in the priestly story. But in raising that question the interpreter is faced with a seemingly insuperable problem. The two Hebrew words translated by "image" in Gen 1:27 play no further role in the priestly account, except in Gen 5:3 and 9:6 where Gen 1:27 is echoed. But if we do not allow ourselves to be governed by narrow limitations of word statistics and structural patterns, we might take into consideration other concepts within the priestly theology in which the purpose of human life is expressed by way of an analogy, an essential likeness, to God. At least one such analogy does exist in the whole of the priestly work. An analogical relation between God and God's human partner is found frequently in the Holiness Code (Lev 19-26) that was incorporated into the priestly corpus. One of the most striking characteristics of this collection of laws, that has provided the name "Holiness Code," is the oft repeated formula "You shall be holy, for I YHWH your God am holy" (Lev 19:2; cf. 20:7, 8, 26; 21:6, 8, 15, 23; 22:9, 16, 32). The language evoked by Gen 1:27 suggesting a mirroring of a subject through the use of nouns like "image, likeness, or picture" is put aside in the Holiness Code in favor of a more abstract analogy and comparability that is found in the essence of God's being, his holiness, and the cultic and moral reality into which Israelites are called because of their exclusive allegiance to YHWH.

I am not suggesting that the author(s) of the priestly creation story had the holiness analogy in mind when the sentence in Gen 1:27 was first written. We have no linguistic or structural hints in the texts that would recommend this connection. But I do mean to propose that the analogy between the holiness of God and the holiness of the Israelite can provide us with a clue of the direction of thought that dominated the priestly mind in the post-exilic period of Israel's history. When the priests thought of an analogy, or an image, of God in the human being, they did not think of some human characteristic that is independent of God, like the physical appearance of a human, or human rationality, or the position of dominance over nature. They thought rather of the consequence of the living bond to their God that establishes the image in the human.

Of course, Gen 1:27 is a statement about creation long before and independent of the existence of historical Israel. But the priestly writers perceived in Israel's cult and demeanor the historical and concrete actualization of the destiny given to human life from its origin in God. The image of God is, then, not a description of the given of human nature in and of itself, but an outflow of the conscious and life-shaping bond to God. The holy human person represents the holy God since this person lives in the power of the holy God and is constantly sustained by his presence. The foremost desire of that kind of human will be expressed in the prayer that the holiness of God may be manifest among us, and with that we reach the NT.

SANCTIFIED BE YOUR NAME

Our thesis stated that the NT proclaims the identity of a specific, historically identifiable human being as the Word, the Son, the Image, the Glory and the Imprint of God, and that the OT, while nowhere claiming an identity of the nature and deed of God with the nature and deed of a human life, nevertheless tells of a number of extraordinary humans who are so captivated by the divine power that they are molded into parables of YHWH. We saw evidence in some OT passages that YHWH is depicted as passionately involved with human partners, a passion expressed in striking forms of anthropomorphic language. On the other side, there are servants of this God who are consumed by a zeal for YHWH that makes aspects of their lives images of God so that they become to some extent theomorph.

In turning now to the NT we ask if the claim for the divine nature and the divine act of the human Jesus might be understood as the completion, the climax, and the surpassing of the lines we traced in the OT. We select to that end the first petition of the Lord's prayer and the Matthean account of Jesus' transfiguration.

The first two petitions of the Lord's prayer are rendered in identical wording in Matt 6:9 and in Luke 11:2: "Sanctified be your name. Your kingdom come."

The extreme brevity of the petitions casts the substance of the prayer into two lean sentences from which no word could be omitted. This concentration on what is absolutely essential causes the modern interpreter difficulties in arriving at an appropriate understanding. It becomes mandatory to set the petitions into the context of Jewish prayers from a time that makes them comparable to Jesus' words and, even more urgently, into the context of the language of the Gospels. When that is done, a great difference between the petitions becomes obvious. The request for the coming of the kingdom is accompanied by a wealth of kingdom sayings and kingdom narratives in the Synoptics which enables us to give precision and range to the meaning of the second petition. With the first petition we find ourselves in a strikingly different position. The "name" of God occurs in the Synoptics, with the exception of Matt 28:19, only in OT quotations (Mark 11:9 and Luke 13:35 with parallels), and the word "sanctify" is restricted to Matt 23:17, 19. The sparsity of the vocabulary of the first petition in Synoptic language does not suggest that its genuineness might be in doubt. But it does necessitate the investigation of comparable wordings from other Jewish sources.

Such investigations of the phrase "sanctify God's name" have led to a fairly definite result.[12] First, the combination of the request for the sanctification of God's name with the petition for the coming of the kingdom is firmly attested in Jewish prayers around NT times, and second, the prayer for the sanctification of God's name echoes phrases characteristic of the prophet Ezekiel.

The collocation of the first two petitions of the Lord's prayer is found in roughly contemporary Jewish prayers. Two of the most important prayers may be quoted. The Qaddish, dated by many before 70 C.E., begins: "Magnified and sanctified be his great name in the world, that he has made according to his will. May he let his royal reign rule in your life and in your days and in the life of the whole house of Israel, in haste and in the near future."

The same coordination occurs in Seder Rab Amram 1 (91) whose succinct wording reminds even more of the Lord's prayer: "Make your name unique in your world, make your royal reign unique in your world." In view of these and other Jewish prayers it can be considered certain that the placement of the first two petitions in the Lord's prayer conforms to Jewish practice. But this common practice, in turn, reflects the emergence of a tradition going back to exilic and post-exilic OT language, especially to Ezekiel.

The "sanctification of God's name" picks up a phrase from Ezek 36:23 where YHWH speaks to the prophet:

> I will sanctify my great name, which has been profaned among the nations, and which you have profaned among them; and the nations shall know that I am YHWH, says ADONAI YHWH, when through you I sanctify myself before their eyes.

The phrase "I will sanctify my great name" at the beginning of this verse has the same meaning as the wording "I sanctify myself" at the end of Ezek 36:23. Here, as often in the OT, the name of God is God himself in his act of revealing himself to those with whom he chooses to communicate. The name of God is God in person as he is known, worshipped, and served by his people.

The conviction that God will sanctify himself (or his name) is characteristically frequent in Ezekiel, although it has earlier antecedents. In Ezekiel it is associated with a cluster of related ideas that give meaning to the prophet's expectation of YHWH's sanctification of himself.

First, the failure to sanctify God's name on the part of YHWH's people results in the profanation of the name before all the nations in the world. It is considered the obligation of the people of God to sanctify God's name first and foremost. YHWH's good name, his honor, is at stake in Israel's obligation to honor the divine name by exclusive devotion to him alone. If Israel fails to do so the name of God is profaned. Therefore, if YHWH spares the transgressions of his people, he does so in order to preserve the honor of his name. God holds back his wrath against Israel in Egypt and in the wilderness because "I acted for the sake of my name that it should not be profaned in the sight of the nations" (20:9; similar 20:22; 36:20-22).

Second, the time is about to come that because of profaning YHWH's name Israel will have to suffer severe judgment at the hands of God, and in that judgment YHWH will demonstrate his holiness. An invasion of Gog from the north will sweep over Israel's territory "like a cloud covering the earth . . . so that the nations may know me, when through you, O Gog, I will be sanctified before their eyes" (38:16, similar on Sidon 28:21).

Third, YHWH's honor will, however, not be fully vindicated by the infliction of a terrible judgment on Israel. The end will not be disaster, but the restitution of all tribes of Israel to their homeland. The restitution of Israel is nothing other than the restoration of YHWH's own honor, his act of sanctifying himself. The litany of Israel's historical failures in the profanation of YHWH's holy name will come to an end "when I bring you out from the peoples, and gather you out of the countries where you have been scattered, and I will manifest my holiness among you in the sight of the nations . . . when I deal with you for my name's sake" (20:41, 44; also 28:25; 39:27).

Fourth, the display of YHWH's holiness is frequently in Ezekiel said to result in the acknowledgment of who YHWH is. God's sanctification of himself (i.e., his name) leads to the insight that YHWH is the sole supreme ruler of history. "I will sanctify my great name, which has been profaned among the nations, and which you have profaned among them; and the nations shall know that I am YHWH, says ADONAI YHWH, when through you I display my holiness before their eyes" (36:23). The oracle "I am YHWH" entails the claim of YHWH's exclusive supremacy. The same claim is stated in an eschatological pronouncement of the prophet Zechariah in which the key notions of the kingdom, the exclusive rule of God, and the name of God are united: "YHWH will become king over all the earth; on that day YHWH will be one and his name one" (14:9).

Fifth, Ezek 36:23 is followed immediately by the expectation that, when YHWH sanctifies his name, Israel will be given a new heart and a new spirit (36:24). God's name will be vindicated not merely in a miraculous reversal of national fortune, but in the fundamental re-orientation of YHWH's people. YHWH's sanctifying of his name will also involve a radical rejuvenation of Israel, a basic change of the nation's internal condition that will enable them no longer to profane but to sanctify the holy name of God.

In summation it may be said that the first two petitions of the Lord's prayer are closely related to Jewish prayers roughly contemporary with Jesus, and that the petition "sanctified be your name" hearkens back to the language of Ezekiel. But what does that mean for Jesus himself? Can we be certain that he associated with the first petition of his prayer all, or indeed any, of the specific ideas the exilic prophet had in mind? The extreme brevity of the first petition does not allow any conclusions for this question, positively or negatively. One can say that some elements that constitute Ezekiel's theology of YHWH's act of exhibiting his holiness, that is sanctifying his name, are in some form present in the Synoptics' picture of Jesus: the judgment on Israel, on the nations, and on the Christian community; the restitution of Israel through the representation of the twelve disciples; the inclusion of Gentiles in the acknowledgment of God; the gift of the Spirit; and the fervor of the eschatological hope. But none of these characteristics of Jesus' teaching and action, is, in the Synoptic gospels, linked expressly to the notion of the sanctification of the name of God.

Nevertheless, the Synoptic tradition does not leave us entirely without a clue. Some narratives in the Synoptics are, more or less overtly, connected to the idea of Jesus' standing good for the honor of God. To these stories belong the accounts of Jesus' temptation, of the cleansing of the temple, of the struggle in Gethsemane, and of the trial before the Jewish and Roman authorities. But, perhaps most clearly of all, it is the story of Jesus' transfiguration that can help to clarify the understanding of the first petition of the Lord's prayer.

The Matthean version of the transfiguration of Jesus on the mountain appears dependent on the account in Mark 9:2-8, but in Matthew's story there appear a large number of references to other sections of the gospel which cannot be found in Mark, nor in the parallel narrative in Luke 9:28-36. Matthew's text is studded with echoes of OT epiphanies to Moses and with hints and allusions that invite the reader to draw connecting lines to Matthew's gospel as a whole, particularly to the baptism and temptation story, and especially to the Easter stories.

The Lukan form of the transfiguration story mentions twice the word "glory." Both Moses and Elijah (Luke 9:31) and Jesus (9:32) are enveloped by the glory of God. Although Matthew, following Mark, does not use the word "glory," there is no doubt that for him also the incident on the mountain is a manifestation of God's glory. The entire episode of the transfiguration tells of a sudden, although passing, appearance of God's glory enveloping Jesus, and this revelation of glory is the point at which the narrative is connected to the petition "sanctified be your name." In the OT the concepts of the holiness and of the glory of God are linked and the verb "to sanctify" can be synonymous with "to glorify." The death of Aaron's sons, Nadab and Abihu, is called an act in which YHWH both sanctifies and glorifies himself (Lev 10:3); in Ezekiel's language the judgment of Sidon establishes the glory and the holiness of YHWH (Ezek 28:22), and in Isaiah's inaugural vision the sanctity of God is insolubly coupled with his glory which fills the earth (Isa 6:3). Consequently, the transfiguration narrative is a declaration of the fulfillment in Jesus' life of the petition "sanctified be your name."

Matthew has linked his account of Jesus' transfiguration to stories of Moses being drawn into God's glory on Sinai. Jesus goes up on a "high mountain," "six days" after he spoke the word of the coming of the Son of Man "in the glory" of his Father. There his appearance is transformed so that his "face shines like the sun," his clothes become "dazzling white," and after Moses and Elijah join the scene, a "bright cloud"overshadows them and the "voice of God" is heard coming from the cloud. It is not possible, in reading Matthew 17:1-8, to miss the connections to the description in Exod 24:15-18 of Moses' reception of the law and to the report of the change of Moses' face at his descent from Mount Sinai in Exod 34:29-35. Exod 24:15-18 tells us that Moses went up on the mountain, the cloud covered the mountain, the glory of YHWH covered it for six days, and on the seventh day YHWH called to Moses out of the cloud. The allusions to the Moses sagas are strengthened further when Matthew, alone among the Synoptics, narrates how Jesus' face "shone like the sun" as Moses' face shone because of his encounter with God (Exod 34:29). The transfiguration story discloses to the three disciples in a brief and passing scene the hidden truth behind the daily contact with Jesus. Jesus shares with Moses the intimacy of companionship with God that transforms his human life into participation with the glory of God.

The allusions to the Moses stories do not exhaust the wealth of connections that are built into Matthew's version of the transfiguration. The high mountain in 17:1 is not only an echo of Mount Sinai but also of other mountain scenes in the first gospel. Matthew's third temptation of Jesus had the devil take Jesus up "on a very high mountain" (4:8), and the Gospel ends with the appearance of the resurrected Jesus on a mountain in Galilee (28:16). If the similarity of the mountain locale were the only point suggesting a link between the temptation and the resurrection stories with the transfiguration, it would be hazardous to read too much into it. But a closer look shows that Matthew's literary artistry is such that his transfiguration story is enriched with details that connect the transfiguration with the beginning and the end of his gospel in several other ways as well.

Critics have proposed that the transfiguration story is a transposed resurrection account.[14] Even if one does not hold to that opinion, it must be recognized that transposition theories can appeal to a number of observations. Jesus' face shining as the sun and the dazzling whiteness of his clothes at the transfiguration (17:2) remind the careful reader of the appearance of the angel at the tomb on Easter morning who looks "like lightning, and his clothing white as snow" (28:3). The company of Moses and Elijah puts two persons together who, either in the OT itself or in Jewish tradition, had been said to have been granted victory over death by their God.[15] Also, the transfiguration story shares definite features with the accounts of Jesus' miracles. But while in all other miracles Jesus is the actor, in the transfiguration narrative he receives a miracle performed on him. It is this passivity of Jesus which again links the transfiguration and the Easter stories. It is undeniable that transfiguration and Easter stories are, especially in Matthew, purposefully connected with each other. In the framework of Matthew's gospel the transfiguration is an anticipatory, and passing, glimpse of a reality that was ultimately revealed in Jesus' resurrection: Jesus lived in the presence and power of the divine glory.

However, Matthew's transfiguration account also reaches backward to the prelude of Jesus' ministry in the stories of baptism and temptation. The similarity of the mountain scene has already been mentioned. But there is also the fact that the voice of God uttered at the time of Jesus' baptism, and the divine voice sounding from the cloud at the transfiguration are identical: "This is my Son, the Beloved, with whom I am well pleased" (3:17 and 17:5 adding "listen to him!"). The transfiguration is, looking backward into Jesus' life, the confirmation of his baptism. He had truly repented in his baptism and accepted the task of bearing the burden of the judgment of God (3:13). Therefore, he is declared from heaven to be the Son of God, the Beloved. His temptation is the test in which his status as God's Son is at stake (4:3, 5). In the three temptation scenes in Matthew, Jesus is presented as the one who remains obedient to God in situations modeled after incidents in Israel's wanderings in the wilderness: Jesus was victorious where Israel failed. The third temptation story on the mountain is like the negative foil of the transfiguration. The temptation on the mountain conjures up the vision of world dominion on condition of acknowledgment that the devil is the god of the world. The transfiguration on the mountain asserts the participation in the glory of God by him who had renounced the devil's claim and, with it, the rule over the world in a manner other than by the sacrifice of his life (20:25-28; 28:18).

That brings us to the last point touching on the context of Matthew's transfiguration story. The transfiguration follows on the heels of Jesus' first announcement of his passion (16:21) and the steely rejection of Peter's view that the passion must, in God's name, not happen (16:22f.). The transfiguration vindicates the resolve of the Son of God to subject himself to rejection and death. This resolve—so abhorrent to Peter, the other disciples, and the readers of the gospel—is disclosed in the transfiguration to be the decision of the Son of God with which God is well pleased, a decision which testifies to his participation in God's glory.

CONCLUSION

In his description of the prophet Hosea, Martin Buber claimed that "only from the world of Israelite faith" could it be understood that "the blood and soul of theomorphous man know about his likeness character, which alone makes possible for him the imitation of God" and that "the theomorphism of man, that is to say, the fact of God's image in him, has been preserved only by God's own becoming anthropomorphous over and over again" in the manner described by Hosea's language of the love of YHWH.[16] The Christian interpreter of Scripture might add to Buber's sentences that his vision of theomorphous human existence in correspondence to the anthropomorphous nature and act of God are not only belonging to the world of Israelite faith, but, far from contradicting or disputing it, they characterize equally the essentials of Christian faith. Life that participates in the glory of God, so the transfiguration of Jesus teaches us, is the life that has as its highest and decisive aim the sanctification of the name of God which releases out of its truth the one true human who is vindicated by God himself as the offspring of God.

NOTES

1. E. F. K. Müller, *Die Bekenntnisschriften der reformierten Kirche* (Leipzig: Deichertsche Verlagsbuchhandlung, 1903), 234.

2. George W. Coats, *Moses: Heroic Man, Man of God* (Sheffield: Academic Press, 1988), 79.

3. Coats traces this dialectic through the entire Moses tradition in the Pentateuch.

4. H. Gross, "Der Glaube an Moses nach Exodus (4.14,19)," in*Wort-Gebot-Glaube: Beiträge zur Theologie des Alten Testaments* (J. J. Stamm, et al., eds.; Zürich: Zwingli, 1970), 57-65.

5. H. Ringgren, "Elohim," *Theological Dictionary of the Old Testament* (eds., G. J. Botterweck and H. Ringgren; Grand Rapids: Eerdmans, 1974), I.280.

6. Gerhard von Rad has traced a picture of the traits of Moses' activity that are emphasized in the major sources of the Pentateuch. See his *Old Testament Theology* (New York: Harper & Brothers, 1962), I.289-96.

7. Basic for this aspect of Israelite prophecy is G. Fohrer, *Die Symbolischen Handlungen der Propheten* (2nd ed.; Zürich: Zwingli, 1953).

8. I have written earlier on the symbolic actions in Hosea and Jeremiah. See *Gottesbild und Menschwerdung: Eine Untersuchung zur Einheit des Alten und Neuen Testaments* (Tübingen: Mohr-Siebeck, 1971), 46-114.

9. H. W. Wolff, *Hosea: A Commentary on the Book of the Prophet Hosea* (Philadelphia: Fortress, 1974), 15.

10. Iain Provan, "To Highlight all our Idols: Worshipping God in Nietzsche's World," *Ex Auditu*, 15 (1999) 25.

11. B. Janowski, "Tempel und Schöpfung: Schöpfungstheologische Aspekte der priesterschriftlichen Heiligtumskonzeption," in *Jahrbuch für Biblische Theologie*, 5 (1990) 37-69, with a great deal of literature on the subject of the link between the account of creation and the Sinaitic laws in the Priestly Code.

12. See particularly the thorough study of Jacques Schlosser in his book *Le Règne* de Dieu dans les Dits de Jésus (Paris: Gabalda, 1980), I.249-255.

13. For other comparable Jewish prayers see Ulrich Luz, *Matthew: A Commentary* (Minneapolis: Augsburg, 1989), 379, note 71.

14. R. Bultmann, *The History of the Synoptic Tradition* (Oxford: Blackwell, 1963), 259.

15. J. Jeremias," Mōusēs," *TDNT*, IV.853-855.

16. Martin Buber, *The Prophetic Faith* (New York: Harper and Row, 1949), 112-113.

PSALM 33 INTERPRETED OF THE TRIUNE GOD

GEOFFREY WAINWRIGHT

"Glory be to the Father, and to the Son, and to the Holy Ghost: As it was in the beginning, is now, and ever shall be, world without end. Amen." Thus the Lesser Gloria or Gloria Patri concludes the saying or singing of the biblical Psalms in the daily office of the Orthodox, Catholic, and Anglican churches. In the early Reformed tradition, a sung trinitarian doxology at the end of the Psalm was known in Scotland from Ninian Winzet's "*Certane Tractates*" and from the "*Gude and Godlie Ballates*"; and the Scottish "*Psalm-Book*" in its 1595 edition contained thirty-two such metrical doxologies to match the various meters in which the Psalms were versified.[1] If, like the hymnwriter Isaac Watts, we wish to make David "speak like a Christian," then we shall have to make him—as Watts himself elsewhere recognized—speak like a trinitarian Christian.[2] In strictly Christian terms, theological interpretation of the entire Scriptures will always be trinitarian, for God did not become Trinity with the Incarnation and Pentecost but is from all eternity Father, Son, and Holy Spirit and acts as such—in differentiated but united ways —towards the world.

That may seem to be moving too fast, historically. So—sticking with the Psalms—let us begin with their christological interpretation from the earliest days of the Church, for the confession of Jesus as the Christ was, of course, the nudge which launched the Church, in the order of knowledge, towards what finally became its full doctrinal formulation concerning, in the order of being, the eternal Triune God. Readers who need no persuasion on this point may move on directly to section III or IV.

I. PSALMS IN THE NEW TESTAMENT

On the Cross, at the height of his Passion, Jesus employed the words of Ps 22 "My God, my God, why hast thou forsaken me?" to invoke the one whom he had consistently in his prayers addressed as "Father" (Matt 11:25-26; Luke 10:21; John 11:41; 12:27-28; 17:1, 5, 21, 24, 25), and whose will he had accepted to the last: "Abba, Father: not what I will, but what thou wilt" (Mark 14:36; cf. Matt 26:38, 42; Luke 22:42). Expiring, Jesus committed his spirit into his Father's hands with the words of Ps 31:5 (Luke 23:46). It seems natural to understand the spirit he thus "gave up" (John 19:30) as his human spirit; however, Jesus was conceived by the Holy Spirit (Luke 1:35), the Holy Spirit was seen to descend on him at his baptism (Matt 3:16; Mark 1:10; Luke 3:22) and to remain on him (John 1:33; cf. Matt 4:1; Mark 1:12; Luke 4:1, 14, 18), so that when Jesus during his ministry "rejoiced in the s/Spirit" (Luke 10:21), we are not sure whether to write "spirit" or "Spirit" (some manuscripts have "Holy," some do not), and the same ambivalence may apply at his surrender of the spirit/Spirit on the Cross. Another psalm verse applied to the Passion of Jesus was Ps 41:9, which was taken at the Last Supper as a prophecy of the betrayal by Judas: "He who ate my bread has lifted his heel against me" (John 13:18).

On the road to Emmaus, the risen Lord Jesus opened the minds of his companions to understand the Scriptures, now that "everything written about me in the law of Moses and the prophets and the Psalms" was being fulfilled (Luke 24:44-49). In his Pentecost sermon (Acts 2:22-36), Peter applied three texts from the Psalms to Jesus as the Christ: he took Ps 16:8-11 as a prophecy by David of the Resurrection (he "was not abandoned to Hades, nor did his flesh see corruption"; see also Acts 13:32-37); he took Ps 132:11 as a prophecy of Jesus' messianic enthronement (God had sworn to David that he would "set one of his descendants upon his throne"); and he took Ps 110:1 as a prophecy of Christ's exaltation and heavenly session and sovereignty: "The Lord said to my Lord, Sit at my right hand, till I make thy enemies a stool for thy feet." Jesus himself had quoted the last-mentioned verse in his own favor as implicitly "one greater than David" (Matt 22:41-45; Mark 12:35-37; Luke 20:41-44; cf. Matt 26:63-64; Mark 14:61-62; Luke 22:66-70), and the same text became a favorite proof of Christ's lordship: 1 Cor 15:25; Eph 1:20-23; Col 3:1; Heb 1:4, 13; 10:12-13; 12:2. In acknowledging the acclamation of himself by the children in the Palm Sunday crowds, "Hosanna to the Son of David! Blessed is he who comes in the name of the Lord!" (Matt 21:9-16; cf. Ps 118:25-26, where "Hosanna" is directed to "the Lord"), Jesus invoked "the mouth of babes and sucklings" who, according to Ps 8:3, praise "the Lord" whose name is majestic in all the earth and whose glory is above the heavens (cf. Matt 11:25-27 for the Father's revelation of the Son to "babes").

The first chapter of the Letter to the Hebrews, in establishing the superiority of Christ the Son over the angels, cites as the Father's words to him Ps 2:7 "Thou art my Son, today I have begotten thee") and Ps 45:6 ("Thy throne, O God, is for ever and ever") and takes Ps 102:25-27 as addressed to Christ the Lord as creator: "Thou, Lord, didst found the earth in the beginning, and the heavens are the work of thy hands" (cf. Heb 1:2: "In these last days [God] has spoken to us by a Son, whom he appointed the heir of all things, through whom also he created the world"). During his earthly life, Jesus "was made for a little while lower than the angels" (Ps 8:5; Heb 2:5-9), while in his very being he never ceases to "bear the very stamp of God's nature" (Heb 1:3).[3]

II. PSALMS BEFORE NICEA

The pioneering study of the christological interpretation of the Psalms in the pre-Constantinian Church was Balthasar Fischer's 1946 inaugural lecture in the Catholic Faculty at Bonn, "Die Psalmenfrömmigkeit der Märtyrerkirche," supplemented by his 1961 address at the Orthodox Institute of St. Sergius in Paris, "Christliches Psalmenverständnis im 2. Jahrhundert."[4] Fischer inclines to the view that the first use of the Psalter in the Church was its reading as a prophetic book, and that the singing of the Psalms came in later as a doctrinally safer alternative to hymns "of human composition."[5] In the earliest Christian centuries, Fischer detects among the fragmentary evidences three principal ways of interpreting the Psalms: they are sometimes taken as divinely voiced witness to Christ in the grammatical third person (the *vox de Christo*), sometimes heard as Christ himself speaking to the Father (the *vox Christi ad Patrem*), and sometimes used by the congregation as its own address to Christ (the *vox Ecclesiae ad Christum*); and, as Augustine recognized, the last two may sometimes be combined so that the whole Body of Christ, head and members, addresses the Father together.[6] This entire complex pattern corresponds to Justin Martyr's answer to the hermeneutical question of whose voices are heard in the prophetic books, among which he reckons the Psalms: sometimes the prophets speak "as in the person of the Father," sometimes "as in the person of the Son," sometimes "as in the person of the people, answering the Lord or his Father."[7]

On the basis of a reexamination of the examples cited by Fischer, some instances may be given here of christological interpretation from the earliest period of the Church. In some cases the emphasis may appear to fall on Christ in his humanity as the typological fulfillment of the vocation and destiny of Israel and indeed the human race; in other cases, Christ receives the name and title by which the Greek OT referred to the God of Israel and all things, "the Lord" (*ho Kurios*). In the later terminology from the ecumenical councils of Nicea I and Chalcedon, Christ is the unique Second Person of the Godhead, the eternal Son of the Father, known and acknowledged by us in two natures, human and divine.

Of the penitential Ps 51, Irenaeus around the year 200 says that "David sang the psalm of confession in expectation of the advent of the Lord who washes and cleanses a man ensnared in sin";[8] and into the "Thou wilt purge me with hyssop, and I shall be clean" of verse 7, a fourth-century manuscript of the Greek Psalter inserts after the hyssop "*apo tou haimatos tou xulou*"—from the blood of the wood/the tree /the Cross.[9] In Ps 96, Justin Martyr in the middle of the second century knows a reading at verse 10—which indeed he accuses the Jews of having suppressed from their manuscripts—that "the Lord reigned from the tree."[10] From the tree and the water of Psalm 1 the second-century *Epistle of Barnabas* draws a reference to baptism undergone with trust in the life-giving death of the Righteous One (cf. Rom 6): "Blessed are those who have descended into water hoping in the Cross."[11] The Lord who in Ps 23 is both shepherd and host ("*Hirt und Wirt*") is interpreted of Christ by Justin, Cyprian, Clement of Alexandria, and Origen.[12]

In the mid second century, the *Epistle of the Apostles* has the risen Christ speak now in the past tense David's prophetic song from Ps 3:5: "I lay down and fell asleep; and I rose up, for God raised me up"; and the same interpretation is given by Justin and Irenaeus, and in the third century by Hippolytus and Cyprian.[13] The second-century *Apocalypse of Peter* applies Ps 24:6-9 (the opening of the gates of heaven for the entrance of the Lord, the King of glory) to the Transfiguration of Christ on the mountain (cf. Matt 17:1-8; Mark 9:2-8; Luke 9:28-36), while the same Psalm is applied to Christ's Ascension by Justin and Irenaeus.[14] From Ps 91:13, the trampling on lion, adder, and serpent as the victory of Christ over Satan was already known to Irenaeus and Tertullian.[15]

III. NICENE DOXOLOGIES

It was in the fourth century that the Psalms entered their heyday as a staple of the daily office. That was the period also in which, during the extended Arian controversy over the godhead of the Son and the Spirit, dispute attended the formulation of the doxologies by which liturgical prayers were concluded. The classic text is the treatise of 373 by Basil of Caesarea, *On the Holy Spirit*.[16] Basil undertook to show that the offering of praise and prayer to the Father "through (*dia*) the Son in (*en*) the Holy Spirit" did not imply, as the Arianizers argued, the subordination of the Son and the Spirit but was rather the "upward" correspondence, in thanks and petition, to the fact that all God's blessings came "downward" from the Father through the Son in the Spirit as the unified action of God. Basil also defended, from Scripture and earlier ecclesiastical tradition, his own employment — as appropriate to God "contemplated in Himself"—of a coordinated form of address "to the Father with (*meta*) the Son together with (*sun*) the Holy Spirit" (which became, of course, the position of the ecumenical council of Constantinople in 381). Further, Basil provides anecdotal evidence for a doxology in which the three Persons of the Godhead are linked by the simple use of "and":

> I once heard a certain Mesopotamian, a man experienced both in language and accurate knowledge, say that in his country it is not possible to say the doxology in any other way, even if one wishes to do so, since the grammatical rules of their language force them to use their equivalent of the conjunction "and." Our Cappadocian dialect is similar; perhaps the Spirit foresaw how useful this word would be, when he gave the gift of tongues to the disciples! What about the entire West, almost from Illyricum to the boundaries of the empire? Does it not prefer this word?[17]

Certainly, the usage is confirmed for Syriac by Aphraates in the early fourth century, who employed the form "Praise and glory to the Father and his Son and his living and holy Spirit from the lips of all."[18] Theodore of Mopsuestia later testified that Diodore and Flavian had introduced a translation of the Syriac formula "Glory to the Father and the Son and the Holy Spirit" into the Greek psalmody at Antioch about the year 350.[19] This became the Byzantine form: *Doxa Patri kai Huiō kai Hagiō Pneumati, kai nun kai aei kai eis tous aiōnas tōn aiōnōn.* And of course in "the entire West" we are familiar with the *Gloria Patri et Filio et Spiritui Sancto, sicut erat in principio et nunc et semper et in saecula saeculorum.*

Given the teaching of the first four ecumenical councils, to interpret the Psalms christologically is already implicitly to understand them in reference to the Triune God. The Church's use of the *Gloria Patri* to conclude the recitation of the Psalms makes that explicit. Without further ado, Ps 33—which is Ps 32 in the numbering of the Greek and Latin Bibles —will now be treated in that way. This Psalm has been chosen because it contains the strongest of what the 1992 *Catechism of the Catholic Church* calls the "suggestions" in the OT concerning the trinitarian action of God in creation:

> The Old Testament suggests and the New Covenant reveals the creative action of the Son and the Spirit [cf. Psalms 33:6; 104:30; Genesis 1:2-3], in-

separably one with that of the Father. This creative cooperation is clearly affirmed in the Church's rule of faith: "There exists but one God . . . he is the Father, God, the creator, the author, the giver of order. He made all things by himself, that is, by his Word and his Wisdom," "by the Son and the Spirit" who, so to speak, are "his hands" [Irenaeus, *Adv. Haeres.* 2.30.9; 4.20.1; PG 7/1:822, 1032].

The Word of God and his Breath are at the origin of the being and life of every creature [cf. Psalms 33:6; 104:30; Genesis 1:2; 2:7; Ecclesiastes 3:20-21; Ezekiel 37:10]: "It belongs to the Holy Spirit to rule, sanctify, and animate creation, for he is God, consubstantial with the Father and the Son . . . Power over life pertains to the Spirit, for being God he preserves creation in the Father through the Son" [Byzantine liturgy, Sundays of the second mode, Troparion of morning prayer].[20]

IV. THE WORD AND THE SPIRIT IN PSALM 33:6

First, the sixth verse of Ps 33 will be examined, since this is what the Catechism alludes to. The historic interpretation of this verse will be displayed, and here I am indebted for some of the patristic references in particular to the two volumes of *La Tradition médite le Psautier chrétien*, and to an article by Bertrand de Margerie.[21] The purpose of surveying the tradition is not simply to establish the fact of widespread trinitarian interpretation of Ps 33:6 but also to pick out those elements in the trinitarian interpretation of the verse that will be valuable in an interpretation of the whole Psalm. All of Ps 33 will, in fact, thereafter be read in trinitarian mode. This exercise is intended as a demonstration of the possibilities for interpreting and using the entire Psalter in this way.

Ps 33:6, and the subsequent and directly related verses 7-9, read thus:

6. By the word [*dabar; logos; verbum*] of the Lord the heavens were made
And all their host by the breath [*ruach; pneuma; spiritus*] of his mouth.
7. He gathered the waters of the sea as in a bottle;
he puts the deeps in storehouses.
8. Let all the earth fear the Lord,
let all the inhabitants of the world stand in awe of him!
9. For he spoke, and it came to be;
he commanded, and it stood forth.

Clearly, v. 6 contains a sort of parallelism. This has led some commentators to take "the word of the Lord" and "the breath of his mouth" as synonymous. However, other commentators, remembering perhaps that the second clause of a "Hebrew parallelism" may also add to, or modify, the first, have taken "Word" and "Breath" as distinct. This provides a linguistic basis for the reading of the verse as a reference to the Father, his Son, and his Spirit—all three. It is these latter interpreters who chiefly interest us.

In *Against the Heresies* 3.8.3, Irenaeus cites Ps 33:6 in explication of Ps 33:9 in order to prove the total transcendence of God who, by a sheer command addressed to his Word, ordered the creation of all things, including the "heavenly powers." He does not in this passage distinguish the Breath from the Word; but elsewhere—though without mention of Ps 33:6 but rather Gen 2:7, 1 Cor 15:45, and Isa 42:5—Irenaeus distinguishes between "the breath of life" (*pnoē zōēs*; *afflatus vitae*), which constitutes the animate nature of man, and the "life-giving Breath" (*Pneuma zōopoioun: Spiritus vivificans*), or divine Spirit, which gives to humankind its spiritual existence. It seems appropriate, therefore, to take in a trinitarian sense the passage in the first book of *Against the Heresies*, where, in expounding "the rule of truth," Irenaeus quotes Ps 33:6 among the scriptural texts to show that it is "by his Word and his Spirit" that God "makes, orders, governs, and gives being to all things."[22]

Origen, in his *First Principles* 1.3.7, cites Ps 33:6 as part of his argument that "nothing in the Trinity can be called greater or less, for there is but one Fount of deity, who upholds the universe by his Word-and-Reason, and sanctifies 'by the Spirit of his mouth' all that is worthy of sanctification, as it is written in the Psalm, 'By the Word of the Lord were the heavens established, and all their power by the Spirit of his mouth.'" Origen was answering the possible misunderstanding that, by limiting the gift of the Holy Spirit to the saints alone, he was exalting the Spirit above the Father and the Son, whose blessings and activities extend to both good and evil, just and unjust. Positively, Origen's views on the respective but unified work of the three divine Persons—reaching from creation through redemption and sanctification to consummation—may come to help in the interpretation of the entire Ps 33. In the immediately ensuing paragraph of *First Principles*, he writes thus:

> God the Father bestows on all the gift of existence; and a participation in Christ, in virtue of his being the Word or Reason, makes them rational. From this it follows that they are worthy of praise or blame, because they are capable alike of virtue and wickedness. Accordingly there is also available the grace of the Holy Spirit, that those beings who are not holy in essence may be made holy by participating in this grace. When therefore they obtain first of all their existence from God the Father, and secondly their rational nature from the Word, and thirdly their holiness from the Holy Spirit, they become capable of receiving Christ afresh in his character of the righteousness of God, those, that is, who have been previously sanctified through the Holy Spirit ....
>
> Thus the working of the Father, which endows all with existence, is found to be more glorious and splendid, when each one, through participation in Christ in his character of wisdom and knowledge and sanctification, advances and comes to higher degrees of perfection; and when a man, by being sanctified through participation in the Holy Spirit, is made purer and holier, he becomes more worthy to receive the grace of wisdom and knowledge, in order that all stains of pollution and ignorance may be purged and removed and that he may make so great an advance in holiness and purity that the life which he received from God shall be such as is worthy of God, who gave it to be pure and perfect, and that that which exists shall be as worthy as he who caused it to exist. Thus, too, the man who is such as God who made him wished him to be, shall receive from God the power to exist for ever and to endure for eternity.[23]

Eusebius of Caesarea, in his commentary on Ps 33:6, declares that the Father's Word and Spirit both "cooperated" in his "establishment" of the heavens and their powers, i.e., the angels. The Word—who is identified with "the Savior"—is the universal creator and brought them into existence; the Spirit simultaneously sanctified them.[24] The passage from Eusebius' commentary was to be echoed and amplified later in the fourth century by St. Basil in his defense of the Spirit's divinity against the Spirit-fighters.

Meanwhile St. Athanasius, in his third and fourth letters to Serapion concerning the divinity of the Holy Spirit, twice quotes Ps 33:6 in order to show both that the Word and the Spirit are distinct and yet that the Spirit always accompanies the Word. After quoting Ps 104:29b-30, Athanasius continues in the first passage:

> Since it is written thus, it is clear that the Spirit is not a creature but that he plays a part in the act of creation; for the Father creates all things by the Word in the Spirit, since where the Word is, there also is the Spirit, and the things that are created by the Word have from the Spirit through the Word their strength to be. For thus it is written in the thirtysecond (third) Psalm: "By the Word of the Lord were the heavens established, and by the Breath/Spirit of his mouth all their power.[25]

And in the fourth letter:

> In the Trinity, in the Father and in the Son and in the Spirit himself, there is but one divinity, and in the same Trinity there is but one baptism, one faith. When the Father sends the Spirit, the Son gives it to his disciples by breathing on them [cf. John 20:19-23], since "all that the Father has is [also] the Son's" [cf. John 16:15]; and when the Word came to the prophets, they prophesied in the Spirit, as it is written and was shown: "By the Word of the Lord were the heavens established, and by the Breath/Spirit of his mouth all their power."[26]

The reference that Athanasius makes back to his own earlier letter ("as was shown") seems to imply that the Psalm itself belongs in the list of the other cases he there cites in order to show that "when the Word came to a prophet, it was in the Spirit that the prophet spoke what he learned from the Word" (cf. Zech 1:6 [LXX]; 7:12; Acts 1:16-20; 2 Cor 13:3 in conjunction with Phil 1:19 and Acts 20:20-24).

St. Basil cites Ps 33:6 three times. In his homily on Ps 33 he follows Eusebius closely and makes two further points.[27] First, he explains that "word" and "breath/spirit" respectively are not to be understood here as "the common form of speech, made up of nouns and verbs" and "vapor dispersed into the air" but rather as "the Word which was in the beginning with God" and "the Holy Spirit which has been given this appellation." Second, Basil elaborates on the cryptic remark of Eusebius that "the angels were not created infants": their sanctification did not await a gradual growth towards worthiness but was rather given them by the Holy Spirit in their first constitution, so that it was hard for them to turn to evil.

In the third book *Against Eunomius* Basil cites Ps 33:6 for evidence of the Spirit's operations which point to his divine nature: "As God the Word is the creator of the heavens, so the Holy Spirit gives to the heavenly powers their stability and firmness."[28]

Basil's most important reference to Ps 33:6 occurs in chapter 16 of the treatise *On the Holy Spirit*. Here Basil is concerned not only to show the superiority of the Holy Spirit over the created angels but also more precisely the Spirit's work in relation to the work of the Father and of the Son—and therefore, at least in some measure, the essential relationships among the three Persons of the Godhead:

> The communion of the Spirit with the Father and the Son may be learned by considering the creation, in the beginning, of the pure, intelligent, and heavenly powers, which are called holy, and indeed are holy, because they possess the holiness that they have received from the grace of the Holy Spirit.... When you consider the creation of them, think first of the principal cause of all that is made, the Father; then of the fashioning cause, the Son; then of the perfecting cause, the Spirit. So the ministering spirits exist by the will of the Father, are brought into being by the work of the Son, and are perfected by the presence of the Spirit. The perfection of the angels is holiness, and their perseverance in it.
>
> Let no one accuse me of saying that there are three unoriginate Persons (*archikas*), or that the work of the Son is imperfect. There is only one Originator of whatever is, who creates through the Son and perfects in the Spirit. The work of the Father, "who works all in all," is in no way imperfect; nor is the Son's creative work lacking if it is not completed by the Spirit. The Father would not have need of the Son, since he creates by his will alone; but he wills to do so through the Son. In turn, the Son would not need help, since he works in the Father's likeness; but he wills to have his work completed by the Spirit. "By the Word of the Lord were the heavens established, and all their power by the Breath/Spirit of his mouth." The word here is not simply a significant movement of air proffered by the organs of speech; nor is the spirit a breath coming out of the mouth from the lungs. Rather, it is the Word who was in the beginning with God and is God [John 1:1]; and the Breath/Spirit of God's mouth is "the Spirit of Truth, who proceeds from the Father" [John 15:26].
>
> You note these three: the Lord who commands, the Word who creates, the Spirit who strengthens. What is this strengthening but perfection in holiness, which manifests itself as an unyielding, unchanging, firm attachment to the good. Such holiness is impossible without the Spirit.[29]

In the rest of chapter 16, Basil immediately goes on to show that, biblically speaking, it is this creative and sanctifying Spirit who, first, makes possible the praise of God and the confession of Christ, whether by angels or by men, and whose work, second, extends in fact throughout the economy of salvation. It is the Spirit who taught the seraphim to chant the appropriately threefold "Holy" (Isa 6:3), who enabled the angels to sing "Glory to God in the highest" (Luke 2:14), and who enables believers to say "Jesus is Lord" (1 Cor 12:3). In the things of old, it was the Spirit who brought to pass the blessings of the patriarchs, the help afforded by the Law, the prophecies and types, the victories in battle, the signs performed by the righteous, the preparation for the Lord's coming in the flesh. It was the Spirit who gave Gabriel the foreknowledge to announce the births of John and Jesus (Luke 1:11-20, 26-38). In the Lord's incarnation, the Holy Spirit rested on the beloved Son (Luke 3:22; John 1:33; Acts 10:38) and was present in all Christ's activity (Matt 4:1; 12:28); nor did the Spirit leave him after his resurrection (John 20:22-23). Moreover, it is the Spirit who orders and organizes the church (1 Cor 12). And the Holy Spirit will accompany the Lord on the day of judgment, to reward and crown with spiritual glory those who were "sealed by the Holy Spirit for the day of redemption and have preserved intact and undiminished the firstfruits of the Spirit which they received" (cf. 1 Cor 15:41-42; Eph 4:30; Rom 8:23).[30]

Theodoret of Cyrrhus, the fifth century exegete of the sober Antiochene school, considers the "surface meaning" of Ps 33:6—which was "suitable for the Jews of old"—to reside in the fact that a word was sufficient for creation, with no time or effort needed on the Lord's part. "True theology," however, "shows us God the Word, with the All-Holy Spirit, having made both the heavens and the heavenly powers." "Blessed David," by "prophecy," was allowed to "anticipate" the teaching of the NT.[31]

Now it is the turn of the West. In a brief interpretation of Ps 33, St. Augustine links our sixth verse with the first by identifying "the heavens" with "the righteous" who are summoned to rejoice in the Lord, "the upright" whom it becomes to praise the Lord:

> "By the Word of the Lord the heavens were established": Not of themselves, but by the Word of the Lord have the upright been strengthened. "And all the power of them by the Spirit of his mouth": And their faith comes from his Holy Spirit.[32]

Augustine has also a much more extensive treatment of the Thirty-Third Psalm.[33] In it, he develops the thought that if, as v. 5 declares, "the earth is full of the mercy of the Lord," then that is due to "those heavens which are nearest to us, that is, God's holy apostles, the preachers of the word of truth." This was predicted in Ps 19:1-4. When the Psalm says that "the heavens that are telling the glory of God" and that "there are no speeches or languages where their voices are not heard," this has been fulfilled at Pentecost when the apostles "spoke with the tongues of all peoples assembled in one place"; and when the Psalm says that "their sound goes out through all the earth, and their words to the ends of the world," this has been achieved when the risen Christ sent his apostles forth to proclaim unto all nations repentance and remission of sins (Luke 24:44-47). The Lord "has sent forth the heavens to pour down rain upon the earth," so that "the growing corn of the Church should spring up and increase."[34]

Reverting to Ps 33:6, Augustine finds reference there to the source of the apostles' boldness and courage:

> How could those heavens of which we speak have dared to go forth with such confidence to become heavens, frail men as they were, but that "By the Lord's Word the heavens were consolidated"? Whence could sheep have shown such valor among wolves, were not "all the power of them *virtus* by the Spirit of his mouth"?

They were armed not with their own strength, "for 'it is not you who speak, but the Spirit of your Father speaking through you' (Matt 10:20), since 'all the power of them is by the Spirit of his mouth' [Ps 33 :6b]." It is "because of the sending of those sheep into the midst of the wolves that we are now keeping sacred the memorials of the martyrs."[35]

Of the divine persons in Ps 33:6 St. Augustine gives in the same lengthy passage a fully trinitarian account, with doxological and soteriological dimensions:

> The Word of God is undoubtedly the Son, just as the Spirit of his mouth is the Holy Spirit ... Did they act without the Father? Who, pray, works through his Word and his Spirit but he to whom the Word and the Spirit belong? This Trinity, then, is one God. This God is worshiped by everyone who has learned how to worship; this God encompasses everyone who has turned towards him. Those who are estranged from him do not seek him; he recalls them from afar, so that when they have been converted to him he may fill them.[36]

It will be remembered that in his "literal interpretation of Genesis," Augustine gave a trinitarian interpretation of the Father's Word and Spirit at 1:1-3, and of the "plurality of persons" in whose image humankind was made "as the image of God" (1:26-28).[37]

Among Latin writers after Augustine, the compilation formerly attributed to Jerome—the *Breviarium in Psalmos*—strongly affirms the trinitarian interpretation of Ps 33:6 as "most manifest": "By the Lord is declared the Father, by the Word the Son, and by the Spirit of his mouth the Holy Spirit." Nor is the Spirit who "proceeds from his mouth" to be considered less but rather equal to the Father and the Son. A double interpretation is given of "the heavens and their powers" as "the visible bodies of the sky" (*visibiles coeli*) and as "the holy apostles" who were created and established by the Word in faith and have their diverse powers (*gratias, virtutes*) by the Holy Spirit, for "we have nothing good but what we have received through him (*nam per nos nihil boni habuimus, nisi per ipsum*)"[38]

In his equally firm trinitarian exposition of Ps 33:6, the sixth-century Cassiodorus also takes up Augustine's point about the apostles and the spread of the Gospel:

> "By the word of the Lord," that is, by the Son of God, "the heavens were established," that is, the apostles or saints were put in place to fill the earth with the preaching of salvation. There follows: "And all the power of them by the breath of his mouth," meaning that their teaching came from the Holy Spirit. "Power" refers both to the miracles they performed and to the law of the Lord that they preached to the nations.[39]

Thomas Aquinas, in his commentary on Ps 32 (33), finds a first connection between verses 6-9 and Gen 1:1-2 through the threefold mention of heaven, earth, and the waters; but the more developed connection is that deriving from the mention of all three divine Persons in each passage: "God" or "the Lord," his Word, and the Breath/Spirit of his mouth. In their undivided work, the Father is the "power" of creation (*potestas, potentia*), the Son as Word is its "shaping idea" (*conceptio, formatio*), the Spirit as Love is "the strength that moves it" (*virtus, motus*). The "literal" interpretation of the heavens in Ps 33:6 concerns the celestial bodies; the "mystical" interpretation applies to the apostles, who were established by Christ the Son and Word (Luke 22:32) and strengthened by the Holy Spirit (Luke 24:49).[40]

In several places Martin Luther offers a trinitarian interpretation of Ps 33:6. The most developed occurs in the "Treatise on the Last Words of David, 2 Samuel 23:1-17." The very beginning of David's declaration as "the sweet singer of Israel" is significant in the matter of the authorship—human and divine—of the Psalms: "The Spirit of the Lord speaks by me, his Word is upon my tongue" (2 Sam 23 :1-2). In the treatise, Luther twice takes up Ps 33:6. Against contemporary Arians on the one hand, who "divide the one divine essence into three gods or creators," and against contemporary Sabellians on the other, who "jumble the Persons together into one Person," Luther maintains the teaching of the Athanasian Creed, which he sees anticipated in David's speech in the psalm:

> The author uses the word "made" only once, saying: "By the Word of the Lord the heavens were made, and all their host by the Breath or Spirit of his mouth." He mentions three distinct Persons, namely, the Lord, his Word, and his Spirit; and yet he supposes only one Maker, without differentiation. All things are made. By whom? By one Maker, who is Lord, Word, and Spirit. The Lord does not do his own work separately, the Word does not do his own work separately, and the Spirit does not do his own work separately. All three distinct Persons are but one Maker of the work of each. And each one's work is that of all three Persons as that of one Maker or Master. For as the Lord makes the heavens, the Word makes the same and no different heavens, and the Spirit makes the same and no different heavens. It is One who creates, and it is one creation that all three Persons create. And again, just as the Lord creates the host of heaven by his Spirit (as the text says: "By the Spirit of the Lord was all the host of heaven made"), so the Spirit creates the same and no other host of heavens, and the Word creates the same and no other host of heaven.[41]

Luther had already said that what applied to the creation of the heavens indubitably applied to the creation of the earth also; and when he reverts later in his treatise to Ps 33:6, he will say that the "all things" of creation "must include and not exclude the exodus from Egypt and whatever else happened in the midst of the people of Israel, yes, all that everywhere has taken place since creation, and still takes place, and will take place." And having found the trinitarian creation in both Moses (Gen 1:1-3) and David (Ps 33 :6), Luther remarks that "Something had to be reserved for the New Testament too, so that in it the Father, the Son, and the Holy Spirit might clearly be named, whom the Old Testament calls the Speaker, the Word, and the Spirit of the Lord"[42]

Calvin is more cautious: he, too, finds in Ps 33 continuity between the initial act of creation and God's ongoing engagement with the world's history, but he cannot bring himself to make a fully trinitarian interpretation of v. 6. Linking that verse with the previous half verse, where the mention of God's beneficence is intended to incite worship, Calvin begins his commentary on verse 6 thus: "That he may stir us up to think more closely of God's works, [the inspired writer] brings before us the creation of the world itself; for until God be acknowledged as the Creator and Framer of the world, who will believe that he attends to the affairs of men, and that the state of the world is controlled by his wisdom and power? But the creation of the world leads us by direct consequence to the providence of God." Taking "the heavens" as "the whole fabric of the world," and "the host of them" as "the stars and planets," Calvin declares that by attributing creation to "the word of God" the Psalmist "greatly magnifies God's power, because by his nod alone, without any other aid or means, and without much time or labor, he created so noble and magnificent a work. But although the Psalmist sets 'the word of God' and 'the breath of his mouth' in opposition both to all external means and to every idea of painful labor on God's part, yet we may truly and certainly infer from this passage that the world was framed by God's Eternal Word, his only begotten Son." But then Calvin, with perhaps a hint of regret, declines—on exegetical, not dogmatic grounds—to go the whole trinitarian hog:

> Ancient commentators have, with considerable ingenuity, employed this passage as a proof of the eternal deity of the Holy Spirit against the Sabellians. But it appears from other places, particularly from Isaiah 11:4, that by "the breath of his mouth" is meant nothing else but "speech." For it is there said concerning Christ "He shall smite the earth with the rod of his mouth, and with the breath of his lips shall he slay the wicked." As powerful and effective speech is there allegorically denominated "the rod of his mouth," so in like manner, for another purpose it is denominated in the immediately succeeding clause "the breath of his mouth," to mark the difference that exists between God's speech and the empty sounds which proceed from the mouths of men. In proving the divinity of the Holy Spirit, therefore, I durst not press this text against Sabellius. Let us deem it sufficient that God has formed the heavens by his Word in such a manner as to prove the eternal deity of Christ. Should any object that these divine persons would not appear distinct if the terms "Word" and "Breath" are synonymous, I answer that the term "breath" is not employed here simply as in other places, in which there is evidently a distinction made between the Word and the Spirit; but "the breath of his mouth" is used figuratively for the very utterance of speech, as if it had been said, As soon as God uttered the breath of his mouth, or proclaimed in word what he wished to be done, the heavens were instantly brought into existence and were furnished, too, with an inconceivable number and variety of stars. It is indeed true that this similitude is borrowed from men; but the Scriptures often teach in other places that the world was created by that Eternal Word who, being the only begotten Son of God, appeared afterwards in flesh.[43]

The Genevan Psalter follows Calvin:

> Dieu par sa parole
> Forma chacun pole
> Et ciel precieus;
> Du vent de sa bouche
> Fit ce qui attouche
> Et orne les cieus.[44]

Isaac Watts, however, is bolder. Both versions of Ps 33 in *The Psalms of David Imitated in the Language of the New Testament* take the trinitarian line. In common meter:

> His Wisdom and almighty Word
> The heav'nly arches spread;
> And by the Spirit of the Lord
> Their shining hosts were made.

And in 8.8.8.8.8.8 structure:

> Justice and truth he ever loves,
> And the whole earth his goodness proves.
> His Word the heav'nly arches spread;
> How wide they shine from north to south.
> And by the Spirit of his mouth
> Were all the starry armies made.[45]

In modern times, the trinitarian interpretation of Ps 33:6 fell out of fashion. Critical exegesis aimed predominantly at recovering the meaning of texts "in their original setting"; and if the question arose at all, it would simply be asserted that the original author of Ps 33, whoever it might be, could not possibly have had an inkling concerning the Trinity.[46] My alternative suggestion sees the Psalm as coming to us laden with centuries of earlier Christian interpretation and use.[47] That fact itself belongs in a trinitarian conception of the history to which the Scriptures bear witness and of which they are themselves a part. The wider framework allows—and even calls for—a trinitarian reading of the Psalm.[48]

V. A TRINITARIAN READING OF PSALM 33

The christological and trinitarian insights gained from the liturgical and dogmatic tradition allow us to glimpse within Ps 33 itself the historical and ontological framework for its interpretation and use. According to the attribution long traditional in both Judaism and Christianity, the Psalms are the "Psalms of David." For the Christian tradition, they are a case of David speaking prophetically on behalf of his messianic descendant. Better yet: through his human ancestor David, the Word is speaking who was to become flesh.[49] If the Psalms are attributed less specifically to David and ascribed more generally to the category of prophecy, they are still open to an early Christian gloss, based on Isa 52:6, which puts on the lips of the incarnate Christ the declaration that "I myself, who was speaking in the prophets, have now come."[50] The followers of Jesus believe that they have been incorporated into the Messiah's people, baptized by the Spirit into the body of Christ (1 Cor 12:13). Thus the typology between the Psalms and Christ and the church is not merely literary but real.[51]

The reality of the typology between the Psalms and Christ and the church is sustained by the Triune God who is the universal creator and has in time revealed himself to humankind for its redemption and final salvation. In the framework of Christian theology, it is possible—and indeed necessary—to hold that the cognitive gap between what was generally made known of the Triune God in OT Israel and what was revealed only through the incarnation, passion and resurrection of the Son and the pentecostal outpouring of the Spirit, is covered in reality by its location in the providential and governmental procedures by which this God is bringing to accomplishment his eternal purposes with humankind and the world. Moreover, Christian belief in the divine inspiration of Scripture implies that the Triune God has overseen the doubtless complex process by which his work has been recorded and interpreted in such ways as to result in the canonical

Old and New Testaments. And now the Spirit of Christ who inspired the prophets and the apostolic preachers of the gospel is available to believers on the way to salvation (1 Pet 1:10-13). Voicing the Psalms in the "Spirit of faith" (2 Cor 4:13) is a component in the process by which we attain to "the chief end of man," which, as the Westminster Catechism puts it, is "to glorify God, and to enjoy him for ever." By picking up their trinitarian hints, we can gain the full sense behind St. Augustine's declaration that in the Psalms "God praised himself in order that men might know how to praise God well."[52] Let us now read Ps 33 in that light. What is offered here is a mere sketch that could accommodate much more detail.

Taken as a whole, Ps 33 is an invitation to the righteous to participate, there and then, here and now, in the praise of the Lord, whose goodness and mercy fills the earth, who governs the affairs of nations and men, and who may be trusted to deliver from dearth and death those who place their hope in him.

More precisely, the first five verses of the Psalm are a summons to the righteous to praise the Lord who is himself righteous in his character, in his word, and in his work, and who looks for righteousness among the people he has made. Who, then, are the righteous? David himself was a sinner, and knew himself for such, as the seven "penitential psalms" make clear (Pss 6, 32, 38, 51, 102, 130, 143). Among the human race, "there is none righteous, no, not one" (Ps 14:13; Rom 3:10-12), for "all have sinned and lack the glory of God" (Rom 3:23). But wait, there is, after all, one who is righteous, Jesus Christ the Righteous (Rom 5:15-20; 1 John 2:1), and he has been made "our wisdom, our righteousness and sanctification and redemption" (1 Cor 1:30). As Saint Paul tells the Corinthians—who have been baptized by the Spirit into the body of Christ (1 Cor 12:12-13)—you "were washed, you were sanctified, you were justified in the name of the Lord Jesus and in the Spirit of our God" (1 Cor 6:11). Having been given the righteousness that comes by faith, believers now may and must live accordingly (Rom 1:16-17 and passim). That will be doxological living, for "praise befits the upright" (Ps 33:1).

Having been placed "in" Christ, we can "in the Spirit" praise the Father, who is "Lord of heaven and earth" (Matt 11:25; Luke 10:21; Acts 17:24); we can also praise Christ "as" Lord (Phil 2:9-11); and we can praise as "Lord" the Holy Spirit, who "with the Father and with the Son together is worshiped and glorified" (Nicene-Constantinopolitan Creed).

Since the kingdom of God consists in "righteousness, peace, and joy in the Holy Spirit" (Rom 14:17), the psalmist's summons of the righteous to praise is also a summons to "rejoice." With Christ, who himself "rejoiced in the [Holy] Spirit" (Luke 10:21), we can "rejoice in the Lord" and rest in the divine "peace" (Phil 4:4-7).

The "new song" of the righteous is "the gospel song" (as Charles Wesley calls it in his hymnic version of Ps 33), the "song of the Lamb" in praise of the slain and victorious Redeemer (Rev 5:6-14; 14:1-3).[53]

Verses 5-9 of our Psalm find in the mighty and gracious work of the Triune Creator of heaven and earth the grounds for "fear" and "awe" as well as praise and joy. The whole world is the product of his will and the object of his love. The consequences to be drawn from that have already been displayed in our survey of the interpretative tradition: the world and its history are under the providence and governance of the one transcendent and universal creator, Father, Son, and Holy Spirit, whose purpose is salvation. Each divine Person plays his part in the unified work of salvation, from the originating Father through the mediating Son to the perfecting Spirit, whose sanctifying energy enables the faithful in Christ to offer their reasonable service to the Father and so live in communion with the Triune God; as the Word of the Lord came to the prophets in the Spirit, so the Spirit has graced the apostles of the incarnate Word that they might carry his gospel to the ends of the earth. In the praise of the coequal Trinity the redeemed join for ever with the heavenly powers, all creatures angelic and astral.

In displaying the creative rule of God, the psalmist in v. 7 calls attention to "the waters." Water has retained an association with the *ruach* of the Lord in the divine work of redemption, from the deliverance of Israel through the Red Sea (Exod 14:21) to the baptismal birth by the Spirit without which no one can enter the kingdom of God (John 3:3-8; cf Titus 3:4-7). It is by water and the Word that the church is sanctified as the body and bride of Christ (Eph 5:25-27).

Verses 10-17 of the Psalm view human history on the grand scale, as though through the eyes of the Lord who "looks down from heaven" on the earth he has made and "sees all the sons of men":

> From where he sits enthroned he looks forth
> on all the inhabitants of the earth,
> he who fashions the hearts of them all,
> and observes all their deeds.

In the affairs of nations, independently made human plans are brought to naught, if they are not in accordance with the eternal purpose of God (vv. 10-11). Salvation is not to be found in the strength of armies or horses (vv. 16-17; cf. Isa 31:1-3); rather, blessing comes from the Lord's own choice (v. 12).

The "counsel" of the Lord (v. 11) is the "mystery" of God's plan to "bring about the obedience of faith" which, having long been hidden, is now revealed in Christ and moves toward completion by the Spirit (Rom 16:25-27; Eph 1:3-14). The incarnate Jesus "knew all men" and "knew what was in man" (John 2:25). He it is who sits at the right hand of the Father until his enemies are made a footstool (Ps 110:1; Matt 22:41-45 and parallels; Heb 1:13; 10:12-13) but who has also "received from the Father the promise of the Holy Spirit" and "has poured out this which you see and hear" (Acts 2:32-36), namely the Spirit of the last days, who enables men and women to call on the name of the Lord and be saved (Acts 2:14-21).

In verses 18-22, the last portion of Ps 33, the attention is focused on the future. Those who "fear the Lord" and "hope in his lovingkindness" may be confident that he will not only "keep them alive in famine" but "deliver their soul from death" (verses 18-19). The latter promise is now made secure by the Father's resurrection of Jesus through the Spirit (Rom 8:11), and Jesus himself will raise at the last day those who, in their hunger and thirst for righteousness (Matt 5:6), have been satisfied by feeding on his body and his blood (John 6:35-59).

The "holy name" (v. 21) in which Christians trust is that of the Father, the Son, and the Holy Spirit that was invoked over us at our baptism. The Lord, in whom resides "our hope" (v. 22), is the Father whom we address as "Abba," who has made us fellow heirs with Christ his Son and given us the first fruits of the Spirit (Rom 8:12-39).[54]

VI. PSALM PRAYERS

Besides the use of trinitarian doxologies to conclude the Psalms in worship, another way in which Christians have appropriated the Psalter is through brief prayers that, by various rhetorical procedures, "insert the Psalms into the mystery of Christ."[55] By latching on to a few key phrases or by summing up the entire Psalm, the prayer may help and guide the application of the text after study and meditation or after recitation in the liturgy. A beautiful trinitarian example is provided for Ps 33 by the fifteenth-century monk from the Netherlands, Dionysius the Carthusian:

> O Christ, Word of the Eternal Father, by whom the heavens were made: Enlighten us with the gift of thy Spirit and stablish us in good works, that we may be justified through faith in the Trinity and through working that which is pleasing to thee, and may, together with the people thou hast chosen for thine inheritance, be glorified for ever; who livest and reignest with the Father and the Holy Ghost, ever one God, world without end. Amen.[56]

The following is a prayer composed by the present writer upon consideration of Ps 33:

> Almighty God, by whose Word and Spirit the world was made and the affairs of nations are governed, we rejoice in your faithful works for the sake of your people. Preserve us, we pray, in the justice of Christ, until your purpose is complete and our hope confirmed, to the praise of your Triune Name. Amen.

For their own use, and staying within the rule of faith, readers are invited to try their hand at formulating such prayers.

NOTES

1. See John A. Lamb, *The Psalms in Christian Worship* (London: Faith Press, 1962), 152-153.

2. Preface to "The Psalms of David Imitated in the Language of the New Testament" (1718), in *Works of Isaac Watts*, volume 4 (1753), p. xviii; cf. "A Short Essay toward the Improvement of Psalmody," ibid., p. 282: "Have we nothing more of the nature of God revealed to us than David had? Is not the mystery of the ever-blessed Trinity brought out of darkness into open light?"

3. For studies on the christological use of the Psalms in the NT, see Pierre Grelot, *Le Mystère du Christ dans les Psaumes* (Paris: Desclée, 1998).

4. Both are reprinted in Fischer's *Die Psalmen als Stimme der Kirche* (Trier: Paulinus-Verlag, 1982), 15-35 and 85-95 respectively.

5. In fact, however, the earliest good evidence extant for the two liturgical uses—reading and singing—is roughly contemporaneous (around 200). The first clear testimony to the liturgical reading of Psalms is found in the homily of Hippolytus, *On the Psalms*, 18. Tertullian is probably referring to the singing of the Psalms at the love feast: "*de scripturis sanctis* vel de proprio ingenio *canere*" (Tertullian, *Apologeticum* 39; PL 1:540); and in Sunday worship: "prout scripturae legen-

tur aut *psalmi canuntur* aut adlocutiones proferuntur aut petitiones deleguntur." (*De anima*, 9; PL 2:701). See Harald G. Buchinger, "Die älteste erhaltene christliche Psalmenhomilie: Zu Verwendung und Verständnis des Psalters bei Hippolyt" in *Trierer Theologische Zeitschrift* 104 (1995) 125-144, 272-298, especially 144, 272-273.

6 See Maurice Pontet, *L'exégèse de Saint Augustin prédicateur* (no place: Aubier; no date [preface 1944]), 400-411.

7 Justin, *First Apology* 36 (PG 6:385). The most detailed work on the "speakers" in the Psalms according to the Fathers—though neglecting *the vox Ecclesiae ad Christum*—is the two-volume "prosopological" study by Marie-Josèphe Rondeau, *Les Commentaires patristiques du Psautier (III—Ve siècles).* Orientalia Christiana Analecta 219 and 220 (Rome: Pontificium Institutum Studiorum Orientalium, 1982 and 1985). Rondeau presents a systematic synthesis of her results in "L'élucidation des interlocuteurs des Psaumes et le développement dogmatique (IIIe - Ve siecle)" in *Liturgie und Dichtung*, eds. H. Becker and R. Kaczynski (Erzabtei Sankt Ottilien: EOS-Verlag, 1983), vol. 2, 509-577. In the same volume (pp. 579-614), a contemporary dogmatic reflection is offered by Leo Scheffczyk, "Vox Christi ad Patrem—Vox Ecclesiae ad Christum: Christologische Hintergründe der beiden Grundtypen christlichen Psalmenbetens und ihre spirituellen Konsequenzen."

8. *Against Heresies* 4.42.2 (ed. W. W. Harvey [1857], 2:240); numbered 4.27.1, in Sources chrétiennes 100 (ed. A. Rousseau, 1965), 734-735.

9. For *xulon* in this sense, cf. Acts 5:30; 10:39; 13:29; Gal 3:13; 1 Pet 2:24.

10. Justin, *Dialogue with Trypho* 73 (PG 6:645). *Ho Kurios ebasileusen apo tou xulou* passed over into the Latin Psalter as *Dominus regnavit a ligno*; cf. already Tertullian, *Against Marcion* 3.19 (PL 2:376).

11. *Epistle of Barnabas* 11 (PG 2:760).

12. Justin, *Dialogue with Trypho* 86 (PG 6:681); Cyprian, *Epistles* 63, 11 (CSEL 3/2 [ed. W. Hartel], 710); Clement of Alexandria, *Pedagogue* 1.7, 61, 3 (GCS 1 [ed. O. Stählin], 126); Origen, *Commentary on the Song of Songs* 2 (GCS 8 [ed. W. A. Baehrens], 138). On the sometimes subtle allusions in these texts, see J. Quasten, "Der Psalm vom Guten Hirten in der altchristlichen Kultmystik und Taufliturgie" in *Liturgisches Leben* 1 (1934) 132-141.

13. *Epistle of the Apostles*, 19 (J. K. Elliott, *The Apocryphal New Testament* [Oxford: Clarendon Press, 1993], p. 569); Justin, *First Apology* 38 (PG 6:385-388); Irenaeus, *Against Heresies* 4.55.4 (ed. Harvey, 2:267), or 4.33.3 in Sources chrétiennes 100 (ed. Rousseau), 838-839; Hippolytus, *On the Psalms* fragment 37 (GCS1/2 [ed. H. Achelis], 153); Cyprian, *Testimonies* 2, 24 (CSEL 3/1 [ed. Hartel], 91).

14. *Apocalypse of Peter* 17 (Elliot, *The Apocryphal New Testament*, 611-612); Justin, *First Apology* 51 (PG 6:404); Irenaeus, *Against Heresies* 4.55.4 (ed. Harvey, 2:268), or 4.33.13 in Sources chrétiennes 100 (ed. Rousseau), 838-839; Irenaeus, *Demonstration of the Apostolic Preaching* 84, in Sources chrétiennes 406 (ed. A. Rousseau, 1995), 196-198; English translation by John Behr, *St. Irenaeus of Lyons: On the Apostolic Preaching* (Crestwood, New York: St. Vladimir's Seminary Press, 1997), 91.

15. Irenaeus, *Against Heresies* 3.36.1 (ed. Harvey, 2: 129), or 3.23.7 in Sources chrétiennes 211 (ed. A. Rousseau, 1974), 462-464; Tertullian, *Against Marcion* 4.24 (PL 2:450-451). For more on the Christian interpretation of the passage see B. Fischer, "Conculcabis leonem et draconem: Eine deutungsgeschichtliche Studie zur Verwendung von Psalm 91 (90) in der Quadregesima," in idem, *Die Psalmen als Stimme der Kirche*, 73-83.

16. St. Basil's treatise *On the Holy Spirit* is found in PG 32:67-217. The Greek text and a French translation are given in Sources chrétiennes 17 bis (ed. B. Pruche, 1968). There is an English translation by David Anderson, *St. Basil the Great On the Holy Spirit* (Crestwood, New York: St. Vladimir's Seminary Press, 1980).

17. Here Basil, *On the Holy Spirit*, 29 (74), in PG 32:208; in Pruche, p. 514-515; in Anderson, p. 111-112.

18. Aphraates, *Homily* 23 (PS 2 [ed. J. Parisot]:128, 14-17).

19. Theodore of Mopsuestia in Nicetas, *Thesaurus* 5, 30 (PG 139:1390); cf. Philostorgius, *Ecclesiastical History* 3.13 (PG 65:501), and Theodoret, *Ecclesiastical History* 2.19 (PG 82: 1057-1060).

20. *Catechism of the Catholic Church* (Mahwah, New Jersey: Paulist Press, 1994), paragraphs 292 and 703, pp. 76 and 186 respectively.

21. *La Tradition médite le Psautier chrétien* appears to emanate from a monastic source and was published by Éditions Téqui in 1973-74. See also B. de Margerie, "Insinuations trinitaires dans le Psaume 33 (32), 6 chez les Pères de l'Église et notamment chez Saint Basile" in *Augustinianum* 40 (2000) 35-41.

22. Irenaeus, *Against Heresies* 3.8.3 (ed. Harvey, 2:29), or in Sources chrétiennes 211 (ed. Rousseau), 94-96; and *Against Heresies* 5.12.2 (ed. Harvey, 2:350), or in Sources chrétiennes 153 (ed. A. Rousseau, 1969), 142-143; and *Against Heresies* 1.15.1 (ed. Harvey, 1:188-189), or 1.22.1 in Sources Chrétiennes 264 (ed. Rousseau, 1979), 308.

23. Origen, *On Principles* 1.3.8 (PG 11:153-155). English translation from G. W. Butterworth, *Origen: On First Principles* (London: SPCK, 1936; New York: Harper & Row, 1966), 37-39.

24. Eusebius of Caesarea, *Commentary on Psalm 32* (33), ad 6 (PG 23:282). Marie-Josèphe Rondeau shows how Eusebius, in various writings, employs Psalm 33:6, 8-9 especially to support, against Marcellus of Ancyra, the distinctions among the divine Persons. See *Les Commentaires patristiques du Psautier (IIIe - Ve siecles)*, 2.177-181.

25. Athanasius, *Third Letter to Serapion*, 5 (PG 26:632).

26. Athanasius, *Fourth Letter to Serapion*, 3 (PG 26:641).

27. Basil, *Homily on Psalm 32* (33), ad 6 (PG 29:333).

28. Basil, *Against Eunomius* 3.4 (PG 29:661).

29. Basil, *On the Holy Spirit* 16 (38) (PG 32:136; Pruche, 376-381; Anderson, 61-63).

30. Basil, *On the Holy Spirit* 16 (38-40) (PG 32:137-144; Pruche, 380-392; Anderson, 63-67).

31. Theodoret of Cyrrhus, *Commentary on Psalm 32* (33), ad 6 (PG 80:1096). English translation by Robert C. Hill in *Theodoret of Cyrus: Commentary of the Psalms (1-2)*, Fathers of the Church, vol. 101 (Washington, D.C: Catholic University of America Press, 2000), especially 203-204.

32. Augustine, *First Sermon on Psalm 32* (33), 6 (PL 36:275).

33. Augustine, *Second Sermon on Psalm 32* (33), especially 2. 1-9 (PL 36:286-290). English translation by Scholastica Hegbin and Felicitas Corrigan in *St. Augustine on the Psalms*, Ancient Christian Writers, volume 30 (Westminster, Maryland: Newman, 1961), especially 117-124.

34. See in particular PL 36:288-289.

35. PL 36:289.

36. PL 36:288.

37. Augustine, *De Genesi ad litteram* 1.4.9-11 (PL 34:249-50), and 1.19.29-31 (PL 34:291-292).

38. Pseudo-Jerome, *Brevarium in Psalmos* (PL 26:821-1270), in particular PL 26:970-971).

39. Cassiodorus, *Expositio in Psalterium*, ad 32 (33):6 (PL 70:227-228). Throughout his commentary on Psalm 50 (51), for instance, Cassiodorus sees David the prophet as knowingly a trinitarian, even "devoted to the undivided Trinity" (PL 70:357-372, especially 366).

40. Thomas Aquinas, *Opera Omnia*, Parma edition (Typis Petri Fiaccadori), volume 14 (1863), 261. The procession of the Spirit is seemingly understood along the lines of the filioque: "Dicitur autem spiritus oris, quia verbo appropriatur os; unde idem est dictum, ac si diceret, Spiritus verbi, quia est spiritus filii et veritatis."

41. WA 54:56-57; English translation from *Luther's Works*, volume 15 (St. Louis: Concordia, 1972), 301-303 (altered). At the first citation of the Psalm verse, Luther's text in the Weimar edition actually bears the curious reading "Der Himmel ist durchs Wort des Herrn gemacht, und all sein Heer *durch den Mund seines Geistes*" (i.e., by the mouth of his Spirit).

42. WA 54:67; *Luther's Works* 15.314; cf. the beginning of the "Sermon on the Gospel for the Main Christmas Service" (WA 10/1/1: 182-186; *Luther's Works* 52:42-45).

43. *Commentary on the Book of Psalms* by John Calvin, translated by James Anderson (1845), volume 1 reprinted (Grand Rapids: Eerdmans, 1949), 540-543.

44. *Psaumes Octantetrois de David, mis en rime francoise par Clément Marot et Théodore de Bèze* (1551), facsimile edition New Brunswick, New Jersey: Friends of Rutgers University Libraries, 1973, 105-110.

45. *Works of Isaac Watts*, volume 4 (1753), 30 and 31. At the end of his Hymns and Spiritual Songs, Watts adds in various meters sixteen versions, shorter or longer, of the Gloria Patri, "to be sung either alone or at the conclusion of another hymn" (ibid., 267-269).

46. Even a scholar so sympathetic to the spiritual reading of the Psalms as Louis Jacquet declares that the "fuller sense" of our verse could have been known "only to the principal author of the inspired document, God Himself, and in no way to the biblical writer"—even if the verse did turn out to be "a providential marker on the way to the NT revelation of the trinitarian mystery"; see *Les Psaumes et le coeur de l'homme: Étude textuelle, littéraire et doctrinale*, volume 1 (Gembloux: Duculot, 1975), 701.

47. In *Die Psalmen I: Psalm 1-50* (Würzburg: Echter Verlag, 1993), Frank-Lothar Hossfeld and Erich Zenger state programmatically that consideration of the reception of the Psalms in the patristic and liturgical tradition is "indispensable" to a hermeneutically and theologically satisfactory commentary on the Psalter (p. 24f.); but in view of the size of the task they defer it to their work in Herders *Theologischer Kommentar*, which (so far as I know) has not yet appeared.

48. For a historical study of a trinitarian approach to the whole of Scripture on the part of one classic theologian, see my article "Wesley's Trinitarian Hermeneutics" in *Wesleyan Theological Journal* (2001); and for a normative systematic approach to the Bible along trinitarian lines, the doctoral dissertation of my pupil Telford Work, to be published in book form by Eerdmans under the title *Living and Active: Scripture in the Economy of Salvation.*

49. A remarkable statement of this view is found in the Psalm-homilies of the late fourth or early fifth centuries by Asterius from Syrian Antioch. In explaining "the secrets of the Son" mentioned in the superscription of Psalm 9 (LXX), Asterius identifies the Son with "the Only begotten God, the Logos, consubstantial with the Father" and then continues: "Whence did David know the secrets of the Son? From the Son's revealing of them to him. He himself [David] says: 'Thou hast revealed to me the unknown things and the secrets of thy wisdom' (Psalm 50 [51]:8). For he told the mysteries to David as his father according to the flesh. And what are the secrets of the Son? The mysteries of his incarnation, which were hidden from all ages and all generations but were revealed to his saints, including David. And that the secret mysteries of the Son were revealed to David, the prophet bears witness when he speaks of the Son's descent from heaven: 'He bowed the sky and came down, and darkness hid him' (2 Samuel 22: 10-12)." See Wolfram Kinzig, "Bemerkungen zur Psalmenexegese des Asterius" in *Christliche Exegese zwischen Nicaea und Chalcedon*, eds. J. van Oort and U. Wickert (Kampen: Kok Pharos, 1992), 104-131, in particular 118.

50. Epiphanius cites the dictum several times in his *Panarion* (23:5; 41:3; 66:42); see Alfred Resch, *Agrapha: Aussercanonische Schriftfragmente* (Leipzig: Hinrich, 1906), 207f.

51. In the twentieth century, the most resolutely christological reading of the Psalms was perhaps that offered, in "pre-critical" mode, by Dietrich Bonhoeffer, signatory of the Barmen declaration and teacher in the Finkenwalde seminary of the Confessing Church: *Das Gebetbuch der Bibel: Eine Einführung in die Psalmen* (1940), in *Dietrich Bonhoeffer: Werke*, volume 5 (Munich: Kaiser, 1987), 104-132; *Dietrich Bonhoeffer Works*, volume 5 (Minneapolis: Fortress, 1996), 155-177. In the perspective of current "canon criticism" and "composition studies," Georg Braulik has argued for the eschatologically oriented "messianic" character of the entire final Psalter on the basis of the structural location of the "royal psalms"; relatedly, Braulik detects a "Davidisation" of the Psalms over the later OT period, so that David ended up as the "Integrationsfigur" of the Psalter. Insofar as the identity of "royal David" was extended to the people, an ecclesiological dimension of the Psalter was also presaged, as well as the christological. See Georg Braulik, "Christologisches Verständnis der Psalmen—schon im Alten Testament?" in *Christologie der Liturgie. Der Gottesdienst der Kirche—Christusbekenntnis und Sinaibund*, eds. Klemens Richter and Benedikt Kranemann (Freiburg: Herder, 1995), 57-86. This article of Braulik's may function as a research report on the treatment of the Psalms by *Alttestamentler* over the latter half of the twentieth century, and especially the last quarter.

52. Augustine, *Sermon on Psalm 144* (145), 1 (PL 37:1869): "ut bene ab hominibus laudetur Deus, laudavit se ipse Deus."

53. Henry Fish and Thomas O. Summers, *The Wesleyan Psalter: A Poetical Version of Nearly the Whole Book of Psalms by the Rev. Charles Wesley* (Nashville: 1855), 89-91. The hymn begins "Righteous souls, rejoice in God."

54. With the entire (anti-Marcionite) Christian tradition, my paper has assumed the identity between "the God of Israel" and "Father, Son, and Holy Spirit." For a wonderfully subtle historic and systematic investigation of that theme in terms of worship, see Bruce D. Marshall, "Do Christians Worship the God of Israel?" in *Knowing the Triune God*, eds. James Buckley and David Yeago (Grand Rapids: Eerdmans, 2000). Marshall would like to find an affirmative trinitarian answer to his question which does not disinherit or disfranchise the continuing people of Israel after the flesh; but he has to leave that issue unresolved at the end of his chapter.

55. On "psalter collects," see briefly Pierre Salmon, *L'Office divin* (Paris: Éditions du Cerf, 1959), 123-130; and for three ancient series of them in Latin, see Louis Brou, *The Psalter Collects: From V—VIth Century Sources*, Henry Bradshaw Society, volume 83 (London, 1949); one of these series is further investigated in Thomas S. Ferguson, *Visita Nos: Reception, Rhetoric, and Prayer in a North African Monastery* (New York: Peter Lang, 1999). The revival of the daily office in the vernacular after Vatican II has stimulated the crafting of new "psalm prayers" to go with the Psalms in the Hours; French compositions are found, for instance, in *Le Psautier de la Bible de Jérusalem* (Paris: Éditions du Cerf) and in *Le Psautier: Version oecuménique, texte liturgique* (Paris: Editions du Cerf, 1977). The Reformed tradition followed another ancient practice, that of summarizing the "argument" of the Psalm; see, for instance, Augustin Marlorat, *In CL Psalmos Davidis, etc.* (Geneva, 1585), and Neil Livingston, ed., *The Scottish Metrical Psalter of A. D. 1635* (Glasgow, 1864). In an appendix Livingston also prints an entire series of "Prayers upon the Psalms" that figured only in the 1595 edition of the Scottish book. The prayer "upon" Psalm 33 runs as follows: "O Eternall God, grant unto us, that thy haly name may alwayes be magnified amangis the middis of us: and that thy mightie and haliee word may sa be imprented in our harts, that we enterpryse nathing against thy godlie will: to the intent that we continuallie depend on thy gude Providence: and be replenishit with that joy, that sall uphald our hope of al thay gud thingis, that thou hes promeist to us through Jesus Christ. So be it."

56. J. M. Neale and R. F. Littledale, *A Commentary on the Psalms from Primitive and Medieval Writers and from the Various Office-Books of the Roman, Moxaribic, Gallican, Greek, Coptic, Armenian, and Syriac Rites* (London and New York, fourth edition 1884), 1.528.

TOWARD RECOVERING THEOLOGICAL EXEGESIS*

BREVARD S.CHILDS

In an important article David Yeago[1] has made a notable contribution in sharply defining the basic issues at stake in recovering a truly theological understanding of Scripture. He has also sounded the strongest challenge to the biblical discipline to put aside the long-standing prejudice of the Enlightenment whose goal was to free the study of the Bible from the so-called heavy-hand of dogma.

Yeago's essay is courageous and bold because it flies in the face of the whole scholarly biblical guild. This is not to suggest that everyone in the guild is doing the same thing or has only one critical agenda. Clearly this is not the case. There are indeed commonly held assumptions shared by most which still allow for different specializations and programs. We are all aware of the tensions between the older historical critics and the newer post-modern literary practitioners. Still the various sub-groups all share the common caricature of the relationship between exegesis and theology in assuming that the former is an independent historical, philological, and literary exercise which follows the established rational rules of critical inquiry, whereas the latter is a dependent, largely subjective construct of a speculative nature. Moreover, it is generally assumed that the interpreter brings to bear on the text his or her own "construal"—whether individual or communal is hermeneutically irrelevant—by which to render an inert composition meaningful for someone. Of course, by shifting the focus of exegesis to the imaginative creation of the interpreter one falls into all the traps of 19th century Protestant liberalism which transformed the theocentric focus of Scripture into anthropology.[2]

The decisive contribution of Yeago lies in correctly insisting that traditional Christian exegesis understood its theological reflection to be responding to the coercion or pressure of the biblical text itself. It was not merely an exercise in seeking self-identity, or in bending an inherited authority to support a sectarian theological agenda. His illustration is fully persuasive that the church's struggle with the testimony to God, found in both Testaments, finally forced a triune formulation of the identity of the one God, even though neither Testament made explicit reference to the Trinity. Thus to suggest that the Christian Church simply in-

*This article originally appeared in *Pro Ecclesia* 6, no. 1 (1997) 16-26. (Published with permission.)

troduced a foreign component of Greek speculation into the Hebrew tradition is a fundamental misunderstanding of the theological process involved in the church's response to the witness of Scripture regarding the identity of God. The one God of both Testaments is surely monotheistic, but not a monolithic monad; rather, God is a dynamic reality in constant inner-communication.

There is, in addition, another aspect of the Scripture's pressure which needs further exploration beyond Yeago's description. The coercion of Scripture also functions critically in relation to Christian dogmatics to fragment and shatter traditional dogmatic structures. Especially in the Reformers' attack on the scholastics one sees how Scripture exerted not only a centripetal, but also a centrifugal force in subjecting all human traditions to radical criticism in the light of the gospel. Right at this juncture one senses a decisive difference between Aquinas and Luther in the use of the Bible.

Now the purpose of this essay, which is fully supportive of Yeago's challenge, is both to outline from the perspective of a biblical scholar some of the major hurdles which still need to be overcome, and also to propose some further historical, hermeneutical, and exegetical reflections which may aid in bridging the enormous gap which presently obtains between serious theological reflection and the current goals and practices of the biblical fields.

THE CONTINUING OBSTACLES TO THEOLOGICAL EXEGESIS

At the outset Yeago has made it very clear that he does not judge a historical critical reading of the biblical text in itself to be antagonistic to theological exegesis. Rather, the issue turns on how the critical enterprise is envisioned and how its analysis is used in interpreting the biblical text. Yeago proceeds to make a logical distinction between judgments and concepts and offers some illustrations of the hermeneutical significance of the distinction. The problem is that this distinction, however valid, is strange and unfamiliar to the majority of biblical scholars and, at the very least, will have to be translated to another idiom if it is to have any serious impact. My own attempt to delineate a similar hermeneutical distinction in terms of canonical function has also not met with widespread comprehension or acceptance within the biblical guild. I am aware that there are other important terms which were developed in the church's arsenal to make such crucial theological distinctions—the Greek Church Fathers' use of skopus would be an example—but most of these have also been lost in current exegesis in spite of the heroic effort of scholars such as T. F. Torrance,[3] and remain virtually unknown within the biblical discipline. In a word, much more effort has to be made by theologians and church historians in rendering the church's venerable exegetical tools comprehensible to a generation largely nurtured and trained within the traditions of the Enlightenment.[4]

There is another sobering point to be made. The field of biblical studies for the last two hundred years has been strewn with countless examples of attempts to recover serious theological exegesis which have not succeeded. This assessment is not to imply that these efforts were totally abortive. One should be truly grateful for those brief moments of genuine illumination even if they could not be sustained before the onslaughts of powerful and learned adversaries. One thinks, for example, of the valiant attempt during the early years of the Oxford Movement to translate into English large portions of the exegesis of the Church Fathers in the hopes that a recovery of the church's exegetical traditions would halt the corrosive effects of historical criticism's entering England both from within and from without. Yet one is deeply saddened to see even in E. B. Pusey's own biblical commentaries[5] how distant he was from the Church Fathers and how he had lost the key to theological interpretation. Or again, W. Vischer's programmatic interpretation of the Old Testament as a "witness to Jesus Christ"[6] not only sounded the alarm for the German church, but also served to offer support during the period of the Nazi threat to a host of hard-pressed pastors who continued to search for a word of God from the Old Testament. However, in the end, Vischer's repristination of Luther's christological interpretation could not be sustained and was soon repudiated even by Europe's most avowedly confessional Old Testament scholars (von Rad, Vriezen, Zimmerli, Wolff).[7]

Finally, Karl Barth's name emerges above all others in the 20th century as providing the most ambitious attempt to construct church dogmatics on the foundation of biblical exegesis. One only has to compare Barth's sustained use of detailed exegesis throughout his dogmatics with Brunner, Althaus, Niebuhr, Tillich and Ebeling, to name only a few, to see what a remarkably different world he had entered from that of his contemporaries. Yet for various reasons Barth's exegesis, for all its brilliant insights and massive stimulus, remained a "virtuoso performance" (the term is Paul McGlasson's) which could not be duplicated and which left little lasting impact either on the biblical academy or on the church. Here the contrast with the enduring biblical contribution of the Reformers is painfully evident.

SOME POSITIVE STEPS FORWARD

In spite of the continuing inability of the modern biblical discipline to enter seriously into the task of theological exegesis, it would give a false impression to suggest that nothing of importance has occurred from the side of the academy. One must gladly acknowledge that there has been some significant hermeneutical progress made on several fronts. Over against J. P. Gabler's misconstrued attempt of 1787 sharply to separate the historical from the theological components of exegesis, it has become increasingly clear to many moderns that the relationship between exegesis and theology is a far more complex and subtle one than earlier envisioned. True exegesis is basically dialectical in nature. One comes to any text already with certain theological (ideological) assumptions and the task of good exegesis is to penetrate so deeply into the text that even these assumptions are called into question, tested, and revised by the subject matter itself.

The implication is that exegesis does not confine itself to registering only the verbal sense of the text, but presses forward through the text to the subject matter (*res*) to which it points. Thus *erklären* and *verstehen* belong integrally together in the one enterprise and cannot be separated for long. The presence of the dogmatic judgment accompanying the exegetical task is in itself far from negative; rather, the crucial issue turns on the quality of both the exegetical analysis and the theological reflection in relation both to text and subject matter.

Then again, recent critical work on the problem of determining a text's *sensus literalis*[8] has made it abundantly clear that the literal sense was never restricted to a verbal, philological exercise alone, but functioned for both Jews and Christians as a "ruled reading" in which a balance was struck between a grammatical reading and the structure of communal practice or a "rule of faith" (*regula fidei).*

Finally, the recent interest in the subject of canon has highlighted certain features of interpretation, which point in a positive direction. There is a broad consensus that it is incumbent on a responsible interpreter not to "Christianize" the Old Testament by reading back into the biblical text later religious concerns, but to do justice to the discrete voice of the Old Testament according to its true historical context. One of the recurrent themes levelled against W. Vischer was that it was "dishonest" to replace an original historical meaning with one which had been imposed from outside onto the text. However, the reason for defending the integrity of the Old Testament "according to its own voice" now rests on a far more profoundly theological understanding than those typical reflexes of the Enlightenment expounded earlier. Contemporary Christian Old Testament scholars in the post-World War II period are more concerned that the Old Testament remains the Hebrew Scriptures of the Jewish synagogue which only secondarily have been appropriated by the Christian Church. In a word, the same biblical text is heard as authoritative Scripture by two communities of faith and practice.

For Christians these Jewish Scriptures, now in the form of a Christian Old Testament, remain authoritative for the church because of their abiding role as prophecy. The New Testament functions as fulfillment of events which had been previously revealed as promise to Israel. The Jewish Scriptures in their received form functioned in this role within the developing Christian Bible without the need of Christian commentary or heavy redaction. To be sure, the ordering of books according to the LXX traditions soon became normative for Christians as revealing more clearly the continuity between the Old and the New within the one divine economy. Moreover, additional books of Hellenistic Judaism formed an enlarged canon for some groups within the early church. As a result of the abiding authority of the Old Testament as an integral canonical entity much of the concern of the Reformers resulted in at least an attempt—at times unsuccessful—to deal seriously with the literal sense of the Old Testament by eschewing allegory. The Old Testament was the voice of Israel to be interpreted at some stage historically and literally, regardless of any other larger theological agenda.

BASIC ISSUES AT STAKE

Right at this juncture the major difficulties regarding theological exegesis begin to set in for most modern biblical scholars. Critical scholarship is committed to an historical reading of the Old Testament in order to hear its own voice commensurate with its cultural setting. This position is further supported theologically by its canonical function within the Christian Bible. How can one then suggest with Yeago that there is a content-derived pressure from the biblical text evoking interpretations which transcend a simple temporal relationship respecting the two Testaments? Does not such a move open the way to uncontrolled allegory?

In response it is important first to recall that it was not just the Church Fathers who sought to relate the message of the gospel to the Jewish Scriptures in a manner which went far beyond asserting a relationship in terms of an historical sequence. The New Testament does not confine itself to just a temporal relationship such as that of prophecy and fulfillment. Rather its use of this temporal pattern does not rule out at the same time moving the discourse to an ontological plane. According to John 1:1 Jesus Christ was the eternal Word who was with God in the beginning. Colossians 1:15 speaks of his being "the image of the invisible God, the first-born of all creation for in him all things were created." Finally, Rev 13:8 makes mention of "the lamb slain from the foundation of the world." Of course, this New Testament usage does not in itself resolve the issue of theological exegesis of the whole Christian Bible, but it does provide a serious precedent for theological reflection, and calls into question the widespread reflex of biblical scholars to dismiss any category other than historical sequence as an illegitimate intrusion from the side of philosophy.

At the heart of the Christian faith lies an apparent paradox in relation to its Scriptures. On the one hand, its canonical form which consists of two Testaments provides a warrant for respecting two discrete voices according to the literal/plain sense of the texts. On the other hand, the Christian Church affirms that its Christian Bible is a unified witness bearing testimony to one Lord, Jesus Christ, who is the divine reality underlying the entire biblical canon. Are not these two approaches in irreconcilable conflict?

THE NATURE OF A MULTIPLE-LEVEL INTERPRETATION

In addressing this issue I would defend the necessity of a multi-level reading of Scripture according to different contexts. This approach does not suggest merely returning to the traditional four-fold interpretive scheme of the Middle Ages which developed some serious theological problems. First, there was always the danger, inherent already in Origen, of regarding the literal sense of the text as peripheral or even as "carnal." Again, the different levels of a text were constructed often in a static and arbitrary manner which resulted in fragmenting the text's unity as exemplified in the exegesis, say, of Bede. Finally, the integral connection of text and subject matter was often seriously blurred and the theological *skopus* was lost in a mass of disconnected observations, as one often finds in Jerome.[9] In the end, the Protestant Reformers became increasingly critical of traditional exegesis because the clear voice of Scripture was compromised by a din of dissonant notes. Nevertheless, in spite of its shortcomings, traditional medieval exegesis correctly sensed the need of interpreting Scripture in ways which did justice to its richness and diversity in addressing different contexts and in performing a variety of functions when instructing the church in the ways of God. The magisterial volumes of H. de Lubac[10] remain unsurpassed in insight in showing how this often-maligned interpretive approach was actually intended to function.

When proposing a multi-level approach to Scripture I am suggesting a single method of interpretation which takes seriously both the different dimensions constituting the biblical text and the distinct contexts in which the text operates.

There is no single hermeneutical principle which would establish a fixed temporal order in exegesis or which would prioritize one entrance into the text. The test of success lies in the ability of exegesis to illuminate the full range of the sense of the text while holding together witness and subject matter in a unity commensurate with its canonical function. For pedagogical reasons I would distinguish three exegetical points of entry.

1. In order to hear the voice of the Old Testament's witness in its own right, it is essential to interpret each passage within its historical, literary, and canonical context. If one is dealing seriously with the Old Testament genre of story as one legitimate form of witness, then in this context to read back into the story the person of Jesus Christ, as Vischer did, or to interpret the various theophanies as the manifestation of the second person of the Trinity, is to distort the testimony and to drown out the Old Testament's own voice. On the story level one cannot fuse promise and fulfillment. In classic terminology the appeal is to the *sensus literalis* of the Scriptures. However, even when restricting oneself to the Hebrew Bible according to its canonical shape, the serious interpreter is still constrained to relate the text's verbal sense to the theological reality which confronted historical Israel in evoking this witness.

2. There is another avenue into the Christian Bible which does not in itself contradict the literal/historical reading, but rather extends it. This reading emerges from the recognition of a two part canon and it seeks to analyze structural similarities and dissimilarities between the witnesses of both Testaments, Old and New. This approach to the two Testaments is neither a phenomenological, history-of-religions comparison of two sets of writings, nor is it merely a descriptive history of exegesis. Rather, it is an exegetical and theological enterprise which seeks to pursue a relationship of content. For example, in terms of an understanding of God, it inquires as to what features the two Testaments hold in common respecting the mode, intention, and goal of God's manifestations. A comparison is made, but not just on a conceptual level. Instead, a theological enterprise is engaged in which neither witness is absorbed by the other, nor are their contents fused. Once again, a theological relationship is pursued both on the level of textual witness and that of the discrete subject matter (*res*) of the two collections.

3. Finally, there is a third entrance to biblical exegesis which arises from the Christian affirmation that the church's Bible comprises a theological unity, even though its form combines two distinct parts, each with a unique voice. The pursuit of the nature of this theological relationship provides the focus toward engaging critically this dimension of exegesis. A level of theological construction is brought together in rigorous reflection in which the full reality of the subject matter of Scripture, gained from a close hearing of each separate Testament, is explored.

Many modern interpreters would probably agree that it is legitimate for a Christian interpreter at some penultimate stage in exegesis to move into a homiletical mode of discourse to accommodate a church audience, and from a subjective, confessional stance join the witnesses of the two Testaments into a kind of Christian biblical theology. The effect of this personal construal, however, lies outside all critical criteria and can be neither proven nor disproven by rational argument. The reader or hearer is often invited to engage in a flight of creative exploration and to enter a world reimaged by liberating imagination. The effect of this interpretive move is to assign the product of this activity to the human creative power of its author and recipients. This understanding of biblical interpretation is precisely what I do *not* have in mind when I speak of a third avenue of exegesis. In my opinion, this approach shares all the assumptions and fatal weaknesses of classic Protestant theological liberalism and, in the end, is a delusion of human *hybris*.

Rather, I am suggesting that confronting the subject matter of the two discrete witnesses creates a necessity for the interpreter to encounter the biblical text from the full knowledge of the subject matter gained from hearing the voices of both Testaments. The interpreter now proceeds in a direction which moves from the reality itself back to the textual witness. The central point to emphasize is that the biblical text itself exerts theological pressure on the reader, demanding that the reality which undergirds the two witnesses not be held apart and left fragmented, but rather critically reunited.

A most obvious example of this pressure from the biblical text is found in the church's formulation of a trinitarian doctrine of God as a response to the biblical testimony, as Yeago has shown. Similarly to speak of the witness of the Old Testament to Jesus Christ (*Christuszeugnis*) is to move beyond the hearing of the Hebrew prophets testifying to a coming royal figure. Rather, in the light of the life, death, and resurrection of Jesus Christ in the history of Israel, the texts of both Testaments in their fragmentary testimony to God's mysterious purpose of new creation take on fresh life. Thus, when the interpreter moves from the reality of God manifest in action back to the Scriptures themselves for further illumination of the divine economy, he or she is constrained to listen for a new song which breaks forth from the same ancient, sacred texts. As a result, in spite of generations of scholarly denial, few Christians can read Isaiah 53 without sensing the amazing morphological fit with the passion of Jesus Christ.

How can one claim to read Isaiah as the voice of Israel in the Hebrew Scriptures and at the same time speak of its witness to Jesus Christ? It is not only possible, but actually mandatory for any serious Christian theological reflection. Because Scripture performs different functions according to distinct contexts, a multi-level reading is required even to begin to grapple with the full range of Scripture's role as the intentional medium of continuing divine revelation.

In the first instance, one seeks to hear the historic voice of Israel in its literal/plain sense. The voices of the prophets testify to a growing future hope of salvation in the very midst of political disaster. These witnesses are often fragmentary, at times contradictory, and always veiled in obscurity. Nevertheless, a literal and historical interpretation of the Old Testament is exegetically crucial especially in revealing just how fragmentary, mysterious, and obscure was the nature of God's messianic promise to Israel which, even following the exile, continued to expand into a host of diverse directions.

In the second instance, one is using Scripture as an authoritative collection of sacred writings which has assumed a unique shape and been given a special role within the Christian community of faith as the continuing vehicle of divine manifestation. In this role the text of Scripture, when infused by the Spirit with the full ontic reality of God, resonates with a fresh voice, and evokes from its readers the response of praise and wonder. This voice which transcends its original historical origins calls forth the hymns, liturgy, and art of the church in ever-changing forms of grateful response. This is the genre of praise and thanksgiving.

The same words of Scripture now perform a different role in instructing the church toward an obedient and joyful life. To project this depth of meaning and experience back into the past as if this interpretation must be coextensive with its original textual sense is not only a basic confusion of genre, but it falsely de-historicizes the canonical witness of the two discrete portions of the Christian Bible. However, to speak of *Christuszeugnis* in the sense being proposed is to describe a text-oriented hearing of Scripture by a Christian community of faith which allows biblical texts to resonate from the force of a divine reality gained through an encounter with the entire Christian Bible. This approach is far removed from Vischer's in that its genre is confession not apologetics, its function is worship not disputation, its content is eschatology not time-bound history, and its truth is self-affirming not analytical demonstration.

In sum, if this description of the nature of truly theological exegesis is to any degree convincing, then the conclusion is inescapable. Our modern critical understanding of the task of exegesis, whether on the left or right of the current theological spectrum, needs major overhauling. Simply to suggest minor adjustments is hopelessly inadequate for doing justice to the true goals of interpretation and will only result in the repetition of past failures. At a very minimum it implies that biblical interpretation cannot continue in its present isolation, cut off from the essential aid of church history, patristics, and dogmatics, but must strive to combine its discipline within the widest possible context of rigorous theological training in the service of church and world.

IMPLICATIONS FOR JEWISH-CHRISTIAN DIALOGUE

A final point to emphasize is that Christianity can make no legitimate theological claim to be superior to Judaism, or that the New Testament is of a higher moral quality than the Old Testament. Human blindness and sin envelop the one as much as the other. Rather, the claim being made is that the divine reality made known in Jesus Christ stands as judge of both religions. This assertion means that Judaism through God's mercy has indeed grasped divine truth in Torah, even when failing to recognize therein the truthful manifestation of God in Jesus Christ. Conversely, Christianity, which seeks to lay claim on divine truth in the name of Christ, repeatedly fails to grasp the very reality which it confesses to name. In a word, two millennia of history have demonstrated that Jews have often been seized by the divine reality testified in its Scriptures, but without recognizing its true name, whereas Christians have evoked the name, but frequently failed to understand the reality itself.

The real task of theological dialogue between Jews and Christians does not lie in exploring the religious boundaries of a lowest common denominator within a secular society, nor does it consist in engaging in common ethical causes—good as the latter maybe. For serious Jews and Christians such endeavors remain, in the end, theologically uninteresting and do not touch the heart of either community. Rather, true dialogue must engage itself with the elements of uniqueness of each group and focus on its highest denominator. Perhaps one place to begin is for Jews and Christians to agree in confessing faith in the one eternal God of Israel who also wills salvation for the Gentiles. Each community will make its own formulation in response to the Bible's pressure to retain Israel's particularity commensurate with the universal rule of God. For the Christian church the continuing paradox of its faith lies in its encounter through the Jewish Scriptures with the selfsame divine presence which it confesses to have found in the face of Jesus Christ.

NOTES

1. David S. Yeago, "The New Testament and Nicene Dogma: A Contribution to the Recovery of Theological Exegesis," *Pro Ecclesia* 3 (1994) 152-164.

2. Cf. the numerous books of Walter Brueggemann which focus on the centrality of creative human imagination for biblical interpretation. Often in this same context one adds the component of "spirituality," but it remains unclear just who or what is meant by "spirit."

3. *Theology in Reconstruction*, London, 1965; *Divine Meaning: Studies in Patristic Hermeneutics*, Edinburgh, 1994.

4. Much of the remarkable success of Hans Frei's book, *The Eclipse of Biblical Narrative* (New Haven, 1974), derived from his choice of hermeneutical categories such as referentiality and narrative function which were immediately illuminating to both theologicans and biblical scholars.

5. *Daniel the Prophet*, Oxford, 1865; *The Minor Prophets*, Oxford, 1877.

6. *Das Christuszeugnis des Alten Testaments*, Bd. I, *Das Gesetz*, Zollikon-Zürich, 1934.

7. Cf. my article "Old Testament in Germany 1920-1940. The Search for a New Paradigm," *Altes Testament Forshcung und Wirkung, Festschrift Henning Graf Reventlow*, eds. P. Mommer and W. Thiel, Bern, 1994, 233-246.

8. R. Loewe, "The Plain Meaning of Scripture in Early Jewish Exegesis," *Papers of the Institute of Jewish Studies, London I*, Jerusalem, 1964, 140-185; B. S. Childs, "The *Sensus Literalis* of Scripture: An Ancient and Modern Problem," *Beiträge zur Alttestamentlichen Theologie, Festschrift W. Zimmerli*, eds. H. Donner, et al, Göttingen, 1976, 80-93; Kathryn Greene-McCreight, *Ad Litteram: Understanding the Plain Sense of Scripture in the Exegesis of Augustine, Calvin and Barth of Genesis 1-3*, Yale University Dissertation, 1994. A very different position is represented by K. E. Tanner, "Theology and Plain Sense," *Scriptural Authority and Narrative Interpretation*, ed. G. Green, Philadelphia, 1987, 59-78, and by R. Williams, "The Literal Sense of Scripture," *Modern Theology* 7, 1991, 121-34. In somewhat different ways both move into the liberal hermeneutical orbit of David Kelsey and are again trapped by his theory of communal "construal."

9. Cf. The interesting correspondence between Jerome and Augustine on certain biblical passages. It is conveniently edited by J. Schmid, *S. S. Eusebii Hieronymi et Aurelii Augustini Epistulae mutuae* (Florilegium Patristicum, XXII), Bonn, 1930. Although Jerome was far more learned than Augustine in respect to the Bible, one comes away from the debate with the sense that Augustine grasped the essential hermeneutical and theological issues far more clearly than Jerome.

10. H. de Lubac, Exégèse Médièvale, 4 vols., Paris, 1959-1962.

ONLY A DISTANT MEMORY: OLD TESTAMENT ALLUSIONS TO JOSHUA'S DAYS

ROBERT L. HUBBARD, JR.

L. Daniel Hawk voices the *Angst* of many concerning the Book of Joshua when he writes:

> The book of Joshua relates the execution of an ancient program of ethnic cleansing, initiated and legitimized by divine decree, and narrated with little expression of remorse save that Israel did not finish the job.... For many readers in an age haunted by violence ... this is an ugly, repugnant story that scarcely deserves retelling.[1]

The violence against native Palestinian peoples in Joshua does, indeed, pose a problem for any Christian doing biblical theology. How does one relate the violence done to Canaan's inhabitants by Yahweh and his Israelite army with Jesus' mandate that his followers eschew it (e.g., Matt 5:39; Luke 6:29; Matt 26:51-54; Mark 14:47; Luke 22:49-51; John 18:10)? Theologically, one's response to the problem shapes (or warps) one's view of the character of God, one's treatment of people of other (or no) faiths, and perhaps one's political policy toward other nations. Sadly, the Bible's influence has wreaked much historical havoc, as Niditch observed: "The particular violence of the Hebrew Scriptures has inspired violence, has served as a model of and model for persecution, subjugation, and extermination for millennia beyond its own reality."[2] According to Gordon Mitchell, in the 1970s and 1980s the Chaplain's Services of the South African Defense Force appealed to the concept of holy war in public statements.[3]

The question is, Does the OT itself, whose prophets foresee a final international harmony under Yahweh, betray any wrestling with the problem?[4] If not, does it at least offer potentially fruitful avenues to pursue for theological reflection on this issue? Elsewhere I have argued that the book of Joshua itself evidences a subtle attempt to justify theologically the survival of the Canaanite Rahab (Josh 2; 6:23-25) and the Gibeonites (Josh 9-10).[5] If true, that phenomenon attests some recognition in Israel of possible exceptions to the divine mandate to exterminate all Canaanites (Deut 7:1-6; 20:16-18). In my view, that recognition reckoned with a reality unforeseen in Deuteronomy—Canaanites who, to some extent, acknowledge the sovereignty of Yahweh. It apparently relativized the mandate's otherwise stern demands. In this paper, I cast my net more broadly by tracking allusions, echoes, or influence to the contents of the book of Joshua in the Deuteronomistic History (DtH) and the prophets, materials whose content or composition one presumes to be chronologically subsequent. My interest concerns how "later" texts present episodes from the Josh era theologically and whether they reaffirm, reformulate, or relativize its problematic aspects.[6]

ALLUSIONS TO JOSHUA IN THE DEUTERONOMIC HISTORY (PART I)

The Deuteronomistic History comprises a long historical work which opens with Deuteronomy and Joshua and ends with 2 Kings.[7] Judges 1:1 ("After the death of Joshua") marks the first post-Joshua mention of Joshua (cf. Josh 1:1; 2 Sam 1:1), while the second mention repeats wording from Josh 24:28-31 to contrast the faithfulness of the previous generation ("The people served the LORD," Judg 2:7) with the apostasy of the next ("the Israelites ... served the Baals," Judg 2:11). Theologically, Judg 2:6-10 traces this covenant breach to absence of relationship with Yahweh ("did not know the LORD") and ignorance of his past interventions for Israel ("the work ... he had done," v. 10). The stark contrast between generations implicitly lauds the faithfulness of Joshua and his contemporaries and contextually continues the indictment of 2:1-5.[8] That apostasy soon followed Joshua's death also might credit Joshua with keeping all Israel faithful. On the other hand, the apostasy distances Israel's relationship with their national God and deprives Joshua of a spiritual legacy after his death. And, despite his positive portrait by DtH (e.g., Josh 3:7-8; 4:14; 6:27; 10:14, 15; 24:31), Joshua suffers a narrative eclipse from Judg 2:23 ("nations ... not handed ... over to Joshua") to 1 Kgs 16:34. After that he completely disappears from the OT except for mention in his father's genealogy (1 Chr 7:27) and a reference to a celebration of the Feast of Booths in his days (Neh 8:17).[9] One wonders what his virtual disappearance says about the Bible writers' assessment of his life and work. Did they see him simply as overshadowed by others of greater stature and achievement (e.g., Moses, Aaron, Elijah, etc.)? Did they even know about him, or was he simply a creation of DtH? Finally, does the eclipse reflect either a desire to distance themselves from his work or the fact that their views had already advanced?

Besides the mention of Joshua, DtH has several allusions to events from his era. In a prophetic oracle, Yahweh explains Israel's current oppression by Midian as divine punishment for their idolatry (Judg 6:8-10). He offers a brief historical résumé—the most common genre in which allusions studied below occur—in the first-person (vv. 8-9): "I led you up from Egypt ... and I delivered you ... from the hand of all who oppressed you, and drove them out before you, and gave you their land" (vv. 8-9). Clearly, the "land" is that which formerly belonged to the Amorites and which Israel now occupies (v. 10)—apparently, Canaan (cf. "all the way to Gaza," v. 4). But the Israelite onslaught victimized Canaanites, so they hardly qualify as those "who oppressed you...." That description might fit the Amorite King Sihon of Transjordan who attacked Israel after they sought peaceful passage through his land (Num 21:21-25), but it best fits the coalition of five Amorite kings whose attack on Gibeon forced Israel, treaty-bound to that city, to rush to its defense (Josh 10). Apparently, they represent all the nations whom Yahweh drove out.[10]

The phrase "I drove out ... and I gave" clearly alludes to conquest under Joshua. "I [Yahweh] gave you (the land)" echoes the ancient, oft-cited divine promise to the patriarchs (e.g., Gen 15:18-21; Exod 13:5; et al.) and probably alludes to the land distribution and settlement. The language has several striking features. An underlying logic unites the pair of verbs: the driving-out must of necessity precede the giving; Yahweh cannot give what other peoples occupy. Also, both verbs are broad, summary terms devoid of details as to how Yahweh "drove" and "gave." They say nothing about Joshua's leadership or about Israel's victories at Jericho and Ai (Josh 2, 6; 7-8) and over southern and northern Canaanite coalitions (chs. 10, 11). Indeed, they speak in retrospect, stressing more the result of Yahweh's actions than the process. "I drove out" fulfills Yahweh's ancient promise (Exod 32:28-31; 33:2; 34:11) and verbally echoes Joshua's historical résumé during the covenant renewal ceremony at Shechem (Josh 24:18). More important, "I drove out" portrays the conquest as expulsion of non-Israelites by Yahweh, not their annihilation (cf. 1 Chr 17:21). Yahweh takes full responsibility for events (as in Joshua) and offers no justification for his actions. His testimony concerns an act of land dispossession by force of one people followed by its gift to the possession of another. It says nothing about the human cost in suffering or loss-of-life for the expulsion, although readers probably understand that.[11] But, in light of the inclusivist spirit of other texts (see below), one wonders if the retrospective use of "drove out" rather than "destroyed" aims to signal even divine backtracking from his earlier harsh policy.

A second historical résumé occurs in Samuel's indictment speech against Israel (1 Sam 12), a speech certainly composed by the Deuteronomist. Verse 8 recalls Jacob's migration to Egypt, the Egyptian oppression, and Yahweh's sending of Moses and Aaron to lead the exodus. Its closing line ("and [Yahweh] settled them in this place") also credits Yahweh with enabling Israel to live permanently in Canaan. Notice that, like Judg 6:9, broad description devoid of detail again dominates but also that, unlike Judg 6:9, this résumé skips over the conquest, moving from the exodus to the settlement and to the judges' era (vv. 9-11). It leaves the impression that Israel left Egypt by force, then easily settled in the land. Further, it credits Moses and Aaron, not Joshua, with settling Israel there.[12] Was Samuel (or the Deuteronomist) someone who did not know Joshua—or at least who did not credit him with any significant role in the settlement?

Probably the statement simply views Moses and Aaron as the key leaders who, notwithstanding their decease long before the settlement, determined its course (see Mic 6:4). According to Joshua the authority to apportion the land derived from Moses for the tribes settled east of the Jordan (Josh 12:6; 13:8-12) and from Yahweh via Moses for those settled west of it (14:1, 5). Thus, it is no stretch to credit Moses with the land distribution and, by implication, the settlement. As for Aaron, according to Joshua, Aaron's son, the priest Eleazar, co-led the distribution of land with Joshua; indeed, that the reports list him ahead of Joshua might imply his preeminence over Joshua (Josh 14:1; 17:4; 19:51; 21:1). Thus, Samuel's comment may simply name Aaron as the paradigmatic priest who represents all his successors, including Eleazar. On the other hand, one still asks why Moses and Aaron eclipse Eleazar and Joshua here. Presumably, the Deuteronomist had his facts straight. Is a literary "halo effect" in play? Does the tradition regard Moses and Aaron so highly (and, perhaps, Joshua so poorly) as to credit them with everything?

ALLUSIONS TO JOSHUA IN THE DEUTERONOMIC HISTORY (PART II)

Far more theologically telling is the allusion to Saul's attempted annihilation of the Gibeonites known to us from Josh 9-10 (2 Sam 21). This marks DtH's first mention of pre-conquest non-Israelite peoples. The author's parenthetical comment (v. 2b) explains, first, that the Gibeonites are not part of the Israelites but part of "the remnant of the Amorites" (i.e., surviving descendants of Canaan's original inhabitants); second, that Israel had "sworn (an oath) to them"; third, that Saul had tried to wipe them out "in his zeal for the people of Israel and Judah." The Bible nowhere records the latter event, so questions remain—i.e., how did Saul proceed, how many deaths resulted, and why did his attempt apparently fail? Likewise, the nature of Saul's motive ("his zeal") remains obscure. Strikingly absent (again!) is any mention of Joshua, despite his key role in the earlier oath-swearing episode. The reference to both Israel and Judah implies an issue of national importance for Saul. Perhaps he saw the Gibeonites—a warrior people (Josh 10:2) along Israel's western border—as a security threat. Certainly, Saul's massacre of the priesthood of Nob confirms his capacity for violence (1 Sam 22:16-19; cf. also 28:3), but there is no evidence to suggest that Saul's zeal sprang from a passion to implement the original Mosaic mandate of annihilation.[13]

Clearly, however, Saul's attack on the Gibeonites (v. 5) violated the oath sworn by Israel under Joshua not to annihilate them (Josh 9:15-19).[14] To remove the bloodguilt and restore blessing to Israel, David sends seven sons of Saul to the surviving Gibeonites (vv. 3, 8), who impale and publicly hang them (v. 9), the standard ancient punishment for treaty-breakers. Later, as a humanitarian gesture toward Saul's family, David has the bones of Saul and Jonathan brought from Jabesh-gilead for proper burial in the tomb of Saul's father, presumably along with the bones of the seven from Gibeon (vv. 11-14; cf. LXX of v. 14). The resumption of answered prayers (v. 14b) and subsequent victories (vv. 15-22) confirm the resumption of divine favor.[15] Several important theological points emerge from this allusion. First, the text implies Yahweh's acceptance, whether grudging or otherwise, of the oath binding Israel and the Gibeonites.[16] At least in my view, that inference makes more sense than to assume that Yahweh would enforce an oath which displeased him. Or, put differently, if Yahweh regarded the Gibeonites as still subject to *ḥērem*, then Saul would have earned approbation not bloodguilt by seeking their annihilation.

Second, the text suggests Davidic endorsement of the presence of non-Israelites within Israel. David clearly acts because he recognizes the ancient oath's validity, and that implies his acceptance of the Gibeonite presence. That implied endorsement is important because DtH portrays David as the benchmark of loyalty to Yahweh for his royal successors (e.g., 1 Kgs 11:6; 15:3, 5; 2 Kgs 14:3; 18:3; 22:2; et al.).

Third, the text may suggest acceptance of the Gibeonites by the editors of DtH itself. If the scholarly consensus is right that the Deuteronomists incorporated rather than composed this pericope, its inclusion as is in DtH suggests at least tacit acceptance of its more inclusivist viewpoint concerning those non-Israelites. If the consensus is also right that the book of Deuteronomy originally introduced

DtH, then this story's incorporation also suggests that the editors of DtH somehow saw the Gibeonites as an exception to that book's *ḥērem* policy. The question now becomes, Were the Deuteronomists or other Israelite theologians willing to extend this ethnic inclusivism beyond the Gibeonites?

One clue comes in parallel reports in Kings and Chronicles that Solomon conscripted non-Israelite peoples for his construction projects (1 Kgs 9:20-21; 2 Chr 8:7-8). Both describe them as "all the people who were left," invoke a typical five-nation list ("the Amorites, the Hittites, the Perizzites, the Hivites, and the Jebusites"), and qualify them as "not of the people of Israel."[17] Both reports also explain their survival, implying awareness of the theological problem it posed. But their explanations differ significantly. Echoing earlier texts (Josh 15:63; 17:12), 1 Kgs 9:21 explains that "the Israelites were unable to destroy [them] completely" (ḥrm) but offers no further accounting (e.g., military inferiority, a lack of effort, unexpected setbacks, etc.). By presuming that explanation to be adequate, the writer also tacitly implies that the presence of non-Israelites is simply a "given," a fact-of-life in Israel which persists "to this day." Further, by listing five nations he extends that acceptance beyond the Gibeonites. Indeed, as a formulaic list, the five-nation schema symbolically includes all Canaan's peoples.

But, apparently troubled, the Chronicler significantly moderated the Kings text by two subtle changes: first, "their descendants" (1 Kgs 9:21) becomes "some of their descendants—i.e., a levy of only some, not all, non-Israelites—and, second, "were unable to destroy completely" becomes simply "had not destroyed"—i.e., the vague piel of *klh* ("to destroy") replaces the more theologically weighted hiphil root *ḥrm* ("to destroy completely," Deut 7:2; 20:17).[18] Thus, the Chronicler sought to downplay both the number of non-Israelites conscripted and the implied failure by Israel. But in so doing, he joins DtH in accepting as a given the presence of non-Israelites in Israel, perhaps even in his own post-exilic era ("to this day"; cf. Ezra 9:1).[19] More important, by minimizing Israel's culpability, he seems to distance himself from the more extreme position of the deuteronomic mandate.

An intriguing reference in Joab's census-taking itinerary shares the same inclusivist attitude (2 Sam 24:5-7). His route swings in a giant arc north from Aroer, east of the Dead Sea, to Dan, then westward past Tyre and south along the coast then inland to Beersheba. In essence, it describes the outer boundaries of David's realm, the limits within which the census tallied its numbers.[20] Verse 7 mentions "cities of Hivites and Canaanites" east of Tyre—apparently, a well-known phenomenon—subject to David's rule. It implies continuing contact within the kingdom between Israel and non-Israelites who were originally subject to *ḥērem*.[21] For our purposes, the important thing is the historical reality which v. 7 assumes—that such non-Israelite cities existed under David (or Solomon, if one prefers that date for the itinerary), that he apparently had not subjected them to *ḥērem*, and that DtH once again reports that reality without apparent criticism.

ALLUSIONS IN THE DEUTERONOMIC HISTORY TO JOSHUA'S CURSE AND LATER POLEMICS

This brings us to 1 Kgs 16:34 and its allusion to Joshua. The text explains that the disaster which struck a certain Hiel of Bethel who "built Jericho" happened "according to the word of the LORD, which he spoke by Joshua son of Nun" (cf. Josh 6:26). In reality, what Joshua spoke was a curse which said that to lay Jericho's foundations and gates would cost the builder, respectively, his oldest and youngest sons. But 1 Kgs 16 fails to clarify whether Hiel sacrificed his two sons as a foundation ritual—an alleged ancient practice attested archaeologically—or suffered their loss as the curse's penalty after completing the construction.[22] Other interpretive issues need not detain us (e.g., the literary intention of this notice with respect to Ahab, its tradition history, etc.). But notice that what Josh 6:26 reports as Joshua's oath 1 Kgs 16:34 now represents as his spoken prophetic oracle.[23] This is no surprise since one of DtH's major themes is the fulfillment of the prophetic word (e.g., 1 Kgs 13:29-32; 2 Kgs 23:17-18). Apparently, DtH saw no theological problem in characterizing "Cursed before the LORD" (Josh 6:26)—a human word invoking divine support—as "the word of the LORD"—a divine word spoken by a human voice. Did DtH find justification in the fact that Joshua once invoked the messenger formula "Thus says the LORD" and spoke as "I, Yahweh" (Josh 24:2-13)? More important, does this imply that DtH now reckons Joshua also among the prophets? Or has DtH simply coopted his oath for ideological purposes? As noted above, however, one thing is certain: henceforth, Joshua virtually vanishes.

Finally, allusions to non-Israelite peoples occur in stereotyped formulae which DtH invokes to characterize religious misconduct during the monarchy. 1 Kings 14:24 sets the tone, indicting male temple prostitutes in Judah for doing "all the abominations of the nations [elsewhere, the Amorites] that the LORD drove out before the people of Israel." The roster of abominators includes all DtH's historical villains: Ahab (1 Kgs 21:26); Ahaz (2 Kgs 16:3; 2 Chr 28:3); the entire northern kingdom (2 Kgs 17:8, 11; cf. v. 15, they "imitated the nations around them"; Manasseh (21:2; 2 Chr 33:2), who even outdid the Amorites in wickedness (v. 11). Clearly, such formulae represent the polemical demonization of Canaan's pre-conquest peoples as paradigms of religious corruption. For DtH, Yahweh regarded anything Amorite as the ultimate abomination. The phrases imply that the Amorites' expulsion was punishment for their idolatrous religion. On the other hand, that DtH elsewhere reflects a more inclusive stance toward non-Israelite peoples suggests that one should regard these formulae as hyperbole, intense rhetoric fueled by frustrated outrage, not at the peoples themselves—they long ago had become history—but at the affront of Israelite idolatry to true Yahwism.[24]

Further, the formula continues the central metaphor of expulsion by Yahweh seen earlier. Yahweh "drove out" the peoples (but here *yrš*, not *grš*); Israel did not "completely destroy" them (Heb. *ḥrm*). Its cultural background comes from the arena of land rights, not cultic sacrifice. The prime role remains Yahweh's not Israel's. Finally, the formula invokes the same broad, general, retrospective description noted above.

ALLUSIONS TO JOSHUA IN THE PROPHETS

Seven prophetic texts allude to events from Joshua's era, three in brief historical résumés of Yahweh's past acts for Israel.[25] Amos 2:9-10 is probably the earliest[26] and forms part of Amos' climactic indictment of Israel for covenant breach (2:6-16).[27] Yahweh's historical résumé clearly alludes to the conquest and settlement:

> Yet I destroyed the Amorite before them, whose height was like the height of cedars, and who was as strong as oaks; I destroyed his fruit above, and his roots beneath. Also I brought you up out of the land of Egypt, and led you forty years in the wilderness, to possess the land of the Amorite.

Yahweh recounts his annihilation of "the Amorite," again a collective personification of the various peoples inhabiting both banks of the Jordan at the time (cf. Gen 48:22; Josh 24:15; Judg 6:10; 2 Sam 21:2). The repetition of "destroy" and the *merism* "fruit above ... roots beneath" connote total decimation, paving the way for Israel to "possess" the land.[28] The Amorite's gigantic stature and astonishing strength mark the event as a stunning, glorious victory of Yahweh the Warrior.[29] Rhetorically, the résumé wields a double-edged sword: by juxtaposing Yahweh's victories for needy Israel with Israel's abuse of needy Israelites it underscores their guilt; by alluding to prior divine judgment it anticipates Israel's own disastrous fate (see Amos 9:8). As with DtH, the allusion is not to a specific event (or events) but to the broad, general result ("Yahweh destroyed"; Israel was "to possess the land"). Also, again Yahweh rightly takes full credit for the victory but omits mention of historic roles which the book of Joshua highlights—Joshua's leadership (3:7; 4:14; 8:18-19, 26), the Transjordanian vanguard (1:14b; 4:12; 22:2-4), and Israel's army (e.g., 8:1-29; 10:11-12, 20-21). Finally, unlike DtH, which prefers the language of expulsion, Yahweh here speaks without apology or justification of violent extermination.

In Micah 6:5 Yahweh offers the second historical résumé in the prophets which alludes specifically to Israel's crossing into Canaan (vv. 3-5). The covenant lawsuit (cf. vv. 1-2) apparently concerns whether Yahweh caused Israel's disaffection (v. 3). In reply, he recalls his liberation of Israel from Egypt and his gift of leaders ("Moses, Aaron, and Miriam," v. 4). In v. 5, he calls Israel to remember his past "saving acts":

> O my people, remember now what King Balak of Moab devised, and how Balaam son of Beor answered him, and what happened from Shittim to Gilgal, that you may know the saving acts of the LORD.

After an allusion to the well-known Balaam narratives (Num 22-24) a terse itinerary follows ("from Shittim to Gilgal," v. 5b). Grammatically, the phrase probably functions as the direct object of the initial imperative "remember" (NRSV supplies "what happened," cf. NIV "your journey"). The allusion reviews Israel's movement from Shittim, their last campsite east of the Jordan (Num 25:1; 33:49 [Abel-shittim]; Josh 2:1; 3:1), to Gilgal, their first campsite west of it (Josh 4:19). But it omits all details, especially the dramatic crossing of the Jordan and Joshua's role in it.

Poetically, the mention of Joshua as the march's leader would have nicely paralleled that of Moses, Aaron, and Miriam in the previous verse (v. 4). Also, allusion to one symbolic episode from the period would have stylistically paralleled mention of the exodus and Balaam episodes.[30] Instead, the prophet quickly advances to Gilgal to make a simple point: nothing stopped the divine juggernaut; through "saving acts" (apparently presumed to be known though unstated) Yahweh got Israel to Canaan as he promised. Once again, the spotlight falls exclusively on Yahweh and his marvelous works for Israel; details of his deeds and his human cohorts require no recitation. Yahweh's deeds are presumed to rebut Israel's complaints against him.

Broad allusion also typifies Jer 2:7, another covenant lawsuit text and the last prophetic historical résumé:

> I brought you into a plentiful land to eat its fruits and its good things. But when you entered you defiled my land, and made my heritage an abomination.

Like Amos, Jeremiah contrasts what Yahweh did ("brought you into ...") with what Israel did ("defiled my land . . ."). Like Micah, the prophet alludes to Israel's entrance but offers no recounting of it. But here the stress falls more on the goodness of Israel's new land and on their defilement of it than on the in-bringing itself.[31] Once again, "brought in" simply alludes to Israel's divinely-led entrance but not to its means. A reader ignorant of Joshua would know nothing of the dramatic river crossing which made it possible (Josh 3-4). Further, the brief, summary-allusion to the latter contrasts the longer reference to the exodus and especially the wilderness period in the preceding verse (v. 6). The prophet leaves the impression that he regards those earlier events as the far greater demonstration of divine care and power—indeed, the far greater achievements—than the land entrance. In sum, of the three historical résumés in the prophets, only Amos 2 mentions the Amorites, none detail events from Joshua's era, and two give more play to the exodus and its leaders than to the conquest and settlement. The latter events seem to have suffered the same eclipse as Joshua did in DtH.

A SPECIAL CASE: EXEKIEL 47-48

Though a vision of the future rather than an allusion to the past, Ezek 47:13-48:7 has thematic connections with Josh 13-19 and, hence, merits consideration. Literarily, the speech by Yahweh reads more like a formal set of lists than a vision report. It lays out the boundaries of Israel's restored land (47:15-20) and orders its division among the tribes (47:21-48:7).[32] In reality, most of the boundary description compares to Num 33:50-34:15; only the southern boundary (Ezek 47:19) has affinities with Joshua (i.e., with the tribe of Judah's southern boundary, Josh 15:2-4).[33] Two things in this description are striking. First, Ezekiel says nothing about a new conquest. Since Israel must return home, one wonders about the reason for this omission. Elsewhere the book says that invading nations will take possession of Israelite houses (7:24) but also portrays Israel's return and resettlement as peaceful (e.g., 28:25-26; 36:8-12, 33-36; 39:25-29). Probably, the prophet deemed the invaders' possession temporary and, hence, a new conquest unnecessary. Second, the "new Israel" excludes the territory east of the Jordan which Moses had allotted to the two-and-a-half tribes (Num 32; Josh 1:12-18; 12:1-6; 13:8-34) and to which Joshua dismissed them with his blessing after the conquest (Josh

22:1-9).[34] In one sense, this exclusion is not surprising since the status of that land depended more on Moses' concession to tribal requests than on Yahweh's ancient promise. Further, Josh 22 reflects ambivalence by some in Israel over its status, if not firm conviction about its ritual uncleanness (see vv. 19, 25, 27). Third, given its northern border, the "new Israel" apparently includes both Philistia and at least southern Phoenicia. Their inclusion along with the exclusion of land east of the Jordan are significant: Ezekiel's vision returns to the land of the original patriarchal promise (47:14; cf. Gen 15:18).[35]

The allotment of territory (47:21-48:8) opens with a surprising prescription (vv. 22-23):

> You shall allot it as an inheritance for yourselves and for the aliens who reside among you and have begotten children among you. They shall be to you as citizens of Israel; with you they shall be allotted an inheritance among the tribes of Israel. In whatever tribe aliens reside, there you shall assign them their inheritance, says the Lord GOD.

As Levenson observed, "This prescription is much more radical than anything else in all the legal corpora of the Hebrew Bible."[36] Granted, the law gave resident aliens the same right to observe Passover as native-born Israelites (Exod 12:48) and mandated that Israel treat them humanely (Exod 22:20; 23:9; Lev 19:10, 33-34; 23:22; Deut 14:29; 24:14-15, 17-22). But they needed legal protection precisely because they stood unwelcome and defenseless outside Israel's tribal structure. And by legalizing the practice of gleaning, the law implied that they could not own land (Deut 24:19-22). But by granting them an "inheritance" (i.e., land), Ezekiel's vision banishes the distinction between alien and natural-born Israelite. In essence, it accords them full citizenship as long as they live in Israel and have fathered children there (i.e., they are permanent residents).[37] Certainly, the prescription also assumes their commitment to trust in Yahweh alone and to obey his covenant. Note, further, that Ezekiel's new policy relaxes the much stricter stipulation of Deut 23:2-9 which admitted only aliens from Edom and Egypt—and only after three generations of residence.[38]

Joshua 13-19 obviously provides the inspiration for the land distribution among the tribes (Ezek 48:1-8). But Ezekiel's allocation plan starkly contrasts that of Joshua. Here no Joshua divides the land on Yahweh's orders nor are lots cast; Yahweh himself decrees the divisions (47:13), and the tribes themselves distribute them ("you" plural, v. 21). Further, Ezek 48 neither details boundary markers nor lists specific cities each tribe is to possess. Instead, it grants each tribe only "one portion," not several portions for a larger tribe as before (vv. 2-7). More important, the north-south length of each tribe's portion is identical, a symbol of the future equality of the tribes, perhaps even an attempt to remedy past inequities.[39] Also, a division of seven northern and five southern tribes replaces the ancient pattern of ten northern and two southern tribes (see 1 Kgs 11:31-36). In other words, the tribes are more evenly distributed north and south of the land's central features, the temple and city. Interestingly, the schema abandons the old concept of scattered Levitical cities (Josh 21), instead gathering the Levites near the temple, perhaps as tangible expression of their status as Yahweh's own "inheritance."[40] The positioning of the other tribes seems dictated both by historical precedent—i.e., Josh 13-19 and Dan's migration (Judg 18)—and by the tribes' genealogical relationships. Per previous history, Dan, Asher, Naphtali, Manasseh, and Ephraim will again reside in the north and Simeon in the south. But it is also apparent that the children of Rachel and Leah enjoy closer proximity to the temple and city than do the children of their two handmaidens (Gen 29-30).[41]

The most surprising placement puts Benjamin and Judah closest to the consecrated area but in reversed locations. Benjamin's southern spot nearest the city might derive from his old association with Jerusalem (Judg 1:21) or from his name's meaning ("son of the right hand" [i.e., south]). Judah's northern setting might accord her a kind of honorary "pride of place" or aim to neutralize old tribal rivalries about prominence, if not actual royal hegemony, by linking him to northern tribes.[42] In any case, the positions both honor the two tribes' traditional centrality and signal the arrival of a dramatically new order. Finally, at the center of the distribution both contextually and geographically is what Zimmerli calls the "thirteenth portion" (vv. 8-22), a provision without precedent in Josh 13-19.[43] It comprises the "consecrated area" for the temple and land portions for priests, Levites, the city, and the "prince," a truly fascinating provision which falls outside our focus.

Instead, I offer several observations concerning this vision. As indicated, the land allotment plan of Ezek 47-48 draws its literary inspiration from its counterpart in Josh 13-19, the latter even dictating the placement of some tribes in Ezekiel's scheme. But there the difference ends. Ezekiel discards Joshua's detailed lists of cities and offers a new genre, what Stevenson calls "territorial rhetoric."[44] In my view, Ezek 47-48 subtly uses Josh 13-19 as a literary foil against which to highlight its differences and their contribution to the prophet's radically new view of future Israel. And nothing is more radical than the new provision for the incorporation of resident aliens who worship Yahweh. Of course, Ezekiel's view parallels that of Isa 56:1-8, although the latter extends the welcome beyond resident aliens to any "foreigners who join themselves to the LORD" but presumes them to reside outside Israel (vv. 6-7). For me this is significant: it goes beyond the far more limited policy of Deut 23. Though the text is not explicit, one may reasonably suppose that the same inclusivism would apply to any believers in Yahweh among peoples who originally fell under the *ḥērem* provision. If so, Ezekiel's view would concur with the view we observed in some texts above.

Finally, I am struck by the dynamic which underlies this new program. I concur with many that it seeks to overcome past wrongs (e.g., tribal jealousies, the oppression of aliens, long-resented royal prerogatives, etc.). I also concur that it offers an ideal new Israel infused with a new spirit—a new ethos, if you will—not a blueprint for temple construction or map for land allocation. But behind it lies a theological freedom, authorized by Yahweh, to abandon the old patterns—*ḥērem* applied indiscriminately (Deut 7; 20), the prohibition of alien land ownership (Deut 23), ancient tribal boundaries (Josh 13-19), the dispersion of landless Levites (Josh 21)—and to pursue new paths. This theological freedom allows Israel to reckon creatively with its past historical experience and with the new realities it faces in the sixth century B.C.E.[45]

Ezekiel's vision works out the logic of Israel's long experience with the person of Yahweh—his compassion toward all peoples, his eventual universal recognition by all peoples—and announces a new way for Israel to be Israel.

CONCLUSION

Christian concern with the violence in the book of Joshua launched this study of allusions to Joshua's era in the OT. Our interest was with how other books viewed Joshua, events from the book bearing his name, and non-Israelite peoples subject to *ḥērem*. Our first discovery is that, after starring in the Pentateuch and in the book of Joshua, Joshua the person suffers a narrative eclipse. The Bible rarely speaks of him—or, put differently, his contemporaries, Moses and Aaron, clearly overshadow him. Given the accolades accorded him, this eclipse is surprising, but we suggested several explanations: that DtH created him (doubtful, in my view), or that later writers simply did not regard him that highly. We also suggested that his eclipse might reflect either their desire to move beyond the violent era of Joshua or the fact that they already had. Our second discovery is that most allusions occur in short historical résumés of Yahweh's past deeds for Israel. Most begin with Israel's slavery in Egypt (only 1 Sam 12:8 opens with Jacob's migration there) and end with Israel in the promised land. Their allusions employ broad general terms (e.g., that Yahweh "drove out" or "destroyed" the nations, or that he "brought you [or Israel] into the land") and stress the result of his work, not the events which finished it. Indeed, in most cases one is hard pressed to know the specific events to which the text alludes. One wonders (but cannot prove) whether the consistent use of nonspecific language also reflects discomfort with aspects of Joshua's days.

Finally, we discovered in some texts an inclusivist spirit toward non-Israelite peoples still living in Israel at the time. The treatment of the Gibeonites in 2 Sam 21 apparently concurs with the book of Joshua in accepting them as an exception to the *ḥērem* mandate, implicitly backed by David's stature and DtH's tacit concurrence. But other texts extend that acceptance to all non-Israelite peoples in the land (2 Sam 24:7; 1 Kgs 9:20; 2 Chr 8:7-8). Indeed, the Chronicler's subtle textual modifications even seem to minimize Israel's culpability for not fully executing *ḥērem*, a reflection perhaps of that writer's misgivings or disagreement with that requirement's harshness. On the other hand, for DtH Israel's worse abomination was to follow (in one case, imitate) the religious practices of Canaan's original inhabitants. Hence, he pointedly mentioned them in formulae indicting his several villains. In my view, however, the above inclusivism suggests that in such cases DtH resorts to hyperbole—that such texts in no way negate the inclusivism. It seems likely that Amorites, the typical pre-conquest non-Israelites, were long dead, absorbed, or too isolated to pose a threat to DtH's agenda.

This inclusivist spirit reaches its radical expression in Ezekiel's vision (chs. 47-48). It not only bypasses the conquest, but remarkably decrees that believing resident aliens may own land and belong to Israelite tribes. More important, Ezekiel's vision leaves behind, loosens, and revises earlier, long-standing biblical practices. I suggested that these moves presuppose a theological freedom which authorized him to announce such changes.

In the last three decades scholars have taken a fancy to the metaphor of a "trajectories."[46] A trajectory is the path which an object take as it moves through space. Applied to scholarly discussions, the metaphor connotes a sense of movement (presumably forward) and direction (hopefully the *right* one!). In my view, the above study has uncovered a subtle theological trajectory within the OT. This trajectory shows movement by some writers away from some of the harsher aspects of the book of Joshua (and, in Ezekiel's case, of several other texts). How it relates to other parallel or contradictory trajectories, and whether it itself spawns other trajectories remains a question for further study. My hunch (if scholars may have "hunches"!) is that this movement emerges as Israelite theologians work out the logic of their theological traditions, on the one hand, and their own historical experience, on the other.[47]

Among the former I would tentatively list Yahweh's kingship of all nations, the prophetic expectation that all nations would one day worship Yahweh, and Israel's hope of a new Davidic ruler. Among the latter I would tentatively list Israel's day-to-day relations with the Rahabs and the Gibeonites of Canaan, i.e., with non-Israelites who to some degree acknowledged Yahweh. We should also contemplate Israel's experience with Babylonians who showed a similar religious openness in exile and their realization that the prophet Jonah got it wrong. Yahweh may extend the compassion Israel received at the exodus to their own enemies, and if to them, why not to their friends or neighbors? Thus, I would argue that the theological roots of the oft-invoked change from the authorized use of violence in the OT to the turn-the-other-cheek ethic in the NT lie in the OT itself. They sprout, in part, as various OT writers come to terms with the era of Joshua.

Finally, how can a Christian pastor make peace with the violent "ethnic cleansing" of the book of Joshua? In my view, that "peace" will dawn when we recognize that, unknowingly, we may have been misreading the book. By "misreading" it I mean that we tend to read it as if it had been written yesterday by a Christian rather than 2500 years ago by an Israelite and as a manual for ethics. We judge it by modern Christian standards of ethics and, on that basis, condemn its Nazi-esque policy toward Canaan. In my view, this approach is unfair to the book because it judges the book by an ethical standard which did not exist when it originated—in other words, to misread it. To read Joshua properly is to read it within its own original context, on its own cultural terms, before screening it by later standards.

What was the original world of the book of Joshua like? While the analogy has its limits, the world of Joshua compares more to the Middle Ages of European history—a cruel, harsh, violent world not yet softened by the ethical teachings and example of Jesus—than to our modern, more humane world. (I fully realize, of course, that our world also has its glaring inhumane examples, but I still affirm the general validity of the contrast I am drawing). In questioning the annihilation of Canaanites, most Christians tacitly assume that God could somehow have arranged for Israel and the Canaanites to share Canaan rather than mandate the killing of the latter by the former. But such a "modern" solution strikes me as naive and as impossible to achieve in Joshua's day as it is in contemporary Palestine. Biblical history certainly undermines its credibility. Both Pharaoh in Egypt (Exod 1-2) and Canaan's allied armies (Josh 9-11) sought Israel's annihilation, making it improbable that land-sharing would have worked. In such a rough-and-tumble neighborhood, the only way for Israel to get good land was to displace other peoples. That is just the way life was back then. More important, theologically the Bible assumes that Canaan was Yahweh's to give to whomever he wished since he owned it (Josh 1:4, 6; Ps 24:1). In the mystery of his will, at that juncture in human history, God chose to give it exclusively to a people called Israel. (I hasten to add that I do not assume Israel's eternal ownership of that land; any such assumption requires biblical justification in light of the subsequent unfolding of God's salvation plan).

But why did God decree the annihilation of the Canaanites rather than their displacement? The simple answer is that since Joshua provides no explanation, we simply do not know. Knowledge of the ancient world, however, suggests that displacement probably had as little chance of success as land-sharing. Where would the Canaanites go—to Philistia or Phoenicia along the coast, east of the Jordan river to Moab or Edom, or south to Egypt? I speculate that, had they remained so near Israel, their hopes of retaking Canaan would have fed into those nations' own dreams of conquering it. Israel would have faced centuries of military harassment, a tragic scenario for Israel since it would have compelled the diversion of precious resources from nation-building to self-defense. In the end, Israel may in fact not have survived.

But this is all risky speculation. We do better to review two theological truths which at least help me to make some rational sense of the harsh annihilation policy. First, it is a biblical truth that God owns humanity and can do with it what he wishes. There is no way to explain his election of Israel and his gift of Canaan other than to appeal to his mysterious will. The same assumption, voiced in the powerful whirlwind scene (Job 38-41), helps me make peace with God's otherwise insane treatment of Job, an individual whose moral character certainly surpassed that of the Canaanites and commended him for better treatment than he got. The second truth is that the survival of any humans this side of the Garden of Eden and the Flood derives from divine mercy, not human dessert. Given awful human sinfulness, God has every justification to annihilate anyone he wishes, and we cannot fault him if he occasionally exercises his justice with some selectivity. To me, the amazing thing is not that God selected the Canaanites for judgment but that he limited himself to them (and to others later in history).

Finally, does the annihilation policy of Joshua set any precedent? May Christians apply it in some other context, say, against militant Muslims, atheistic communists, or present or future pharaohs? Definitely not! In my view, one major implication of the present paper is that the Bible views Joshua's policy as limited to a very unique moment in history—Yahweh's conquest of Canaan and Israel's settlement there. Once Israel settles, that purpose is achieved, the mandate expires and cannot be applied elsewhere without divine warrant. As I argue above, the trajectory of God's plan for humanity points Israel in an increasingly inclusive direction. It heads toward a future day in which all people will worship Yahweh, a day in which God's people will comprise ethnically international and inclusive members. In other words, the target of the trajectory is the assembly of "a great multitude that no one could count, from every nation, from all tribes and peoples and languages …" (Rev 7:9).

Finally, how can a Christian pastor make peace with the violent "ethnic cleansing" of the book of Joshua? In my view, the first step toward that "peace" is to recognize that, unknowingly, we may have been misreading the book. By "misreading" I refer to the tendency to read it as if it had been written yesterday by a Christian rather than 2500 years ago by an Israelite. We judge it by modern Christian standards of ethics and, on that basis, condemn its Nazi-esque policy toward Canaan. In my view, this approach is unfair because it judges the book by an ethical standard which did not exist when it originated—in other words, to misread it. To read Joshua properly is to read it within its own original context, on its own cultural terms, before screening it by later standards. While the analogy has its limits, the world of Joshua compares more o the Middle Ages of European history—a creuel, harsh, violent world not yet softened by the ethical teachings and example of Jesus—than to our modern, more humane world. (I fully realize, of course, that our world also has its glaring inhumane examples, but I still affirm the general validity of this point.) Of course, to read Joshua within its own ancient context does not "solve" the problem we have with its violence, but it at least reminds us that the book well reflects the situation of its own day.

But the truly tough question is, What do we do about the character of God who decreed the mandate that so troubles us? We do well to remember threee relevant and instructive theological truths which may help us make some rational sense of Joshua. First, the Bible stresses that God's way of doing business does not always make sense to us. In Isaiah 55:9, God declares, "as the heavens are higher than the earth, so are my ways higher than your ways and my thoughts than your thoughts" (Isa 55:9). God claims to be the God of the Higher Ways and Higher Thoughts, a claim which warns us to expect that occasionally divine activity may seem mysterious, iorrational, and perhaps ethically problematic. However hard to accept, I suggest that Joshua's ethnic policy marks one such strange and mysterious divine activity. Second, it is a biblical truth that God owns humanity and can do with it what he wishes. There is no way to explain his election of Israel and his gift of Canaan other than to appeal to his mysterious will. The same assumption, voiced in the powerful whirlwind scene (Job 38-41), helps me make peace with God's otherwise insane treatment of Job, an individual whose moral character certainly surpassed that of the Canaanites and commended him for better treatment than he got. The same assumption also undergirds the mysterious election of the Church of Jesus Christ and my own totally undeserved membership in it. The third truth is that the survival of any humans this side of the Garden of Eden and the Flood derives from divine mercy, not human dessert. Given awful sinfulness, God has every justification to annihilate anyone he wishes, and we cannot fault him if he occasionally exercises his justice with some selectivity. To me the amazing thing is not that God selected the Canaanites for judgment but that he limited himself to them (and to others later in history).

Finally, does the annihilation policy of Joshua set any precedent for today? Absolutely not! I strongly oppose any appeal to Dueteronomy and Joshua to justify political or military policy today. This applies to claims to the ancient land of Canaan and to the treatment of any of its current inhabitants. Those thorny issues require thoughtful biblical exegesis and attention to matters of justice rather than a sweeping, imprecise appeal to ancient biblical claims. If my thesis holds, to appeal to Joshua to support land claims today is to reinstate an ancient policy which the Bible's writers long ago replaced. Further, in my view, the teachings of Jesus forbid Christians from applying Joshua's policy in some other context—say, against militant Muslims, atheistic communists, or present or future pharaohs—and from supporting those who appeal to it to justify their policies. On the contrary, this paper argues that the Bible views Joshua's policy as limited to as very unique moment in history—Yahweh's conquest of Canaan and Israel's settlement there. Once Israel settles, that purpose is achieved, the mandate expires and subsequently cannot be applied anywhere without divine warrant, even in Canaan itself.

More important, the trajectory of God's plan for humanity points Israel in an increasingly inclusive direction. It heads toward a future day in which all people will worship Yahweh, a day in which God's people will comprise ethnically international and inclusive members. In other words, the target of the trajectory is the assembly of "a great multitude than no one could count, from every nation, from all tribes and peoples and languages..." (Rev 7:9). Instead, the book of Joshua itself and both the Old and New Testaments model and comment a far better way for the treatment of fellow humans. And they do so on behalf of the God who created all peoples, gave them the scriptures, and intervenedin human history to b ring them salvation.[48]

NOTES

1. L. D. Hawk, "The Problem with Pagans," in *Reading Bibles, Writing Bodies: Identity and the Book* (eds. T. K. Beal and D. M. Gunn; London and New York: Routledge, 1996), 53.

2. S. Niditch, *War in the Hebrew Bible: A Study in the Ethics of Violence* (New York: Oxford University Press, 1993), 4.

3. G. Mitchell, *Together in the Land* (Sheffield: Sheffield Academic Press, 1993), 9 (an appeal "... disgusting enough to overcome my lethargy" and to inspire his Ph.D. research topic). For Christian preaching on war in support of war, especially early wars against Native Americans, see Niditch, 3-4.

4. For prophetic texts, see Isa 2:1-5//Mic 4:1-5; 19:18-25; 25:1-8; Zech 2:11; 14:16; Mal 1:11; et al.

5. R. L. Hubbard, Jr., "'What Do These Stones Mean?': Biblical Theology and a Literary Motif in Joshua," *Bulletin for Biblical Research*, forthcoming.

6. For background on my methodology, see B. D. Sommer, *A Prophet Reads Scripture: Allusion in Isaiah 40-66* (Stanford, CA: Stanford University Press, 1998), 6-31; cf. the so-called "inner-biblical exegesis" of M. Fishbane, *Biblical Interpretation in Ancient Israel* (Oxford: Clarendon Press, 1985). Sadly, my focus leaves out of consideration allusions in nine psalms.

7. Unless indicated otherwise, all scripture quotations below cite the NRSV. For a convenient discussion of the theory concerning DtH, see T. Fretheim, *The Deuteronomic History* (Nashville: Abingdon, 1983); and A. H. W. Curtis, *Joshua* (Sheffield: Sheffield Academic Press, 1994), 30-35. I have excluded 1 Kgs 8:56 from consideration below, although it shares the phrase *lōʾnāpal dābār ʾeḥād mikōl* ("not one thing failed of ...") with Josh 23:14. In my view, the deuteronomists reused the phrase without apparently intending to link the two texts.

8. Did "who did not know the LORD ... or the work that he had done for Israel" (Judg 2:10) allude to the Pharaoh "who did not know Joseph" (Exod 1:8, my rendering)? If so, the reader would expect Judg 2:10 to read "who did not know *Joshua*," thus paralleling Joseph with another human leader whose absence marked a radical change in Israel's situation. The phrase "did not know Yahweh and the work . . . for Israel" would thus sound ironic. In Egypt Pharaoh did not know Joseph and enslaved Israel; in Canaan (the land of divine promise) Israel forgot Yahweh and enslaved themselves to other gods. Cf. T. J. Schneider, *Judges* (Berit Olam; Collegeville, MN: Liturgical, 2000), 30. In my view, however, the "work" in mind here probably encompasses all Yahweh's mighty acts from the exodus to the conquest.

9. He fares better in the Apocrypha, especially Sir 46:1-8 (cf. 1 Macc 2:55; 2 Macc

12:15; 2 Esdras 7:107). But the NT only mentions him twice (Acts 7:45; Heb. 4:8) although ironically Rahab earns three mentions (Matt 1:5; Heb 11:31; Jas 2:25). I am grateful to Professor Geoffrey Wainwright for pointing out that the Church Fathers connected "Jesus" and "Joshua" because of the common Greek.

10. If "Amorites" (Judg 6:10) includes all Canaan's subgroups, then the reference might also incorporate the coalition of northern kings which Jabon King of Hazor rallied against Israel at Merom (Josh 11:1-14). Among the defeated coalition were the Amorites, Hittites, Perizzites, Jebusites, and Hivites.

11. If amended according to the LXX (so NIV; NRSV), David's later prayer similarly refers to Yahweh's having driven out nations and, interestingly enough, "their gods" (2 Sam 7:23).

12. BHS notes that many Hebrew manuscripts read *wayyōšibēm* ("he [Yahweh] settled them"), as does LXX. The current MT offers the harder reading, however, and is to be retained (so NRSV and NIV).

13. Cf. R. P. Gordon, *I & II Samuel: A Commentary* (Grand Rapids: Zondervan, 1986), 299: ". . . the Gibeonites were an affront to Saul's brand of nationalistic Yahwism, and the fact that they were settled in Benjaminite territory cannot have helped." For attempts (unpersuasive, in my view) to link the Gibeonite killings with Saul's massacre of the priests of Nob (1 Sam 22), see P. K. McCarter, Jr., *2 Samuel* (Garden City, NY: Doubleday, 1984), 441.

14. Note that the phrase "swore to them" only occurs in Josh 9:18 and 2 Sam 21:2.

15. Cf. H. W. Hertzberg, *I & II Samuel: A Commentary* (Philadelphia: Westminster, 1976), 385 ("The last word is that of the grace of God").

16. Elsewhere I argued the same point from the thematic structure of Josh 7-10. That is, ignorant of Yahweh's anger, Israel attacked Ai and failed because of Achan's hidden sin. When Israel covenants with Gibeon without consulting Yahweh (9:14), the reader expects similar failure when Israel comes to that city's rescue (10:7). But when Yahweh promises and delivers victory instead (vv. 8-43), I infer his acceptance of the Israelite-Gibeonite covenant; cf. Hubbard, "'What Do These Stones Mean?'."

17. For the latter phrase, see also Judg 19:12; 2 Sam 21:2. The texts of Kings and Chronicles differ in details. In 2 Chr 8:7 the Hittites precede the Amorites in the list, and the phrase "were not from the people of Israel" (1 Kgs. 9:20) reads simply "not from Israel."

18. S. Japhet, *I & II Chronicles: A Commentary* (Louisville: Westminster/John Knox, 1993), 624; H. G. M. Williamson, *1 and 2 Chronicles* (Grand Rapids: Eerdmans, 1982), 230 ("a slight alleviation of a possible embarrassment"); Fishbane, 204; but cf. the caution of S. L. McKenzie, *The Chronicler's Use of the Deuteronomistic History* (Atlanta: Scholars Press, 1984), 97 ("the similarity in the verb forms ... is too great to dismiss the possibility of unintentional variation").

19. Cf. Japhet, 204, who believes the Chronicler simply copied "to this day" from his source in Kings.

20. Hertzberg, 412; A. A. Anderson, *2 Samuel* (Dallas: Word, 1989), 285. McCarter, 530, provides a convenient map of the itinerary (map 10). For an assessment of its relationship to fluid political realities and its probable antiquity, see H. J. Stoebe, *Das zweite Buch Samuelis* (Gütersloh: Gütersloher Verlagshaus, 1994), 520-522. First Chronicles 21 omits it but not for ideological reasons since the itinerary contains nothing which the Chronicler "would have found offensive or adverse to his purpose" (McKenzie, 68).

21. The location of these cities roughly corresponds to the description of various groups in Josh 11:3.

22. Fishbane (500-501) offers the intriguing idea (improbable, in my view) that Hiel and others read the curse as specifying the conditions required to rebuild Jericho rather than warning of the terrible results for doing so.

23. The deuteronomic formula invoked here ("according to the word of the LORD, which he spoke by the hand of *X*") always refers to prophets (1 Kgs 14:18; 15:29; 17:16; 2 Kgs 24:2).

24. Of course, rhetorically the formula functions as an implied threat against Israel: if Yahweh drove those nations out, a similar fate awaits those like them—as Israel's subsequent history shows.

25. Isaiah 17:9 is too textually problematic for inclusion here. I have also left Ezek 36:11 out of consideration since the allusion is unclear. In addition, Levenson has shown that Ezek 44:6-10 does not have the Gibeonites in mind (cf. Josh 9:27) and, hence, requires no treatment here; cf.

J. D. Levenson, *Theology of the Program of Restoration of Ezekiel 40-48* (Missoula, MT: Scholars Press, 1976), 135-136. Finally, the interpretive ambiguity of Heb. *kĕna*ʿănî in Zech 14:21 (NIV "Canaanite" [footnote: "merchant"]; NRSV "traders") dictates its exclusion from this study. But cf. the case for "Canaanite" and a possible inclusivist interpretation by C. L. Meyers and E. M. Meyers, Zechariah 9-14 (New York: Doubleday, 1993), 489-492, 506-507.

26. For the discussion and bibliography, see J. Jeremias, *The Book of Amos* (Louisville: Westminster/John Knox, 1998), 39.

27. The background of this oracle is the covenant trial scene; so S. M. Paul, *Amos* (Minneapolis: Fortress, 1991), 87. The context sharply contrasts the abuse of the needy by "they" (i.e., Israel, vv. 6-8) with the constant aid provided them in dire need by "I" (i.e., Yahweh, vv. 9-11), all in violation of the covenant.

28. For biblical and extra-biblical usage of cedars and oaks singly and paired together, see Paul, 88-89.

29. Elsewhere biblical tradition remembers the Canaanites as frighteningly tall (Num 13:28; Deut 1:28; 2:10, 21; 9:2; Josh 14:12, 15; 15:14).

30. Besides the miraculous Jordan crossing (Josh 3-4), other memorable "saving acts" from this period include the plague that Yahweh sent for Israel's idolatry at Shittim and Phinehas' fabled heroism (Num 25; cf. Ps 106:30), the defeat of Midian (Num 31), and the two stone memorials made by Joshua in the Jordan and at Gilgal (Josh 3-4). As the base from which Israel launched many subsequent victories across Canaan (9:6; 10:7; 14:6), Gilgal certainly symbolized Israel's arrival in the land. Finally, recall that at Gilgal the provision of manna stopped and Israel ate from the land's produce (Josh 5:12). All of these potentially offered the prophet a rhetorically suitable allusion.

31. Ezek 20:27-28 makes the same point, albeit with more details of the defilement. For other divine recounting of the in-bringing with *bōʾ* in the hiphil, see Josh 24:8; Judg 2:1.

32. For the text's possible compositional history, see W. Zimmerli, *Ezekiel 2* (Philadelphia: Fortress, 1983), 526; L. C. Allen, *Ezekiel 20-48* (Dallas: Word, 1990), 278; D. I. Block, T*he Book of Ezekiel* (Grand Rapids: Eerdmans, 1998), 2:703-705, 720-722. Cf. R. M. Hals, *Ezekiel* (Grand Rapids: Eerdmans, 1989), 287 ("we are left with a definite impression of the inadequacy of the structure of chs. 40-48").

33. Cf. Zimmerli, 530 ("a mild reduction of the series of fixed points in Josh 15:2-4").

34. Also excluded are northern territory conquered by David and Edomite territory once part of Judah whose southern point was Ezion-geber; cf. T. Renz, *The Rhetorical Function of the Book of Ezekiel* (Leiden: Brill, 1999), 127.

35. Hals, 344; Zimmerli, 542.

36. Levenson, 123.

37. Note that "the tribes of Israel" (v. 21) has two subcategories, "yourselves" and "the aliens" (v. 22). By implication, the text considers the latter among the "tribes," i.e., assumes their full membership in Israel. That the latter are to receive "their inheritance" in the Israelite "tribe" where they settle (v. 23) reinforces that assumption.

38. Zimmerli, 532.

39. Block, 722; Hals, 345; Zimmerli, 542 ("the rule of the just portion is to prevail"). The width of each portion, of course, would vary with its eastern and western borders. But, the east-west orientation yields two benefits over the old allotments: it more equitably distributes the desirable and undesirable lands among the tribes and avoids granting a monopoly to any tribe over the best areas; cf. M. Greenberg, "Idealism and Practicality in Numbers 35:4-5 and Ezekiel 48," *Journal of the American Oriental Society* 88 (1966) 63-66.

40. So Levenson, 116-117.

41. For further discussion, see Levenson, 116-121; but cf. the caution of K. R. Stevenson, *Vision of Transformation: The Territorial Rhetoric of Ezekiel 40-48* (Atlanta: Scholars, 1996), 82, n. 6 ("It is difficult to see any kind of consistent relationship between priority of birth and proximity"). For maps of the allotment and consecrated area, see Zimmerli, 535, 537.

42. Cf. Zimmerli, 541. For the pride-of-place view, cf. G. Ch. Macholz, "Noch einmal: Planungen für den Wiederaufbau nach der Katastrophe von 587," *Vetus Testamentum* 19 (1969) 335; for the neutralization view, cf. Block, 724. Cf. also Levenson, 118 ("a concern that the royal tribe not oppress the North, that the North have a share in the House of David, and the House of David a share in the North").

43. The closest analogy would be the provision of towns for the Levites (Josh 21), but it distributes no land and makes no provision for priests or for a temple.

44. Stevenson, 143, 149-151. By "territorial rhetoric" Stevenson means a rhetoric which invokes human geography as a symbol in order (in this case) to affirm Yahweh as Israel's only king and to preserve Israelite identity from cultural assimilation. Other scholars speak of Ezek 47-48 as "theological geography," i.e., a kind of symbolic, ideal Israel; cf. Macholz, 331; Block, 723; Allen, 285.

45. Cf. Levenson, 124: "The central motivation of these reforms lies not in a doctrine of equality, but in a concern for the realization in social, even visible form of the relationships defined by *Heilsgeschichte*"; cf. Allen, 286: "The covenant clearly has implications for human relations."

46. E.g., J. M. Robinson and H. Koester, *Trajectories Through Early Christianity* (Philadelphia: Fortress, 1971).

47. For a similar approach, albeit with some differing emphases, see R. P. Knierim, "Israel and the Nations in the Land of Palestine in the Old Testament" in R. P. Knierim, *The Task of Old Testament Theology* (Grand Rapids: Eerdmans, 1995), 309-321.

48. For further reflection on these issues, I highly commend M. Prior, "Confronting the Bible's Ethnic Cleansing in Palestine," *The Link* 33/5 (December, 2000)1-12, which unfortunately came to my attention too late to incorporate in this paper.

MARY GOES TO REFORM SCHOOL: A REFORMER, A REFORMED, AND REFORMING MEET MARY

KATHRYN GREENE-McCREIGHT

There is no rose of such virtue
As is the rose that bare Jesu:
Alleluia.
For in this rose containèd was
Heaven and earth in little space:
Res Miranda.
By that rose we may well see
There be one God in Persons Three:
Pares forma.
The angels sang: the shepherds too:
Gloria in Excelsis Deo:
Gaudeamus.
Leave we all this worldly mirth
And follow we this joyful birth:
Transeamus.

(Medieval: Author unknown)

What would a Protestant biblical theology of Mary look like? Can it include a feminist vision? My working assumption will be that in order to do biblical theology, one needs to pay attention not only to the biblical texts but also to interpreters who have gone before us who have been successful biblical theologians, with the assumption that they may have much to teach us. In constructing a biblical theology of Mary, we need first to look at the main NT texts about Mary. In addition we must at least mention the dogmas codified by the Roman Catholic Church regarding Mary, because whether for the Catholic or Protestant, these have shaped Western understandings of Mary. We will then examine two reformers who are noted biblical theologians, the Reformer Martin Luther, and the Reformed Karl Barth. Then we will turn to the "new Reformation," that is, the feminist theological debate about Mary, in particular to the work of Rosemary Radford Ruether (who is, paradoxically, Roman Catholic!). Finally, we will attempt to sketch the beginnings of a biblically-grounded theological appraisal of Mary which will engage feminist concerns.

MARY IN THE NEW TESTAMENT

Briefly, the NT texts in which Mary appears are Matt 1-2; 12:46-50; 13:55; Mark 3:31-35; 6:3; Luke 1-2; 8:19-21; 11:27-28; John 2:1-12; 6:42; 19:25-27; Acts 1:14 and Gal 4:4. These can be grouped into 5 broad thematic categories. The first category is the infancy narratives, Matt 1-2 and Luke 1-2, where Mary appears as mother and wife. Secondly comes Jesus' relativizing of the ties of motherhood and family, as in Mark 3:31-35; "Whoever does the will of God is my brother, and sister, and mother" (cf. also Matt 12:46-50; Luke 8:19-21; 11:27-28, the last where Jesus responds to "blessed is the womb that bore you ..." with "blessed rather are those who hear and keep the word of God"). The third category is Mary's presence at distinct moments of revelation, such as her presence at Jesus' first sign and at his last breath in John 2:1-12; 19:25-27. The fourth category presents Mary as believer, praying with the disciples after the resurrection (Acts 1:14) and Mary as first disciple, as she "kept these things in her heart" (Luke 2:19; 2:51) believing even where she could not see. Fifth, Mary appears as theological datum for Paul (Gal 4:4 born of a woman, born under the law), where Mary grounds Jesus' humanity and our election.

MARIAN DOGMAS

The Roman Catholic Church has four basic dogmas about Mary. The first is Mary as the bearer of God, or *theotokos*. This was first formulated at the Council of Ephesus in 431. Because Jesus is both God and man, his mother can be said to be God-bearer just as much as human-bearer. This dogma, in part because it is the oldest of Marian dogmas, is understood by most Reformers as being necessary, but their arguments in favor of its importance are usually christological rather than mariological.

The second dogma is the Perpetual Virginity of Mary. This was accepted as dogma by the Lateran Council in 649. This posits that Mary was a virgin before conception took place, that she remained a virgin through Christ's birth, the hymen remaining intact, and that she had no other children after the birth of Jesus and had no sexual relations with Joseph. The first formal definition which had all three parts was codified as dogma under Pope Martin I, and Trent confirmed this in 1555 under Pope Paul IV. Interestingly enough, this was directed not against the Reformers but against Socinians. The classical Roman theological statement is: *semper Virgo, ante partum, in partu et post partum.* As regards the *ante partum,* the NT provided the doctrinal basis for this in Matt 1:18 and Luke 1:26-34. For the *in partu* the claim is made for the ability of the church to interpret Scripture in this fashion. The *post partum* is based on a body of tradition in the *Protoevangelium of James,* with its story of a gynecological exam proving Mary's virginity after the birth. In addition to the *Protoevangelium of James* a few Bible texts are cited in proof, such as "A garden enclosed is my sister, my spouse; a spring shut up, a fountain sealed" (Song 4:12); "This gate shall be shut, it shall not be opened, and no man shall enter in by it, therefore it shall be shut, it shall not be opened, for the Lord, the God of Israel, has entered by it" (Ezek 44:2); and the jar in which Moses tells Aaron to keep the manna (Exod 16:33) "throughout all generations" is understood to be a type of Mary's uncorrupted womb.

The third dogma is the Immaculate Conception, which was promulgated by Pope Pius IX in 1854. Technically this does not refer to the moment of conception but when God infused the soul into the body[1] "in view of the merits of Jesus Christ, the Saviour of the human race, [Mary] was preserved free from all stain of original sin." In other words, by the retroactive power of Christ, Mary is understood to have been exempted from original sin. Duns Scotus was the father of this dogma, with his theory that it is "fitting", along the lines of Eadmer's dictum, *Potuit, Decuit, ergo Fecit* (God could, should and therefore did do it). There are no biblical texts given for this, except a possible mistranslation of the curse on the serpent in Gen 3:15: "she (*ipsa* in place of *ipse*, he) shall bruise your head and you shall bruise his heel." The dogma has a checkered career. Up to 1140 the testimonies of the Fathers were opposed to the Immaculate Conception. Pelagius mentions the idea, as does Radbert (d. 860), but Anselm of Canterbury denies it as does Bernard of Clairvaux (d. 1153) who calls the Immaculate Conception a novelty "of which the rites of the Church know nothing, that reason does not approve, and ancient tradition does not recommend" (Bernard, *Epistola* 174). Thomas Aquinas (d. 1274) said, as did Bonaventure (d.1274), that Mary did indeed have the effects of original sin.

The fourth dogma, that of the Bodily Assumption, was promulgated by Pope Pius XII in 1950 in *Munificentissimus Deus*. It posits that Mary was taken up into heaven and that Mary's body is not under the laws of nature of decay and corruption. This dogma rests on doctrinal considerations rather than historical or biblical accounts. Epiphanius was the first to mention Mary's death in his *Panarion* (355) where he says that no one knows anything about it, a statement which itself adds nothing except that people were wondering about the circumstances surrounding her death. In the fifth century and later, we find the legend *Transitus Maria* mentioned by Pope Gelasius I (492-496) as being unsuitable for reading. She is mentioned also in *De Gloria Martyrum* written around 590, and from Gregory the Great onward the legend enters the official Church. The liturgical feast of the Assumption was celebrated in the east and introduced in the west by Pope Sergius (687-701). Even Aquinas, who rejected the Immaculate Conception, favored the Assumption as pious hypothesis.

In addition, there is a body of "pious beliefs" which are known as the Marian Theses. These are not dogmas binding on the faithful, but a body of beliefs which are acknowledged by the Magisterium. These are 1) Mary as Coredemptorix with Christ; 2) Mary as Mediatrix; 3) Mary as the Dispensatrix of All Graces; 4) Mary as the Queen of Heaven; 5) Mary as the Prototype of the Church.

MARTIN LUTHER

Having briefly reviewed the NT texts and the Roman Catholic understandings of Mary, we can now turn to our Reformers. Martin Luther (1483-1546) was a friar and scholar trained in Scholastic theology and a professor of biblical studies. In other words, he is one for whom biblical theology was an active concern. He was especially suspicious of the Pelagian tendencies in Roman doctrine and popular theology and was concerned about the Church's Marian dogmas, even though he was in many ways a Marian theologian. He preached about 60 sermons on a number of Marian feasts, e.g., for the Immaculate Conception (Dec 8, 1520), for Mary's nativity (Sept 8, 1522), for her Assumption (Aug 15, 1523), for the Annunciation (March 25, 1540), for the Visitation (July 2, 1544), and for her Purification (Feb 2, 1544).[2] The doctrinal development of Luther's theology is mirrored in his theology of Mary and "the devotion which a Christian should have to the Mother of God is a small-scale representation of his entire religious accomplishment."[3] Luther's own religious personality can be said to contain two sources of his recasting of medieval Mariology. The first was his suffering under popular devotional abuses, such as the veneration of the saints. A second factor was Luther's personal theological struggle. Justification by faith alone, a grace which was Christ's pardon from sin and which freed one from the slavery to merits and from the intercession and the accomplishments of the saints, could not but "lead to a new frame of reference for Mary, the exemplar of the Catholic Christian and the first among the saints."[4]

His commentary on Psalms, which he was working on from 1513 to 1516 is where he first expressed doubts about any theological emphasis on Mary even while lauding Mary:

> The Blessed Virgin sees God in all things.... Although Elizabeth with great perception sees Mary to be the mother of God, even more perceptively the Virgin sees God in all things; he alone is great. Therefore the most pure venerator of God is the Blessed Virgin, who magnifies God above all things; she has no idols. She boasts of nothing herself, nothing of merit, no work; she is, by her own admission, purely passive and a receiver, not a doer of good works. (W.A. 1.61, 77-79).[5]

In 1517 Luther spoke of Mary's sinlessness, in 1519 he advised calling on Mary when facing death, but in 1520 his concern for Marian abuses was growing (W.A. 4.634). In his sermon that year on the Feast of the Assumption he said that if devotion to Mary in any way detracted from devotion to Christ "then we must practice christocentric moderation. Mary must be honored, but Christ must be the matrix of this veneration. Mary exists for Christ alone, and this is the view of the Bible" (W.A. 4.634).[6]

He also wrote a commentary on the Magnificat, which is where we find the meat of his understanding of Mary (LW 21.297-358).[7] This was composed for the education of one of Luther's supporters (John Frederick, 1502-1554, the nephew and eventual successor of Luther's chief protector, Duke Frederick the Wise of Saxony, 1463-1525). Luther began the commentary in early 1521 and completed it while at Wartburg in the early fall of that year. The Dedicatory letter gives us an idea of what one can expect when reading the Magnificat. Luther says that from the Magnificat one will have "wholesome knowledge and a praiseworthy life." In it even Mary gives wisdom: "May the tender Mother of God herself procure for me the spirit of wisdom, profitably and thoroughly to expound this song of hers" (LW 3.119-200).[8]

The commentary is relatively early, but by the time he began it, a number of Luther's propositions had been condemned by Leo X (on June 15, 1520, *Exsurge Domine*), and he himself was excommunicated before he actually began the commentary (Jan 3, 1521, *Decet Romanum Pontificem*). However, at this point

Luther has not yet been so sharpened by polemic, and this commentary is an example of this somewhat softer work. He does believe justification of the soul to God is only through faith and not through works and that all doctrine must stand before the bar of Scripture which is the judge of all sacred teachings. However, he maintains the *theotokos*, that Mary is the bearer or mother of God, and Mary's perpetual virginity. One of the main points which he stresses is the paradox that God chooses the lowly for his exalted service, and understands that "humility is the highest of virtues." He regards the Virgin Mary to be an example of this humility and lowliness and as such she is the "foremost example of the grace of God."[9] Of course, he gets this motif from the Magnificat itself, a motif which is found elsewhere throughout Scripture as well (e.g. Matt 18:1-6; Phil 2:7-11; 1 Cor 1; etc). In keeping with Luther's emphasis on justifying faith, he sees Mary's response to God ("let it be unto me . . .") as an example of faith for Christians to follow.

For Luther, Mary is Queen, she is free of sin, and she can impart wisdom. But he also warns against an incorrect Mariology which has issued in idolatry:

> I say Mary does not desire to be an idol; she does nothing; God does all. We ought to call upon her that for her sake God may grant and do what we request. Thus, also, all other saints are to be invoked, so that their work may be every way God's alone.[10]

Mary and the saints, like ourselves, are weak and have no special claim on God. In 1522, Luther is still speaking of Mary's sinlessness, and retains this belief for another five years. Between 1522 and 1527 his opinion on the Immaculate Conception begins to change. In 1522 he preaches on the Feast of the Assumption and takes for granted this belief, and yet in the same year, in his Sermon on Mary's Nativity he affirms that "we are just as holy as she, for that she has a greater grace is not due to her merit." Even so, he still allows his followers to pray for her intercession (W.A. 7.118-193).[11] In 1527 when he preaches on the feast of the Immaculate Conception, he indicates that Mary's body had the effects of original sin and that she was conceived in the ordinary way. In 1530 he argues that it is an aspect of the "hypocritical church" which should be eliminated. In 1532 he denies any notion of a special conception of Mary: "Mary is conceived in sin just like us . . ." (W.A. 36.141).[12] In 1544 he regards the feast of the Assumption as "totally papist, full of idolatry and without foundation in the Scriptures" (W.A. 52.681).[13] Up until that point he kept the celebration of the feast on its traditional day, Aug 15. But even after 1544, he still affirms that Mary was in heaven, whether in her body or out of her body he is not sure, for Scripture is silent on this. He says that what is important is the celebration of the Ascension of Christ, by which and through which Mary also is understood to be in heaven with her son.

Eventually Luther retained three Marian feasts: The Annuciation (March 25), the Purification (Feb 2) and the Visitation (July 2), the first two preserved as feasts of Christ, the third being "totally papist" but allowed anyway. He left this advice: "Mary should be minimized in three areas. We should not overestimate her personal gifts, for her grace and her relation to justification is the same as ours. Secondly, her intercessory prayer has no special efficacy. Finally, she should be imitated in those Christian virtues of humility, obedience, trust, and above all, faith" (W.A. 15.478).[14] Not surprisingly, Mary is an example of justification by faith. "She should be, and herself gladly would be, the foremost example of the grace of God" (LW 21.323), and "Mary, therefore, calls God her Saviour or her Salvation, even though she neither saw nor felt that this was so, but trusted in sure confidence that He was her Saviour and her Salvation" (LW 21.309).

Luther's *pro me/pro nobis* is also found in his Mariology, in his sermon on Christmas where he says of the nativity that it is important to understand Mary to bear the Son of God "for me."

> Mary, you did not bear this child for yourself alone. The child is not yours; you did not bring him forth for yourself, but for me .... I have a greater honor than your honor as his mother. For your honor pertains to your motherhood of the body of the child, but my honor is this, that you have my treasure, so that I know none, neither men nor angels, who can help me except this child whom you, O Mary, hold in your arms (W.A. 32.354).[15]

But even here he qualifies his Mariology for the sake of christology and says "I am to accept the child and his birth and forget the Mother, as far as this is possible, although her part cannot be forgotten, for where there is a birth there must also be a mother .... We dare not put our faith in the mother, but only in the fact that the child was born" (W.A. 32.252).[16] The grace of God in Christ eclipses Mary to an extent, even though as he says, "her part cannot be forgotten" (W.A. 32.252).[17]

KARL BARTH

To consider Protestantism today one would think that Mary is non-existent both liturgically and theologically. Insisting that Mary not eclipse Christ has issued in the almost complete suppression of Mary. The Swiss theologian, Karl Barth, is an exception to this, and yet in a sense he is the exception that proves the rule. His main discussion of Mary the Mother of the Lord comes, appropriately, in his section on "the Mystery of Revelation" (the third paragraph of Part II, "The Incarnation of the Word", in CD I.2, *the Doctrine of the Word of God*). Why is this appropriate? Because fundamentally any statement about Mary is a statement about her "fruit," Jesus. That is, as was the case for Luther, so it is for Barth, that any statement about Mary must be a christological statement. To this extent, the Church must, even while disavowing Mariology, hold to the confession of Mary as the "Mother of the Lord", *theotokos*. Holding Mary to be *theotokos* is "a test of the proper understanding of the incarnation of the Word" (CD 1.2 138). Barth notes that in Luke 1:43 Mary is addressed by Elizabeth as "the mother of my Lord." This is essentially a "twofold assertion," says Barth. First, in the incarnation of the Word we are not dealing with a *creatio ex nihilo* but with a birth from a woman (Gal 4:4). Here as elsewhere, the birth of Jesus from Mary grounds his humanity. Secondly, in being born of the Virgin Mary, Christ was not a "second thing," in addition to the Son of God, but his humanity and divinity are both asserted at the same time. Thus the two elements of the Chalcedonian formula, that Jesus is fully human and fully divine, hold together in the title of Mary as the Mother of God. Barth points out that Luther fully agrees that Mary is *theotokos* and that Reformed Orthodoxy also upholds the *theotokos*.

However, for Barth, Mary in and of herself is not a theological datum:

> The content of the biblical attestation of revelation does not give us any cause to acknowledge that the person of Mary in the event of revelation possesses relatively even such an independent and emphatic position as to render it necessary or justifiable to make it the object of a theological doctrine that goes beyond the one statement made . . . . Mariology is an excrescence, i.e., a diseased construct of theological thought. Excrescences must be excised. (CD 1.2 139)

That every statement about Mary should be a christological statement and not an excresence is true of all of the statements about Mary in the biblical stories, even the scene between Mary and the angel Gabriel in Luke 1. Like John the Baptist, Mary points ever away from herself to Jesus. Both figures are the "climax of the Old Testament penetrating into the New, and the first among humanity to receive Jesus. 'Behold I am the handmaid of the Lord; let it be to me according to your word.' (Luke 1:38)" (CD 1.2 139). Here Mary is the first to receive the miracle of revelation and the first to take up the call to discipleship: "Behold, I am the handmaid of the Lord ...." Mary represents the disciples in her receptivity to the divine Word.

Barth agrees with Luther insofar as he understood the greatness of Mary to consist in the fact that all interest is directed away from her to the Lord. She is the handmaid, not the demi-goddess. Barth points out that this was a common feature of early interpretation of Mary. Ambrose made it clear in his dictum: "Mary was the temple of God, not the God of the Temple" (*De Spiritu*, III.11, 80; CD 1.2 140). The dogmatization of the *theotokos* at Ephesus (431) and confirmation by Chalcedon (451), says Barth, must be upheld. These councils take an expressly christological interest in Mary. The entire scene between Gabriel and Mary points away from Mary to Christ. Barth says:

> We reject Mariology, 1) because it is an arbitrary innovation in the face of Scripture and the Early Church and 2) because this innovation consists essentially in a falsification of Christian truth .... [Mariology] is the central doctrine of the Roman Catholic Church, the dogma from the standpoint of which all their important positions are to be regarded and by which they stand or fall ... . In the doctrine and worship of Mary there is disclosed the one heresy of the Roman Catholic Church which explains all the rest. The "mother of God" of Roman Catholic Marian dogma is quite simply the principle, type and essence of the human creature co-operating servantlike (*ministeraliter*) in its own redemption on the basis of prevenient grace, and to that extent the principle type and essence of the Church (CD 1.2 143).

Barth is basically saying that Mariology amounts to Pelagianism, which formed one of the greatest struggles which Augustine faced and which arose again as one of the principle problems of the Protestant Reformation. This chief heresy of Roman Catholicism, according to Barth, presumes that in Mary as the head of all creatures humanity has an openness or receptivity to God simply by dint of being human. This receptivity brings with it in Mary's case her own capacity for redemption, and she becomes "co-Redemptorix." Barth again quotes a Catholic explication of Mariology (E. Przywara, quoted in CD 1.2 145):

> The profoundest meaning, the greatest richness of redemption, is that it raises the creature endowed with reason from the infinite remoteness of its natural impotence, and from the abysmal forlorness of sin, into the living divine tide, and thereby enables it, while preserving its essential creaturely condition, to co-operate in the work of redemption . . . . Thus in a measure all humanity enters the sphere of the living divine powers. To that extent it is not merely an object, but also a subject of the divine redemptive activity.

Barth points out that this means that Mary shares in the work of Christ, thereby engaging the human creature also as co-redeemer, which, says Barth, is a "relative rival with Christ" (CD 1.2 145). Here then is Barth's objection to Mariology: that the statements which see Mary as doing anything other than pointing away from herself and toward Christ fall into the Pelagian mode which sets the creature on par with Christ as co-redeemer. This inner link which is created between Mary and Christ in the work of redemption is then passed on to the Church:

> Like Mary ... the Church also possesses a relatively independent place and function in the redemptive process. It, too, vies with Christ ... not only is it born of Christ but, particularly in the eucharistic center of its life, Christ is also born of it. Not only does it need Christ but in all seriousness Christ also needs it .... The Church in which Mary is venerated is bound to regard itself as it has done in the Vatican decree [of papal infallibility, 1870, which, Barth notes, together with the dogma of the Immaculate Conception (1854), was promulgated under Pius IX] (CD 1.2 146).

The Protestant (or Evangelical, as Barth would call it) answer to this must be that:

> Jesus Christ, the Word of God, exists, reigns, and rules in as sovereign a way within the created world as He does from eternity with the Father, no doubt over and in man, no doubt in His Church, and by it, but in such a way that at every point He is always Himself the Lord, and Man, like the Church, can give honor only to Him and never, however indirectly, to himself as well. There can be no thought of any reciprocity or mutual efficacy even with the most careful precautions. Faith in particular is not an act of reciprocity but the act of renouncing all reciprocity (CD 1.2 146).

Having given his biting caution of Mariology,[18] Barth proceeds with the theological work ahead of him, which is the Chalcedonian formula, "very God, very man." He points out that "born of the Virgin Mary" and "suffered under Pontius Pilate" both serve to underscore Jesus' humanity. Both the Virgin Birth and the Empty tomb belong together as a "single sign" (CD 1.2 182; notice he does not say the cross!) which marks this life from its beginning to its end off from all others. Throwing light, then, on the words "truly human," the Virgin Birth also "eliminates the last surviving possibility of understanding the *vere Deus vere homo* intellectually ... it leaves only the spiritual understanding of the *vere Deus vere homo*, i.e. the understanding in which God's own work is seen in God's own light" (CD 1.2 177). In the Virgin birth the initiative is solely with God. There is no explanation of how, or even why, but simply the "that," and all from God's side. "The Virgin Birth denotes particularly the mystery of revelation. It denotes the fact that God stands at the start where real revelation takes place—God and not the arbitrary cleverness, capability or piety of man" (CD 1.2 182). The empty tomb denotes the "revelation of the mystery ... [that God] has no need of human power and is free from all human caprice" (CD 1.2 183). In the Virgin Birth, man is "the object of sovereign divine action ... God Himself and God alone is Master and Lord" (CD 1.2 186). The Virgin Birth is "an event in this world of ours, yet such that it is not grounded upon the continuity of events in this world nor is it to be understood in terms of it" (CD 1.2 187). Here is where Barth shows how the Virgin Birth as biblical doctrine functions exactly the opposite of how the dogma functions in Roman Catholicism. It shows that there is no capacity in human nature to become "the human nature of Jesus Christ," i.e., the place of revelation (CD 1.2 188). "The virginity of Mary in the birth of the Lord is the denial, not of man in the presence of God, but of any power attribute or capacity in him for God" (CD 1.2 188). It is upon this human nature, the nature that is so distorted by sin that it has no point of contact for union with God, that this "mystery must be wrought ... in its receiving the capacity for God which it does not possess" (CD 1.2 189). This mystery is signified by the Virgin Birth. This is why the Virgin Birth excludes the sexual act: "the sinful life of sex [since the fall] is excluded as the source of the human existence of Jesus Christ not because of the nature of sexual life nor because of its sinfulness but because every natural generation is the work of willing, achieving, creative, sovereign man" (CD 1.2 192).

This theme of the willing and achieving of the assumedly sovereign creature is of course one of Barth's pet peeves. That it should find place in the discussion of the Virgin Birth is no surprise. Barth states that the capacity of the creature for God is simply not a possibility: "There is no plane upon which the meeting between God and man can be possible or real except in virtue of the mystery of the divine mercy" (CD 1.2 195). It is not that Jesus is conceived of the Virgin Mary because women are naturally less in need of conversion than men (so Schleiermacher, CD 1.2 195) nor because Mary herself was free from sin. Rather, she was a fallen creature like all others, and her virginity does not exclude her from the taint of original sin. If this were not the case, a way to Mariology would be opened. But as it is, "human nature ... is made worthy to be a partaker of the divine nature by grace and by a miracle of grace" (CD 1.2 196). The *natus ex virgine* means, then, "the inconceivable act of creative omnipotence in which He imparts to human nature a capacity, a power for Himself, which it does not possess of itself and which it could not devise for itself" (CD 1.2 201). The Virgin Birth is thus an instance of the reformation concept of *sola gratia*.

FEMINIST THEOLOGICAL DEBATE

Some of the newest reformers to meet Mary head-on are feminist theologians. Feminist theologians are quick to point out what should be obvious, but which has great repercussions once stated: that most theologians have been men. The claim is made that men approach the theological task differently from women, with "male categories" such as "a focus on the cerebral or the abstract, the building of theoretical systems and the construction of specific hermeneutical principles."[19] The claim is also generally made that men have divorced theology from experience, at least and especially from the experience of women. This theology, which has been cordoned off into the arena for the academic elite, has its own "language structure and its own networks, and can be communicated through theological texts and university departments without beginning to affect the way we actually experience day-to-day reality."[20] What is needed, then, so it is claimed, is a female-experience based theology. This is not simply because female-experience based theology is "better", whatever that might mean in this case, but because justice demands that the female experience have its say. Male theology, as Elaine Storkey puts it:

> sees and interprets theological phenomena through male eyes. It begins from the assumption that to be male is the norm, and that somehow theological systems all uphold this norm of maleness. Thus theology incorporates a male-defined reality into liturgy, church government and organisation and scriptural interpretation. Such theology by its very definition and development excludes women or relegates them to being the passive recipients of truths handed down by men. As historically developed it also inevitably passes on misleading and inacccurate "feminine" stereotypes. So feminist theology is that which specifically attempts to challenge the idea that the male is the norm.[21]

When feminist theologians turn then to one of the few important feminine figures of the NT, Mary, there is a spectrum of responses.[22] For our purposes we can understand one pole to be represented by figures as distinct from each other as Elizabeth Schüssler Fiorenza, Elizabeth Cady Stanton, and Mary Daly, on the one hand, and the other by Ann Loades and Rosemary Radford Ruether and others. Ironically this team of scholars is drawn from both Protestant and Catholic ranks and are nevertheless Reformers of the new type insofar as they seek to reform Christian theology from the standpoint of women's experience. For Fiorenza, Mary cannot be useful to the feminist project because she has been so distorted by male theology which has focused on her virginity and her image as ideal mother[23] so that she is of no service to feminist theology.[24] Fiorenza finds Mary Magdalene to be a better role model because she typifies women's proclamation of the Easter message, but finds no positive theological use for Mary the Mother of our Lord. In a similar tone Ann Loades quotes Elizabeth Cady Stanton who, in her *Women's Bible,* states that she finds the doctrine of the Immaculate Conception to be "profoundly troublesome to women" and the Virgin Birth to be a "slur on all the natural motherhood of the world" because it presents the birth of Jesus as "something higher, sweeter, nobler than ordinary motherhood."[25] (Here Stanton herself apparently unknowingly confuses the Immaculate Conception with the Virgin Birth but this does not affect her rhetoric.) In accord with this, she quotes *Redemptoris Mater*:

> In the light of Mary, the church sees in the face of women the reflection of a beauty which mirrors the loftiest sentiments of which the human heart is capable: the self-offering totality of love; the strength that is capable of bearing the greatest sorrows; limitless fidelity and tireless devotion to work; the ability to combine penetrating intuition with words of support and encouragement.[26]

This is the ideal of womanhood presented to faithful women in light of Mary. For

Mary Daly too, the "impossible ideal of Virgin-Mother has ultimately a punitive function, since no actual woman can live up to it, throwing all women back into the status of the first Eve, and essentially reinforcing the universality of women's low caste status."[27]

On the other hand, the idea of the Virgin Birth/Immaculate Conception can be understood as negating the myth of feminine evil. Ann Loades wonders:

> if, however, we could retrieve the association of "virgin" with autonomy, but carefully balanced with a sense of co-inherence and without the abasement of a woman's visual image, and if we could bypass sugary-sweetness and dizzy immoblisation on a pedestal, then Mary might be re-associated with the affirmation and not the negation of what women discover themselves to be, and we might re-connect Mary to present needs… .[28]

Likewise, Mary's virginity can be seen as freedom from male power and can be a positive element to that effect. Ruether therefore, also like Loades, sees a more positive role for Mary. She (implicitly) adopts the idea that pagan goddess-worship prepares the way for veneration of Mary, or is its "prototype"[29] and then "the ancient mother goddess was eventually repressed in Hebrew worship, but images associated with her survived in hidden or allegorical ways."[30] This is true of the portrayal of Israel as God's bride. In the Wisdom literature, another aspect of feminine symbolism appears, where according to Ruether this "second 'person' of God" is not male but female, not a divine son but a divine daughter.[31] All of this imagery presents a feminine face of God which then is taken up in the imagery of Mary in the NT, and Mary serves as the feminine face of the Church, the soul open and humble before God. She then posits that three kinds of relationships can be gleaned from her study. They are: "1) the believing community is seen as God's feminine companion; 2) an aspect of God at work in his creation—his Spirit, Presence, or Wisdom—can be received as feminine; and 3) the feminine can symbolize the soul's openness and receptivity to God's initiatives."[32] Her main thesis is that "as the development of feminine religious imagery in the cultures that came into Christianity … neither a male nor a female symbol was entirely lost. Each was translated and reinterpreted in new ways in the Old Testament and then in Christianity."[33] This then has an impact on Christian theology particularly in the figure of Mary: "Mariology is a later development that uses the figure of the mother of Jesus as the person around whom to regroup this theology of feminine experience."[34] According to Reuther, there are aspects of Protestant thought which were particularly important in reducing Marian devotion: "First there is the protestant devotion to the Bible… then there is the abolition of monasticism and the rejection of virginity as the highest expression of Christian devotion … . Marriage is the normal state for the Christian, both clergy and laity."[35] "The third element in Protestantism diminishes the role of the feminine as a symbol of human nature of the church in relation to God … . Neither the church nor Mary as its symbol can be seen as a cooperator in the drama of salvation."[36] Protestantism is thus the "bad guy" which discourages the feminization of baptized pagan beliefs and practices.

Surely for a feminist biblical theology, Mary cannot be neglected insofar as she is a biblical figure, indeed arguably the most theologically important biblical figure vis-á-vis Jesus. However, her significance cannot be adduced from her utility as a feminine principle. She will be sought on the basis of the biblical passages which bear her and in terms of her relationship to Jesus.

Even though Reuther admits that "Mariology has acted as an extension and safeguard of the doctrines of Christ's uniqueness"[37] this is not enough for her. She needs Mariology to function on its own terms in the theological realm. Thus she says, "Mariology can allow that male to experience himself as 'feminine' or to experience what is called his 'feminine side.' Even the most patriarchal theologian is able to experience himself as the passive, receptive vassal of divine activity and grace, since all people in the church are thought of as 'feminine' in relation to the dominant 'masculine' ego of 'God'."[38] Thus Mariology can heal patriarchy if men are thereby enabled to see their feminine side, because "when only one side, the male, is active, and the other side, the female, is receptive, women never learn to be real people and men never learn to listen to and help others. Real reciprocity between people is destroyed by this sexist model of male activity and female receptivity. This means that the very possibility of genuine relationship is destroyed."[39] Reuther understands this use of Mary to be fruitful for the humanizing of the Church, for bringing men to see their feminine side.

However helpful this may be, this is to put the cart before the horse. A biblical theology needs to move from the *res* of Scripture to its benefits to humanity, and not vice versa, for the very fact that one seeks the *res* of Scripture means in traditional terms that one trusts Scripture to form us in health. We cannot look to Mary for anything other than what the biblical witness paints for us, and yet this is just what Ruether does. This is also what the dogmas of the Perpetual Virginity, the Immaculate Conception and the Assumption do. That is, even while these dogmas may be, from one point of view anyway, helpful to women insofar as they portray Mary as powerful and free from the confines of the marriage bed and indeed beyond sin, their lack of attestation in the Scriptures will not allow us to include these elements in a feminist biblical Mariology. Can we truly have a feminist biblical Mariology? Maybe Mariology is too exalted of a word. What images, therefore, of Mary can we offer for a feminist biblical theology of Mary?

Mary can be seen as an example of the foremost of the disciples; indeed, she beat the disciples to it. She trusted God even at the very conception of Jesus. She thus portrays obedience: "I am the handmaid of the Lord; let it be to me according to your word" (Luke 1:38). Mary becomes the key example and prototype not only of the disciples but also of unmerited grace.[40] She believed before she knew and obeyed before she saw, and was chosen apart from any merit of her own. She showed us the very pattern of discipleship, the humbling of the self before God. This is in itself not another example of a woman taking the backseat, a weak-willed unfulfilled *Hausfrau*, but she represents in her subjecting the self before God the very strength of the Christian disciple—"for when I am weak, then am I strong" (2 Cor 12:10). A biblical feminist theology of Mary will need to take seriously what this motif means for women, this finding in weakness one's strength. Feminist theory and theology would cry a loud warning about such a kind of "strength." But would accepting this strength in weakness necessarily end in relinquishing any small trophies won by and for women, as much of feminist theory would indicate? Does this mean subjection under the load of patriarchy? It certainly need not be so, for this motif in the NT makes for the strong and the great. Here a feminist biblical theology has a choice to make: does it make use of even this motif, insofar as it is present on the lips of Mary and attested throughout Scripture, or does it decide to bring in the assumptions of feminism as a foundation, advising against this notion of servanthood?

As for themes which the feminist biblical theologian can take from Mary, the first is her compassion. Mary was present at Jesus' first and last breath (John 19:26). Thus she holds within her heart the whole span of Jesus' earthly life, in compassion and care. At the cross she realized that Simeon's prophecy had come true, that a "sword will pierce through [her] own soul as well" (Luke 2:35). This is the height of compassion, literally to suffer with. As such she is again a model for us; we too in our turn must be compassionate nurturers, especially "to the least of these" for "as you did it to one of the least of these, my brothers and sisters, you did it to me" (Matt 25:40). Certainly this cannot be taken as license to saddle women alone with the nurturing. But Mary's role regarding Jesus was certainly in part as nurturer.

In addition, Mary is in solidarity with the poor, which is a prominent feminist theological theme.[41] In Mary's Magnificat she praises God for he has "scattered the proud in the imagination of their hearts, he has put down the mighty from their thrones, and exalted those of low degree; he has filled the hungry with good things and the rich he has sent empty away" (Luke 1:51-53). The fact that Mary says these things is significant, but it must be noted, as is often not the case in liberation theologies in general and in feminist theologies in particular, that Mary is not the agent here. She is praising God for his agency.

She "kept all these things, pondering them in her heart" (Luke 2:19, 51). Even though she could not understand, she believed, and remembered. She did not understand the shepherds' gloria and Jesus' words that he must be about the work of his Father, but neither did she deny them. Instead she tucked them away, precious souvenirs for another time when they might mean something more to her. How like this is Augustine's dictum, "I believe in order that I may understand." Even when the circumstances seem contrary to the facts at hand, faith means a suspension of unfaith until such a time as circumstances will seem fitting. So, with Mary as our model, we too must keep these things, pondering them in our hearts.

As the mother of Jesus she is the mother of God. While this may not be immediately "biblical" it certainly is "scriptural". We cannot, then, ignore the importance of Mary as *theotokos* (Ephesus 431). Since Jesus is fully human and fully divine (so Chalcedon, 451), Mary could not be mother to one and not the other, for both are fully present in the one man of Nazareth. So she is, as according to Catholic dogma, the mother of God. But even here Jesus qualifies this role: "Whoever does the will of God is my brother, and sister, and mother" (Mark 3:35). Also in response to the cry "Blessed is the womb that bore you and the breasts that you sucked," he answered, "Blessed rather are those who hear and keep the word of God" (Luke 11:27-28). Even Mary's motherhood is not an untouchable privilege reserved for her alone. The importance of this for the feminist should be obvious: as mother of God Mary has a function which none of us will repeat. Yet that place can be repeated not in biological but in theological, doxological motherhood.

What of Mary's virginity? This is, at least her virginity before the birth, arguably biblical. The last two clauses of the perpetual virginity are not. But can a feminist theology account for the virginity of Mary, even for the reduced biblical account? Why does virginity need to be such an impossible obstacle for feminists? Clearly in the ancient and medieval world, virginity meant independence from men. Would a feminist discussion of Mary need to exclude her virginity? If it were to be a biblical feminist theology, this would have to be accounted for somehow.

What do we make of her life with the disciples at prayer in Acts 1:14? She is not excluded from the gathered community after the resurrection, but is mentioned alongside the men, and some other women. Certainly one gleans from this that as women they are considered important for the life of prayer of the whole community. The women are not shunted off to the side to their own place of prayer. A feminist account of Mary could include her own spirituality as valued even by the men of the New Covenant.

But as for the feminist quest for Mary, in the end we must ask whether the search for a Mary who is a user-friendly feminist prototype is a search we are willing to make. Elaine Storkey's early definition of biblical feminists is interesting here. They are:

> feminists who do not take their cue from the autonomy of the Enlightenment but from a Christian view of people under God; a view which recognizes the fact of sin and the need for salvation. But it is not an individualist belief for salvation does not merely affect "personal" or "moral" life but needs to be worked out in fear and trembling in all areas, including sex and gender.[42]

This makes it sound like Christian interpretation and theology can be compatible with feminist theology and interpretation. Yet in her later work she seems to imply that the goals and values of feminism in some degree must eclipse Christian theology and interpretation and that the feminist nature of the work must take precedence over the theological nature. Is there a happy medium with regard to Mary? Certainly some feminists such as Mary Daly, Elizabeth Schüssler Fiorenza, and others, would say no, that there can be no medium, no compromises. Along with Marshall McLuhan they would say that the only thing in the middle of the road is yellow lines and dead possum. There can be no compromising with the male-dominated theological world.

Yet one wonders what such a project is in its own interiority. That is, what is it, on its own, apart from its struggle against patriarchal theological constructs that bind women to their second-class status? Ultimately one must ask whether there is any substantive difference between their project and what Barth warned of in Roman Catholic Mariology. Is this type of feminist theology in essence a re-creation of Pelagius' project? Of the creature struggling to assert itself in the arena of the divine? Another version of claiming its own qualifications, its own status, its own merits? This question would need to be grappled with for a feminist biblical theology of Mary.

How far can we take Mary theologically without turning her into 1) a horror for women with her being raised to a pedestal which defies the abilities and faculties of human women; or b) a horror for the church insofar as it entails raising the creature to a cooperator with divine grace? Because of the second reason Protestant Christians have usually rejected any serious thought about Mary, and now some wish to reject Mary for the first reason. The fact is that Mary as present in the NT cannot be ignored as simply a Roman Catholic saint and depository of prayers. She must have a function for Protestants and for the reforming sisters as well. Mary can be reckoned with for the feminist biblical theologian only in such a way that prioritizes the overarching story of Jesus and makes a secondary claim along feminist lines. This is because being a biblical theologian does not mean being merely interested in biblical texts, or using biblical motifs as they are useful, which may or may not be the case, but it means to be both constrained and impelled by the central narratives of the Christian Bible which portray the life, death and resurrection of Jesus in the NT and the patterning forth of these in the OT. There can be no dual allegiances. This does not mean that Mary cannot be seen to be a powerful figure for women, but in the end, the utility of Mary for feminist theology must always play a secondary role. But one thing is certain: Mary cannot be neglected if one is to be a true biblical theologian. Roman Catholics may have the market on devotion to Mary, but, nevertheless, biblical theologians need to reclaim her as a key theological figure in the life of Jesus and therefore in the life of the church.

NOTES

1. Stephen Benko, *Protestants, Catholics and Mary* (Valley Forge: Judson Press, 1968).

2. Eric W. Gritsch, "Embodiment of Unmerited Grace: The Virgin Mary According to Martin Luther and Lutheranism," in *Mary's Place in Christian Dialogue*, (ed. Alberic Stacpoole; Wilton, Conn: Morehouse-Barlow, 1982), 133.

3. Thomas O'Meara, *Mary in Protestant and Catholic Theology* (New York: Sheed and Ward, 1966), 113.

4. Ibid., 114.

5. Also quoted by O'Meara, 116.

6. Also quoted by O'Meara, 116.

7. See also his "How to Preach on the Annunciation of Mary" (1533) in his *Table Talk*, LW 54.85, n. 494.

8. See George Tavard, *The Thousand Faces of the Virgin Mary* (Collegeville, Minn: Liturgical, 1996), 110.

9. Ibid., 111 and 119. See A. T. W. Steinhaeuser, *Works of Martin Luthe*r (Philadelphia: Holman, 1930), 3.119-200.

10. O'Meara, 117; *Martin Luther's Commentary on the Magnificat* (St. Louis: Concordia, 1960), 34.

11. See also Hilda Graef, *Mary: A History of Doctrine and Devotion* (New York: Sheed and Ward, 1965), 2.9.

12. O'Meara, 118.

13. Tavard, 119.

14. See O'Meara, 124.

15. Tavard, 114; Timothy Lull, ed., *Martin Luther's Basic Theological Writings* (Minneapolis: Fortress, 1989), 23.

16. Lull, 228.

17. Tavard, 113.

18. One wonders what Barth's argument would have looked like if by this point he had known of the statement of John XXIII that "the Madonna is not pleased when she is venerated above her Son." Of John XXIII we do have record of Barth having said, "It seems to me remarkable that this old Angelo Roncalli has in fact shown the papacy to be so rich. After a man like that one cannot continue to argue as insistently against this institution as one could in the past. He was a good man." See Eberhard Busch, *Karl Barth: His Life from Letters and Autobiographical Texts* (Philadelphia: Fortress, 1976), 467.

19. Elaine Storkey, "The Significance of Mary for Feminist Theology," in *Chosen By God: Mary in Evangelical Perspective* (London: Marshall Pickering, 1989), 184.

20. Ibid.

21. Ibid., 185.

22. Els Maeckelberghe, *Desperately Seeking Mary: A Feminist Appropriation of a Traditional Religious Symbol* (Kampen, The Netherlands: Pharos, 1991), 13-39.

23. Storkey, 188.

24. Elisabeth Schüsssler Fiorenza, *In Memory of Her: A Feminist Theological Reconstruction of Christian Origins* (New York: Crossroad, 1983).

25. Ann Loades, "The Virgin Mary and the Feminist Quest," in *After Eve* (ed. Janet Martin Soskice; New York: Collins, 1990), 159.

26. Ibid., 160. See John Paul II, *The Mother of the Redeemer: Redemptoris Mater*, Encyclical Letter of March 25, 1987 (Washington, D.C.: United States Catholic Conference, 1987).

27. As quoted by Loades, 166.

28. Ibid., 172.

29. Rosemary Radford Ruether, *Mary: The Feminine Face of the Church* (Philadelphia: Westminster Press, 1977), 18.

30. Ibid., 21.

31. Ibid., 25.

32. Ibid., 43.

33. Ibid., 45.

34. Ibid., 48.

35. Ibid., 71.

36. Ibid., 73.

37. Ibid., 51.

38. Ibid., 78.

39. Ibid., 79.

40. Gritsch, "Embodiment of Unmerited Grace: The Virgin Mary According to Martin Luther and Lutheranism," 132.

41. Daniel L. Migliore, "Mary: A Reformed Theological Perspective," *ThTo* 56 (1999) 346-358.

42. Elaine Storkey, *What's Right with Feminism?* (Grand Rapids: Eerdmans, 1986), 137.

RESPONSE TO GREENE-McCREIGHT

Vincent Bacote

I would like to state my appreciation for a paper so thought-provoking that I have decided to begin my classes on Christology with a discussion of Mary. The mention of Mary, the mother of our Savior, does not provoke tepid responses, as she is nearly worshipped by some Roman Catholics and almost reduced to the level of "just another sinner" by Protestants who feel nausea when faced with Mariology. This paper helps us to see the significance of Mary in unexpected places, such as in the thought of Martin Luther and Rosemary Radford Reuther. Even though Luther moved away from high Mariology, our Reformed father tells us she cannot be forgotten, as I fear she is in most of the Protestant world, except for Christmas time, of course. While not free from the problem of subjecting Mariology to her feminist presuppositions, Reuther did articulate a positive perspective on Mary that could create potentially constructive dialogue between the sexes. I was surprised to learn of this positive view of Mary from a leading light of feminist theology.

As one "guilty" of forgetting Mary, much less perceiving that she has any theological significance, I now ask how do we move forward to an appropriate appreciation of Mary? While I certainly agree that we must ask if feminist theology and biblical theology can meet in Mary, I would suggest that we go further and ask if there is a way to free Barth from his solitude as theological interpreter of Mary and articulate a Protestant theology of the mother of our Lord that is not a polemic against Rome. While refraining from titles like "Queen of Heaven" and dogmas such as the Immaculate Conception, what direction should Protestants take to arrive at a respectful theology of Mary?

Greene-McCreight gives us clues in the themes she finds for feminist biblical theologians. Compassion and solidarity with the poor are themes universal in scope which need not be left to our sisters. Christ himself urged the church to develop the character and demonstrate the virtue which Mary exemplifies so well. Additionally, much room exists for Protestant theological reflection in Greene-McCreight's insight regarding Mary's example in Luke chapter two. When Mary "kept all these things, pondering them in her heart," it is suggested that she believes in order to understand. Even though she does not understand, she believes and remembers. Is it possible that we as Protestants do not understand Mary's significance, whether we are blinded by anti-Roman prejudice or simply uninformed? Do we need to believe in order to understand? Could it be that there is something that we must tuck away for a time, and then retrieve it when we have matured or increased in knowledge? Certainly one must ask what it is about Mary that merits further reflection? As a start we could ponder the significance of the designation *theotokos* for Protestant theology, particularly those streams of tradition that are non-Anglican. This Chalcedonian designation stands at the root of all orthodox Christology, yet I, and maybe many other Protestants (lay, if not clergy) stumble over this term. We could also reflect on Mary's paradigmatic role as a disciple. Development of this perspective on Mary keeps us from high flights of Mariology but also presents us the opportunity to ponder a unique example of humility and submission to the Lord as Mary played the dual roles of mother and disciple.

Another helpful area of reflection would be pneumatology. Though recently various authors such as Moltmann, Pinnock, Dunn, and McIntyre have written on this neglected member of the Trinity, the need for increased reflection on the Spirit remains. A Protestant theology of Mary can be helpful in this regard. We can ask how deeper thinking about the conception of Christ can elevate the Spirit to a truly equal member of the Trinity in our theology. Gary Badcock's work suggests that the Spirit's role in Jesus' conception and life on earth reveals a more reciprocal relationship between Jesus and the Spirit, and further that the Spirit is at the center of the entire divine drama, rather than a literal "third wheel" added on at some later time. (See his *Light of Truth and Fire of Love: A Theology of the Holy Spirit,* Grand Rapids: Eerdmans, 1997, esp. ch. nine.) I would by no means suggest that a Protestant theology of Mary would greatly reduce the mystery which surrounds the Spirit's work, but I do think it would enhance, strengthen, and broaden our sparse pneumatology as Protestants.

What of the feminist concerns raised in the paper? I take issue with the feminist claim that men generally have divorced theology from experience. I would rather argue that such a tendency comes from White Eurocentric men, who, it is true, have written the bulk of theology in the West. I would add that African-Americans and Hispanics generally would agree with the feminist concern about the suspicion of experience in most theology. At the very least, these two minority groups have echoed the same complaint and have urged theologians to resist absolutizing European male experience in theological method and results. While one certainly would not want to develop a biblical theology that starts with experience, against which the paper warns, it is important that our theology pay heed to all aspects of our humanness. As much as we may want to be logical and rational, we must acknowledge that our minds are as fallen as the rest of us.

I found it intriguing that Mary' virginity, prior to birth, could serve as a possible contribution to feminist theology. One way I think this could be helpful is in relationship to the independence virginity afforded medieval women. In this era, the maintenance of chastity prior to marriage seems to be a great challenge, yet there is an opportunity here for those women who would label themselves Christian, even apart from any feminist label. Mary's virginity and discipleship can serve women by strengthening the resolve to resist the objectification of women so prevalent in this world. (One only need look at the advertising industry or Seventh Avenue in Manhattan during fashion week to see this). A commitment to virginity prior to marriage may preclude what some consider sexual liberation, but it does provide liberation from social mores which implicitly and explicitly tell women that their value lies in their ability to attract predatory males in college frat houses and late night rave parties. Is it possible for biblical and feminist theology to meet in Mary? Greene-McCreight tells us yes, but only when our social agendas place themselves second to Christ. I am thankful that this paper brings Mary to our attention as Protestants. We need to make sure that Mary comes to Reform school, instead of relegating her to Vatican City. In fact, we need to do our best to get to know Mary as our sister, instead of reducing her to one or two dimensions.

"YOU WHO ONCE WERE FAR OFF HAVE BEEN BROUGHT NEAR": REFLECTIONS IN THE AID OF THEOLOGICAL EXEGESIS

R. R. RENO

The challenge of theological exegesis is not altogether different from other situations of reading and listening. The difficulties of interpretation rest in the problem of hearing what is said. For a number of reasons we are often very distant from what is spoken, and as a consequence, it is difficult to hear. For example, my daughter is often in the basement reading a book, and she only vaguely hears me yell for her to go and clean her room. She hears, but does not hear. One must be rather close to children in order to get them to pay attention.

When we read the Scriptures, of course, the text is not on one floor, yelling, while we are distracted on another. Yet, the situation is similar. The text has something to say, or more precisely, as a written artifact, it is forever saying what it has to say. We, on the other hand, often fail to hear. Even when the Scriptures are open before us, as near as the desktop, we remain at a distance. What is being said is not always clear. Like my daughter, we often respond to Scripture's word with a pregnant "What?"

At the most basic level, hermeneutics is the discipline of attention that help us overcome this distance. After all, Hermes was a messenger. He bridged the chasm between the gods and human beings. He traveled the distance from the divine speakers to the human listeners. For this reason, no matter how much theoretical heavy machinery is brought to bear on the problems of interpretation, hermeneutical reflection is always practical. It involves acquiring the knowledge and skill necessary to reach the goal of listening: to hear what is being said. It is in a sense the knowledge and skill of a traveler, someone who can find a way to overcome the distance that so often mutes, obscures, and even silences. Any biblical hermenuetic worth its salt will provide guidance for negotiating what I call the "problems of distance." It must inculcate the knowledge and skill necessary to get from where we are to what the Scriptures are saying.

These remarks will advance the following thesis about the hermeneutical task of bridging the distances that separate us from the Word of God. The most important and debilitating distance that separates us from what Scriptures are saying should be understood spiritually. For all our worries about history, as well as those about the limitations of finite language and culturally conditioned texts, our difficulties in relation to the biblical text are not historical or metaphysical. More precisely, those difficulties are but subsets of the fundamentally spiritual reason why paying attention to Scripture is such a challenge. The Word of God is near to us, but even as it is before our eyes and on our lips, *we* are far. Only the cure of our souls will bring us to hear the Word of God. But now *I* am speaking cryptically and at a distance. What, exactly, do I mean by "historical," "metaphysical," and "spiritual" distance?

THE DISTANCES OF TIME AND FINITE FORM

The notion of historical distance is familiar to anyone who has taken a course in modern biblical criticism. For the modern reader of the Bible the challenges to understanding are severe. The Scriptures were written a long time ago, and as a result, the context, semantic use, and the very languages of the texts stand at a distance. This makes it easy for us to confuse anachronistic readings with accurate readings as we substitute assumptions about the present for the realities of the past.

A great deal of the angst of modern Christian biblical scholarship rests in the historical distance created by the passage of time and the challenges it poses. One of my colleagues is emphatic: the distance is nearly unbridgeable. The NT, he insists, was written in a "high context" social matrix of Mediterranean agrarian culture. It cannot be understood by students raised in a "low context" Northern European industrial culture. His way of formulating the historical problem of distance is idiosyncratic, but the basic judgment is widespread. The currents of history carry us so far from the original context that only heroic efforts allow for recovery. In order to pay attention to what is actually being said in Scripture, rather than projecting onto the text what we imagine or would like it to say, the hard work of traveling back in time must be undertaken. Theoretical aides, schemes of reconstruction, ambitious expeditions of textual archeology—these and many other vehicles carry the biblical critic across the distances created by the passing of time.

The metaphysical problem of distance receives less articulate attention among historical critics, but it is even more pervasive and threatening to modern readers of the Bible. Here, the difficulty rests in the fact that the depths of meaning are fundamentally greater than the limited forms of speech. Finite signs and utterances cannot capture the fullness of what is said. The problem is exacerbated when words seek to speak of God. How can the infinite be represented by the finite? How can spiritual truths take effective form as carnal or fleshly sounds in the air formed by our throats, or marks on the page formed by our hands? How can the array of ancient texts that we call the Bible, written by and for members of a small tribe of ancient people and the messianic movement they spawned, be the Word of God?

More often than not, modern interpreters treat this metaphysical distance as the nub of difficulty. What we often refer to as "historical context" is not just a challenge to our historical understanding. It is also a challenge to our religious imaginations. To cite a now widespread example, many contemporary readers are anxious to separate the patriarchal form of the biblical witness from its spiritual message. The finite form of the witness, wrapped in the historical and cultural limitations of its own cultural milieu, must be distinguished from the timeless and spiritual message it seeks to communicate. The biblical interpreter often must reformulate the message of Scripture so that the modern reader "gets it."

Like traveling across historical distance, the distance between representation and that which is represented must be traversed. New words must be spoken, even new texts written, so that the eternal Word might shine forth in our new age. For most twentieth century academics, the word "hermeneutics" refers to theories of communicative interaction that guide our efforts to parse meaning from medium, and thus guide effective interpretation. A general account of what words and texts can and cannot do directs the journey from what is said to what is meant. The itineraries vary. For some, we must navigate the difficult terrain that separates the finite form of signs from the fathomless depths of consciousness (Ricoeur) or from the effective power of texts (Gadamer). For others, we must renounce such journeys as futile and instead prepare ourselves to be pilgrims devoted to following the swerves and twists of semiotic play (Derrida) or the forward movement of communal consensus (Rorty). For still others, we should gird our loins for the adventures of strong misreading (Bloom) or discipline our souls to endure the prison of language (De Man). In each case, metaphysical distance defines the journey.

My descriptions of historical and metaphysical distance give the impression that these are uniquely modern problems. This is not so. The Church Fathers were very aware of both. Origen did not assemble the text-critical apparatus of multiple versions of the OT, the Hexapla, in order to meditate. He did so because he was very aware of how the exigencies of history can corrupt the texts. The passage of time requires the transmission and dissemination of the written word, which is the visible form of memory, and in this process copyists make mistakes that must be identified and corrected. Origen's judgment about how to discern and remedy these mistakes may lack the reliability of modern methods, but he certainly understood an important aspect of the historical problem of distance. In the same way Ireneaus did not commend the succession of teachers stretching from his time back to the apostles in order to provide a foundation for later catholic polity. He did so in order to identify the reliable basis on which believers can bridge the distance between his own time and the apostolic age. The public memory of the community, expressed in the doctrine of qualified teachers and buttressed by signs of holiness, provides effective guidance to our efforts to gain accurate knowledge of apostolic teaching.

The metaphysical problem of representation and the distance it entails was even more pressing for the Fathers. At a systematic level Augustine famously distinguished between signs and things, and in so doing, gave conceptual form to the problem facing all biblical interpreters, both ancient and modern. Not only is there an inevitable slippage between signs and things, as we all experience in both the multiple referents of words and their varying uses, but more importantly, the "thing" of which Scripture seeks to speak is God, and God transcends all signs. As Augustine says, when he speaks of God he enters into the paradox of not saying what he wishes to say, for he wishes to speak of the unspeakable (*De doctrina Christiana* I.6). The reality of God is so much greater than the finite forms of language that the most true thing that can be said is that he is ineffable. The metaphysical problem of distance knows no clearer expression. Without doubt, then, the ancient church was sensible of the historical and metaphysical problems of distance. What the Scripture says is difficult to hear. Time separates us from what is said, and the finite form of all signs and texts makes the Bible a peculiar instrument for speaking about God. However, to say that the Fathers were cognizant of the historical and metaphysical problems of distance does not mean that they approached them in the same way as most modern readers. Indeed, the solutions they offered are very different from the ones we typically think appropriate. We want historical methods to solve the problems posed by history. We want metaphysical theories of meaning to solve the problems posed by the fact that we use words to talk about things, texts to communicate realities. In contrast, the Fathers offered spiritual or theological guidance for navigating the distances created by time and the finite form of language. For them the challenges of interpretation, many as they are, revolve around a spiritual problem: the distance between sin and righteousness, the chasm that separates fleshly existence according the exigencies of "the world" from holiness.

For this reason, the Fathers treated the difficulties posed by history, as well as divine transcendence of language, as particular manifestations of this more fundamental distance between the ways of the world and the ways of the Lord. For example, Ireneaus does not dwell on the evidential value of public transmission of apostolic teaching. Instead, he draws a sharp contrast between the willfulness of heretical innovation and the obedient submission of orthodox teachers to the doctrine entrusted to their care. Reliable guidance across the distances of time requires affiliating oneself with the community of the faithful in visible continuity with the apostles and adopting its Rule of Faith. What we might now call canonical interpretation, guided by the living magisterium of the church, preserved in her creeds and alive in the consensus of the faithful, is an appropriate and accurate gloss on Ireneaus' method for preparing ourselves to hear the testimony of Scripture.

Augustine's approach to the distances created by finite language is no less theological in character. For Augustine the soul seeks that which transcends time and finitude. Such a journey, however, is beyond our power. Augustine takes the metaphysical problem of distance very seriously indeed. "We would not be able to do this," he continues, "except that Wisdom Himself saw fit to make Himself congruous with such infirmity as ours ..." (*De doctrina Christiana* I.11).[1] The Incarnate Word journeys to us so that we might journey with and to Him. "He wished to assume flesh," writes Augustine, "not only for those arriving at their estate but also to prepare the way for those setting out at the beginning of their journey ..." (I.34). His form is fleshly, and encoded with the signs and language of prophecy, he dwells amidst the limitations of finitude. Here, the relation of Jesus to the Father is not governed by a general theory of mediation, either metaphysical or hermeneutical. Following Jesus' path we acquire the habits of a traveler along his way, habits of faith, hope, and love, and thus are we carried across the metaphysical distance from creature to Creator.

BIBLICAL ASSUMPTIONS ABOUT TIME

The ways in which the Fathers analyze our hermeneutical situation can seem impossibly "pre-critical." Surely historical distance cannot be overcome with the waving of some magical wand, as if prayer and fasting can substitute for the critical tools of modern textual analysis. The problems of historical distance must be treated independently of so-called theological exegesis. The limitations of historical context must be acknowledged! Something that scholars like to call "historical consciousness" cannot be gainsaid! Responsible exegesis must depend upon intellectual and not spiritual discipline! Similar reactions worry that this spiritual turn ignores the real and enduring problems of representation. Surely we must not confuse words about God with God! Surely we should avoid being idolaters of the letter of Scripture! Unless we gain some sophistication about words and their function as representations, then we will confuse what is said with what is meant!

I cannot begin to answer these objections, common as they are. A full-scale defense of patristic hermeneutics would require a genealogy of modern historical inquiry, as well as close analysis of the ways in which the metaphysics of representation was understood by the Fathers. The Fathers inherited and modified a complex and sophisticated Platonic tradition that nests with the Old Testament's dual structure of polemic against idolatry and affirmation of the power of divine presence in both Temple and prophecy. Unpacking this interaction of Platonism with exegesis requires heavy lifting in the realm of metaphysics.[2] I have a perhaps unhealthy tendency to spend a great deal of time in the theoretical gymnasium. To avoid overtraining, I wish to set aside, for the moment, concerns about representation. Instead, I will digress to consider a theological assumption behind the usual historical-critical objections to pre-critical exegesis. This assumption is best described as historical pessimism, the assumption that time is a curse (or a blessing, if one wishes to wipe the slate clean) because it creates an unbridgeable gap between past and present. The passage of time wears away at our connection to the past, and the erosion is unstoppable. This assumption needs to be examined, for the Scriptures themselves advance a theological judgment at odds with the modern view.

Consider the way in which the LORD blesses Noah after repenting of the desire to end the cycle of generations. The blessing opens and closes with a commandment: "Be fruitful and multiply, and fill the earth" (Gen 9:1, 7). The passing of generations turns the unmarked passage of time into human history. Genealogy is the archetypical biblical form of encompassing the distance from past to present. Clearly, then, the Scriptures neither deny nor efface the passage of time, and in that sense the biblical witness affirms and promotes "history," as innumerable modern commentators on the OT have noticed. Nonetheless, unlike the pessimism of modernity, the Scriptures do not treat historical distance as corrosive and corruptive; it is the medium of spiritual life, not an alien impediment. The space between past, present, and future creates room for blessing and curse. Time can be filled up and held together by covenant and faithfulness.

In the OT faithfulness is bound up with memory. However, the mnemonic challenges are not simply technical or intellectual, as if proper critical techniques might suffice for, or even be relevant to, the problem of historical distance. My daughter forgets that I have told her to clean her room on Saturday mornings because she would rather read or play. We fail to remember because we are tempted to forget, and in this sense, the ability to bridge the distances of time depend upon a moral and spiritual discipline, not intellectual techniques.

Second Kings 22 and the discovery of the book of the law suggests such a situation. The scene is very much about "history" and the distances it creates, but the sentiments are antithetical to modern historical sensibilities. A lust for evil has darkened memory and corrupted the disciplines necessary to keep the past ever before the eyes of the present. A series of bad kings mark eclipse of the past. This makes the discovery of the books of the law a dramatic moment, and King Josiah's reaction is telling. He does not muse about the odd religious views of an archaic culture; he does not consult with critics to discern the *Sitz im Leben*. Instead, "when the king heard the words of the book of the law, he rent his clothes" (2 Kgs 22:11). He is a good king, and he has the eyes to see that which is written, to hear that which is spoken. The passage of time is a challenge to memory, but it is the drama of sin and righteousness that determines our connection to the past.

Paul's reflections on the fate of carnal Israel assumes and deepens the view of history we find in 2 Kings. The passage of time creates a stage for the drama of God's promises and the outworking of his redemptive will, not only in the triumphs of memory, but also in its failures. For Paul the mysterious unbelief of Israel conforms to the OT pattern of blindness and forgetfulness. Quoting from Isaiah, Paul interprets the Jewish rejection of Jesus as the consummating form of Israel's blindness. The organs of memory—eye and ear—are disabled (Rom 11:8). Yet, for Paul the very distance of carnal Israel from the fulfillment of the promise that is her birthright—she is cut off—allows for the nations to enter into the drama of history. They are grafted onto the genealogy of Israel that, as promised to Noah, will fill up the distances created by time and its passing. "I want you to understand this mystery," writes Paul, "a hardening has come upon part of Israel, until the full number of the Gentiles has come in" (11:25). Israel's inability to hear, as did King Josiah, the word that, however distant in time or form, "is near you, on your lips and in your heart" (10:8), establishes the very conditions for the elongation of time. Time and the historical distances it creates is for Paul the gift that Jewish unbelief gives to the Gentiles. Or more precisely, this time before the end of all time is God's gift, which he gives, mysteriously, through his providential hardening of the heart of carnal Israel. I do not intend these brief exegetical digressions as sufficient for understanding the scriptural view of time. Nonetheless, I hope both examples cast doubt on the historical pessimism that characterizes so much of modern scholarly reading of the Bible. From the perspective of the Scriptures themselves, history does not necessarily or inevitably distance us from the word of God. In 2 Kings, as in so much of the OT, history offers both the opportunity to draw near and the risk of falling away. For Paul the continued passage of time after the fulfillment of God's promises in Jesus extends and intensifies that opportunity, as one form of falling away makes possible another form of drawing near. Thus, the distances created by time are very real. Neither the author of 2 Kings nor Paul have any interest in denying the reality of historical time. Quite the contrary, both insist upon its reality, both as the medium for memory and as the stage upon which divine promises find their fulfillment. What is important, however, is that in both cases, the distances of time are set within the broader problem of spiritual distance. What matters most is the relation of our souls to the LORD; the crucial issue is the distance at which we stand from that which is near.

TWO EXEGETICAL TECHNIQUES

If my brief meditation on the biblical view of history has given cause to reconsider the typical modern pessimism about time and its passing, then I would be pleased. If the suspicion is growing that, as the Father's so consistently taught, questions of historical distance, like those of metaphysical distance, are best considered under the greater and more fundamental problem of spiritual distances, then we have come a good way toward rethinking the notion of biblical hermeneutics. Yet, neither the biblical view of history nor the patristic account of the fundamental distances that separates us from the word of God adds up to hermeneutics. As indicated earlier, to have a hermeneutics is to have the disciplines of hearing that help us overcome the distance between what we hear and what is said, and these disciplines are just that, disciplines or practices that train our ears and eyes. Hermeneutical skill does not stem from investigation of the biblical views on any particular subject, even a subject as central to modern interpretation as history. Nor does that skill result from sympathy with the larger, spiritual outlook of the Fathers. Instead, if one is beginning to think that the Fathers are right, that the difficulties of interpretation revolve around a fundamental problem of spiritual distance, and if one wishes to address the exegetical challenge at that level, then one must acquire the skills of reading that characterize patristic exegesis. One must read as the Fathers did.

I can no more provide the acquisition of patristic skills of reading than I can offer a full-scale defense of pre-critical exegesis against critical objections. Indeed, I can be of even less help, for the acquisition of a skill requires the tutelage of a master, not the observations of a scholar, and I am no master of the particular methods and techniques of reading that characterize patristic exegesis. Nonetheless, I can offer two brief performances, one keyed to the problem of history, and the other directed to the problem of representation. Both are methods of spiritual reading that have dominated the exegetical practice of Christians for centuries, and they have been so influential and long-lived because they succeed in overcoming distance.

Figural reading is one way in which the Fathers traversed the distances that separate us from the text. Just what is involved in figural reading is a matter of endless debate. Nonetheless, Christian figural exegesis has a recognizable form. Jesus Christ functions as the disclosing antitype, and he illuminates the meaning of events both before and after his life, death, and resurrection. This illumination occurs because events or persons have a shape or form that outlines a common "figure." One common instance is the deliverance of Israel from the Egyptians through the Red Sea. The deliverance through water prefigures redemption in Christ, a redemption sealed in our passage through the waters of baptism. Here, an event in the past, separated from the reader by the distances of time, is brought near through figural conformity to events in the present. An event in Exodus is drawn through Christ into present ecclesial practice. In this way figural exegesis overcomes distance. What happened to the Israelites has happened to each of us.

The Red Sea—redemption in Christ—baptism figural constellation is widespread in pre-critical exegetical works, but its very conventionality tends to disguise the dynamics of figural reading. Better, then, to undertake something more adventurous. Consider this particularly powerful figural interpretation that I draw from the work of Ephraim Radner.[3] It involves three historical moments. The first is the division of Israel into Northern and Southern Kingdoms, the weakening entailed in this division, and then the slow slide toward defeat, enslavement, and exile. These events serve as the background for the prophetic books, and they, in turn, are central to the Christian interpretation of the identity of Jesus as the Christ. Moreover, this sequence is not simply historical background to particular prophetic passages that are fulfilled. The sequence of division, diminishment, and exile is recapitulated and intensified in Christ: his betrayal, the scattering of his disciples, his diminishment and affliction in arrest, and his God-forsaken death. In Jerusalem, Jesus alone is the remnant of holiness, reduced to death by the afflictions due to the unrighteous.

Here, the second historical sequence of events—the fate of the man, Jesus of Nazareth—enters into an illuminative relationship to the first historical sequence. The relation of type to antitype discloses more fully the redemptive suffering of those few faithful, who, bound to the body of Israel, were borne into the captivity that is rightly due to the unfaithful. Now, the power of the covenant is more fully visible. The union of the righteous to the body of the nation, like Jesus' union with carnal flesh, cannot be sundered, and this union subjects the righteous to an undeserved and yet redemptive suffering. Under the burdens of exile, the remnant carries forward the disciplines of memory that make possible the return to Jerusalem and restoration of the Temple, just as Christ, enduring the final burden of death, rises and makes possible our return to the Lord in restored worship. Furthermore, to pursue the figure, neither return simply restores; both intensify and sharpen the disciplines of holiness. The books of Ezra and Nehemiah are characterized by a redoubled, rather than relaxed, restoration of cult and Torah. Paul as well preaches the power of the risen Christ as spiritual worship and discipline that intensifies and fulfills.

The power of figure does not just extend from Christ backwards to the history of Israel. It extends forward to the history of the church. The church is Christ's body, and as such, she participates in the figural sequence of exile and restoration. This forward lean of figure is primitive to Christian interpretation of present times. First Peter, for example, is addressed to the "exiles of the Dispersion" (1:1) who "suffer various trials" (1:6), all of which purify and refine so that a remnant of holiness might be called out of the darkness and into divine light (1:9). But the figure does not jump from Old Israel to New Israel. Instead for the author of 1 Peter, Christ is the illuminating center of the figural sequence. The desolation of trial, the afflictions of exile, should be embraced. "Rejoice," exhorts the author, " in so far as you share in Christ's sufferings, that you may also rejoice and be glad when his glory is revealed" (4:13). Israel, Christ, and Church are three historical moments in figural relation.

First Peter establishes a pattern of reading that invites subsequent interpreters to place the history of the church into the figural sequence. The Fathers did this at every turn. We can do so as well. As Ephraim Radner suggests, the divided churches in the West, fragmented by the Reformation, suffer the same fate as the two kingdoms of ancient Israel. One need but visit a German or a French or an English church to feel as though 1 Peter speaks to the present. Truly, the few who gather are exiles in the Dispersion. They are a remnant that clings to the disciplines of memory that keep Christian faith alive in the enclosing darkness of a post-Christian culture. For just this reason Radner urges us to complete the figural sequence. We suffer the failures and weaknesses of our churches. Yet, such afflictions are none other than the suffering that shapes the church into the body of our Lord, so that she might share in his suffering. Still further, if we press the figure from the present into the future, then we can look to the narratives of Ezra and Nehemiah for a pattern of ecclesial resurrection in Western culture. Given this pattern, we should hope that the church will come to weep bitterly in penitent confession of faithlessness, and, in redoubled zeal for holiness, that she will put away her foreign wives and children.

We need to be clear about how this figural sequence functions. In the first place this way of reading is *not* a matter of matching up prophetic passages with christological fulfillments that are, in turn, connected to specific ecclesial doctrines or practices. Instead, this figural approach takes historical events and brings them together. The division of Israel, the conflict between the two kingdoms, the diminishment and decline that follows, the vulnerability to captivity and affliction, the persistence of a remnant, the return and redoubled restoration enters into an illuminating relation to a parallel pattern to the present sequence of events in the Christian church in the West, and it does so through the prism of the passion, death, and resurrection of Jesus. These entities share a common figure or form that makes events that are historically distant come together. Of course, they do not merge. The historical sequences are very real. Neither a second century reader who thinks Ezra and Nehemiah and the synoptic gospels are utterly reliable accounts of what actually happened, nor the most sophisticated modern reader who has all the latest critical tools at his disposal, has ever imagined that these two sequences of events are not separated by the distances of history. Nor do any imagine that the more recent history of the church is any closer, in time, by virtue of figural interpretation. The point is that their figural association allows the reader to bridge the very real and enduring distances of time through an interpretive coordination. Each historical sequence says the same thing about the way of faithfulness. For this reason figural reading is the essence of Christian "historical" exegesis. The illuminating form of Christ provides the basis for understanding how the word of God is revealed in events and practices that stand at a distance from each other.

Intensive reading is another and very different skill that was no less dominant among the Fathers. Unlike figural interpretation, which deals with patterns and sequences that make up historical events and practices, intensive reading focuses on the semantic plentitude of particular scriptural signs or episodes. Patristic commentary on the Gospel of John is paradigmatic. Origen, for example, gathers up many meanings of *logos*, and he does so not to sift through them in order to settle upon a single and univocal meaning, but in order to arrange the many meanings around the christological focus of the Johannine text.[4] In this way Origen engages the problem of metaphysical distance. He follows the many threads of meaning, making progress across the difference between representation and reality, between the sign "*logos*" and the One who is signified.

I do not propose to reproduce Origen's reflections. Instead, I wish to illustrate the intensive approach by considering John 6:39, a verse that I have long found puzzling because of its play of pronouns. Jesus teaches that he does not do his own will, but the will of the Father. In this discourse, the will of the Father, very much the crux of the passage, is semantically ambiguous. Jesus says, "This is the will of him who sent me that I should lose nothing of all that he has given me, but raise it up at the last day." The passage perplexes me because "all" and "it" are words or signs that represent something central to Jesus' message. Yet, they are pronouns that hold the place for something else. They are the open variables in an equation. Some *x* is given to Jesus. He shall lose nothing of this *x*. He shall raise up this x at the last day. Precisely because they have semantic openness—pronouns are wonderfully fungible parts of speech—the passage generates more questions than it answers. What is given to Jesus, and what will he raise up?

The immediate context of the passage suggests the proper referents for the pronouns. The very next verse tells us that all who believe in the Son shall have eternal life, and that Jesus will raise them up at the last day. By this reading, the "all" and "it" refer to the faithful. This reading is reinforced by Jesus' emphatic affirmation of the saving power of his flesh and blood later in the discourse (6:54). The Father has given followers to Jesus, and the Father has given Jesus the power of redemption, manifest in the eucharistic ritual. Joined to his body and blood in the sharing of the consecrated bread and wine, we participate in his death and resurrection.

The reading seems right, but I am not sure that we have cracked the nut of this puzzling verse. Why would the verse say that the "all" given to Jesus is an "it" that he will raise up? I do not wish to suggest that we are not given to Jesus, and that he will not raise us up on the last day. I only wish to point out that the particular and carnal form of the signs used, that is to say, the difference between impersonal and personal pronouns, invites further exegetical reflection. Perhaps the Father has given Jesus the power of life. Then, with this as the x in the passage, we can see that nothing of the power shall be lost, even if Jesus is betrayed, arrested, and crucified. This reading is also strongly reinforced by the immediate context. Jesus is the bread of life. Unlike the manna in the wilderness that sustains a few and only for a time, Jesus gives life to the world (6:33). Therefore, on the cross, on his last day, he raises up the power of life. His flesh and blood is for all and forever.

These pronouns can shift yet again. Maybe the x represented by "all" and "it" is neither the faithful nor the power of life. Maybe the x represents the flesh that the Father gives to the Son by sending him to us as the Incarnate Lord. The Son will lose nothing of this gift, and for just this reason, the Eternal Logos will experience destitution, suffering, and death. Nothing of carnal life is left out or lost. All of "it" is raised up on the cross in the form of the dead man whose flesh is pierced. For just this reason, you and I, flesh from flesh, are neither left out nor lost in the risen Lord. Christ will let go of nothing. As he bears the marks of the nails and the wound of the spear—nothing of the flesh is lost—he raises us to light and life.

The point of this kind of reading is not to decide which referent is the right one. Instead, the skill involves allowing the very distance between sign and signified to motivate us to undertake interpretive effort. In this case, I drew attention to the way in which the semantic openness of pronouns can open rather than close questions. This openness does not frustrate. Instead, the difficulty of settling on a particular interpretation forces us to look again and again at the possibilities. Looking again and not elsewhere is the reason way the Fathers did not view metaphysical distances created by representation with regret; such ambiguity stems from the plenitude of sense that is an inevitable consequence of the fact that the words of Scripture are effective but inadequate signs. They are inadequate for the reason Augustine identified: they seek to speak to us of the ineffable mystery of God. Yet they are effective because these signs are not mute and sterile but vocal and fecund. The "failures" of representation—in this case, the "defect" of semantic openness characteristic of pronouns—lead us toward the fathomless depths of that to which all the scriptural signs point: the mystery of Christ. Thus, the metaphysical distance between sign and signified is no more collapsed by intensive reading than historical distance is collapsed by figural reading. Instead, exegetical travel is undertaken, and that which seems impossibly distant comes into view in just the right way.

THE ASCETICAL CORE OF THEOLOGICAL EXEGESIS

Hermeneutical skill is the ability to understand words; it requires the virtues that sustain travel across the distances between what we hear and what is said. I hope that my brief illustrations of the figural and intensive reading have provided a small degree of insight into classical Christian methods for overcoming distances. If we acquire the ability to see figural sequences, then we can travel across the distances of history. If we cultivate an appreciation of the plentitude of sense, then we can travel along the distance between sign and signified. These skills, however, are not isolated. In both cases, a spiritual discipline undergirds the practices of reading. On the central role of spiritual discipline, Origen is perhaps the most lucid and direct of all the Fathers. Origen is as emphatic as the most hard-nosed evangelical preacher. "There is no possible way," he writes, "of explaining and bringing to man's knowledge the higher and diviner teaching about the Son of God, except by means of those Scriptures which were inspired by the Holy Spirit, namely, the gospels and the writings of the apostles, to which we add, according to the declaration of Christ himself, the law and the prophets" (*Peri archon*, I.3.1).[5] Yet, unlike a great deal of modern conservative reaction to the very real problems of historical and metaphysical distance that have come to dominate the academic study of the Bible, Origen is no proponent of easy perspicuity. The Scriptures are full of obscurity, contradiction, and offense. The examples Origen gives could just as well come from a contemporary introduction to historical critical study of the Bible. Some passages of Scripture are patently mythological (e.g., when Genesis speaks of God as walking in paradise); some are culturally conditioned (e.g., Jesus' commandment to his disciples not to possess shoes); some are morally repugnant (e.g., the Septuagint rendering of Gen 17:14 which requires the uncircumcised infant to be destroyed after the eighth day); some entail contradiction (e.g., the synoptic and Johannine treatments of Passover in relation to Jesus' passion). The distance between us and the text is very real indeed.

However, for Origen such distance is not a curse. Quite the contrary, "Divine wisdom," Origen writes, "has arranged for certain stumbling blocks and interruption in the historical sense ... by inserting ... a number of impossibilities and incongruities, in order that the narrative might as it were present a barrier to the reader" (IV.2.9). Our distance from the Scriptures is part of the pedagogy of salvation. "By shutting us out and debarring us," continues Origen, God "might recall us to the beginning of another way, and might thereby bring us through the entrance of a narrow footpath, to a higher and loftier road and lay open the immense breadth of divine wisdom" (IV.2.9). The more sensible we are of the distance between what we hear and what God wishes to say, the more accurate will be our sense of the arduous and difficult nature of traversing that distance. Reading rightly will require the surest of guides, and here, for all his intepretive inventiveness and potentially dangerous theological speculation, Origen is utterly opposed to the complacent strategies of reading that seek to find relevance or that depend upon the inner resources of the reader. The ability to traverse the distance, the power to read rightly, rests only in "that rule and discipline delivered by Jesus Christ to the apostles and handed down by them in succession to their posterity ..." (IV.2.2). Only as we are formed by the common life of the church, her ancient teachings, her ceaseless prayer, and her patterns of self-discipline and mutual service, can we read rightly. This is the most fundamental form of the patristic theory of hermeneutics.

The present age founders on the problems of history and representation because we are unwilling to enter into the spiritual discipline necessary to travel the distance between what we hear and what is said. The ways in which the Fathers read Scripture are alien, because their discipline is now alien. We no longer submit ourselves to the common life of the church, not only because our modern souls fear authority, not only because intellectual life has come untethered from ecclesiastical reality, but because Western Christianity has such a severely fragmented common life. The prayer of the church is cacophonous. Her doctrines are defined in the spirit of mutual condemnation not mutual service. What Origen thought so indispensable, we now seek to recreate through ecumenical endeavor. Not surprisingly, then, the practices of spiritual reading are suspect; the communal conditions for their disciplined use exist only in part.

Equally important, spiritual reading gains little traction because the moral and ascetical practices that the Fathers thought essential to the Christian life are now divorced from intellectual training. Who would imagine that fasting might contribute to exegetical insight? To a certain degree, modern historical study has inculcated moral discipline. Pursuit of truth requires the courage to consider all the evidence. Moreover, loyalty to truth engenders humility, especially the humility of a historian who knows that historical judgment traffics in likelihood and possibility, not certainty and necessity. Yet, even these virtues are in decline. Postmodern "methods" put few demands upon the souls of their practitioners or the students they train. Nothing could be further from the patristic atmosphere of interpretation. For Augustine the ambiguities and uncertainties that finite signs produce does not yield a "play of difference." We cannot turn what is hard into something easy. Instead, interpretation is difficult, and for Augustine, "this situation was provided by God to conquer pride by work and to combat disdain in our minds, to which those things which are easily discovered seem frequently to become worthless" (*De doctrina Christiana* II.6). Here, the patristic outlook is clearly expressed. Hermeneutical discipline is no different from spiritual discipline. "The mind should be cleansed," writes Augustine, "so that it is able to see [divine] light and cling to it once it is seen. Let us consider this cleansing to be as a journey or voyage home" (I.10). To read rightly will both require and lead to humility; it will both require and lead to a love of that which God wishes us to hear.

This assimilation of hermeneutical skill to spiritual virtue can seem pious and preachy. It is both, but that is because piety and preaching seek to bring us to exactly that which words seek to achieve: understanding that which is said. I wish to conclude with an exchange that typifies this truth.

When I graduated from college, I lived in New York City, near Harlem. One day, on the way home from the subway stop, I tarried briefly to listen to a man harangue a small group that was gathered at the corner. His voice was filled with urgency; his eyes were aflame. What he said I cannot reconstruct, but I vividly remember the way he ended nearly every sentence. He would say, "Do you hear my, brothers? Do you hear me?" He had no doubts about the volume of his voice. He was not wondering whether his listeners had their hearing aides turned on. He was asking them if they would allow what he was saying to gain leverage over their lives. Were his listeners with him? Would they undertake to travel with him toward that which he saw and sought? This was the hermeneutical challenge he posed, and it is, I think, the most fundamental challenge of anyone who wishes to hear something genuinely important and true. Our relation to the Scriptures is no different, for they seek to speak the most important and pressing truth. Few wish to hear. Most wish to stand at a distance. No technical or intellectual aides will bring us near. Only spiritual discipline will carry us toward something which, however, crowned in glory, is flavored with the bitter taste of vinegar and gall.

NOTES

1. I follow the translation of *De doctrina Christiana* by D. W. Robertson, Jr. (Indianapolis: The Library of Liberal Arts, 1958).

2. For two contemporary efforts to do this heavy lifting in metaphysics, see Nicholas Wolterstorff, *Divine Discourse* (Cambridge: Cambridge University Press, 1995) and Jean-Luc Marion, *God Without Being* (Chicago: University of Chicago Press, 1991). These two Christian philosophers draw on radically different philosophical traditions, but both undertake to "solve" the problem of distance created by the fact that Christianity requires the use of signs.

3. See Radner's essay, "The Cost of Communion: A Meditation on Israel and the Divided Church," in *Inhabiting Unity: Theological Perspectives on the Proposed Lutheran-Episcopal Concordat* (ed. Ephraim Radner and R. R. Reno; Grand Rapids: Eerdmans, 1995), 134-152, as well as his extended uses of this figural interpretation throughout *The End of the Church: A Pneumatology of Christian Division in the West* (Grand Rapids: Eerdmans, 1998).

4. See Origen's *Commentary on the Gospel According to John*, Book One.

5. I follow the translation of *On First Principles* by G. W. Butterworth (Gloucester, Mass.: Peter Smith, 1973).

RESPONSE TO RENO

TODD E. JOHNSON

The story is told of an autumn afternoon when the theology department of a prominent university gathered for its fall colloquium. The discussion for the afternoon was the nature of a theology department. All dutiful graduate students were present with most of the faculty. The meeting was lead by a well respected patriarch on the faculty, a systematic theologian and Catholic priest. The sage began his presentation with a quote from Baron Friedrich von Hügel, emphasizing that what identifies a true theologian is that a true theologian prays what he or she studies. Dutiful graduate students nodded with agreement as he elucidated the distinction between a religious studies department and a theology department, with the former emphasizing disinterested objectivity, the latter rooted in reflection and study from within the context of belief and practice. As he finished his presentation all dutiful graduate students felt justified with their choice of graduate programs. "This is a perspective on the theological task I can own," they said to themselves.

Then the responses began. The faculty and students became polarized by this talk in ways that no dutiful graduate student had anticipated. The response came swift and firm from the Scripture scholars and historians: one must step outside of one's faith if one is truly to exegete a text. Beginning with explicit presuppositions of faith will more likely lead to eisegesis, not exegesis, they argued. The volley continued as the other half of the department came to the good father's defense arguing that a theology department is at the service of the church and must operate within the context of the faith. There they were, a department with a methodological line clearly drawn in the sand, biblical scholars and historians on one side arguing for objective scholarship, and liturgists, ethicists, and systematicians on the other furiously invoking the holy trinity of Augustine, Aquinas, and Rahner in defense of the dual foundation of faith and reason. The initial feeling of appreciation for studying theology was polarized by the area of study of each of the dutiful graduate students.

Reno's paper has awakened the memories of this story. More than reminding me of the divisions separating many theology departments, Reno has made obvious the line in the sand that exists in the academy over the relationship between faith, theology, and the interpretation of Scriptures. Reno, sitting firmly on "my side of the room"—where faith and reason work hand in hand—has reminded us of the patristic insistence on the prayerful interpretation of the sacred texts. Likewise he has underscored the spiritual discipline required of any who seek properly to interpret the Scriptures, amplifying the echo of Augustine's charge to cleanse one's mind that one might "see the divine light and cling to it once it is seen." He has offered us concrete examples of this approach (his "figural" and "intensive" readings) which will lead to a lessening of hermeneutic distance in the interpretation of the text, a goal and an approach for which I have general sympathies.

But what about "the other half of the room"? How would they respond to such a proposal? I would like to offer by way of response, the critiques that I anticipate from the other side of the room. The purpose of this is to focus our conversation on the issues at stake not just for this conference but for churches and academic guilds of which we all are a part.

Reno begins his paper with an image that runs throughout, that of distance limiting one's ability to hear and/or to understand. This raises the initial question: is the issue of exegesis one of hearing, listening, and understanding or of appropriating the text?

Reno continues by describing the process by which this distance is bridged as a hermeneutic task. He then subsumes the hermeneutic task under the auspices of spiritual discipline or spirituality. This raises a tremendous issue in the larger academy, as no discipline is in more flux than that of the study of spirituality in all its forms. What spirituality is, as well as what it is not, has been at the center of recent meetings of the Society for the Study of Christian Spirituality, and we have arrived at no consensus as of yet.

Although Reno only defines the term "spiritual" or "spirituality" operationally, he does provide some clues as to the direction he wishes to go with this term. First, spirituality is a set of which both history and metaphysics are subsets, which implies a very broad definition of the term. It appears to begin with the acknowledgment of the divine/human dichotomy, specifically the recognition of a sinful humanity and a holy God. Although implicit, his sources often reflected a Platonic or Neo-Platonic framework which has certainly been the mainstay of a good deal of Christian spirituality. It has an existential element to the extent that it assumes that faith is rooted in memory, as well as preserving the sensibilities of Evagrius of Pontus with his emphasis on ascetic practices related to hermeneutics, what he called apotheia. For hermeneutics to be located as a subset of spirituality, as Reno has done along with history and metaphysics, a clearer definition of spirituality will be required for dialogue with the larger world of theology and Scripture scholarship.

Reno has also raised the chicken and egg question of the relationship between Scripture and faith. He is fairly consistent that faith is required for the proper discernment of the text. Although I do not presume that he suggests one cannot become convicted or come to faith by the reading of the text, that is not entirely clear. The answer to this query will necessarily be put into dialogue with his assertion that the hermeneutic discipline is no different from a spiritual discipline.

Historically, Reno's hermeneutic canon is located in patristic exegesis. He is definitive, "One must read as the Fathers did." I can see the fire in the eyes of the historians on the other side of the room now: "Only the Fathers? What about other periods? What makes the patristic hermeneutic any more reliable in the interpretation of the text than say the scholastics?" Or maybe they would say, "Are the patristic writings any less distanced from us than the Scriptures themselves?"

And I certainly imagine a good dose of skepticism that we could ever read as the Fathers did today, or that all the Fathers read the text the same way. Certainly Tertullian, Theodore of Mopsuestia, Augustine, and Chrysostom did not have a single hermeneutic approach among them. As Reno himself states, the task of defining and defending patristic exegesis is a complex one. It is a front which this position will have to defend however.

There are suggestions for reinforcements Reno might consider for his defense. For example, the approach of many theologians to consider Christ as God's Word, and the Scriptures as the Word of God only as a derivative of this christological assertion. In this way a typological reading is rooted both in the nature of God and the doctrine of revelation, as the Scriptures ultimately reveal Christ. Similarly, his description of the intensive reading of Scripture, not to find one best meaning but to work with the "many threads of meaning" is very similar to the agenda sacramental theologians have been working on the past fifty years. In particular, Reno's work might want to follow Alexandre Ganoczy's identification of the loss of symbolic competence and the suggestions for its recovery he and others have offered. (See Ganoczy's *An Introduction to Catholic Sacramental Theology*, New York: Paulist, 1984.)

This last piece suggests another tack that might be taken in regard to Reno's defense. What would this proposal look like if hermeneutics were supplemented with sacramentality as a theological paradigm for "spiritual interpretation"? Could one add to the concept of spirituality the sacramentality of the Spirit? Is it compatible to consider the story of God's people as the moving of the Spirit through the human sphere in space and time? This moving of the Spirit could then be seen as recorded by people responding to the same Spirit and the validity of their interpretation validated by the Spirit led community. The Spirit is likewise still active and present, pointing to Christ's redeeming work and empowering the on-going ministry of the body of Christ in the world. The Spirit likewise assists in the interpretation of the texts of Scripture, as well as the evolving texts of the faithful which would imply the reduction of the distance between the sign and signified, past and present, the Divine and Human.

Reno's paper has obviously spurred a great deal of thought and sympathy on my part and is deeply provocative concerning the role of the spiritual life in the task of interpretation. I am prodded by his work to consider further the work of the Spirit in this process invoking a divine human synergy in the process of both revelation and interpretation.

A BRAZEN FAITH

JOHN 3:14-15

STEPHEN CHAPMAN

Gracious God, Source of all true speech, now complete and perfect my thoughts, that your Word may be preached and heard in what I say, not only in fulfillment of my best intentions, but even in spite of them. Amen.

What a strange thing for Jesus to say! "And just as Moses lifted up the serpent in the wilderness, so must the Son of Man be lifted up, that whoever believes in him may have eternal life."

A Pharisee named Nicodemus had gone to Jesus by night, seeking for an explanation of the wonderful things he had seen Jesus do. But when Jesus told Nicodemus about life in the new kingdom of God, a life so different that it is like emerging a second time from the womb, Nicodemus became thoroughly confused. "How can these things be?" he protested. In good rabbinic style, Jesus answered his question with a question: "Are you a teacher in Israel, and yet you do not understand these things?"

At this point the language of the passage condenses and one feels the words of Jesus merge together with the testimony of John and the early church. "We speak of what we know and testify to what we have seen," the text continues, "yet you [the Greek verb is now plural!] do not receive our testimony." Between the lines of the narrative about Jesus and Nicodemus, John is apparently addressing the rejection of apostolic teaching in his own generation. In effect, "If you all cannot understand something as basic as life in the kingdom of God, how will you ever understand the really profound, heavenly things of the faith?" And what are these "heavenly things"?—That only the Son of Man has ascended into heaven and descended again; that the Son of Man must be lifted up in fulfillment of what was enacted by Moses long ago; that only in this way is life in the kingdom of God made possible. It is in the "lifting up" of the Son of Man that the kingdom of God breaks in upon the world.

Strange; these "heavenly things" are still mysterious to us today—opaque, disconcerting, even jarring. Faced with their weird logic we all become like Nicodemus, all over again.

None of the other gospels includes this serpentine saying. John, however, makes it central to his proclamation of Christ. While the other gospels portray several occasions on which Jesus predicts his own death, the Gospel of John contains three episodes in which Jesus tells of "the lifting up of the Son of Man"

(John 3:14; 8:28; 12:32). In John 12:33, we are finally told what this "lifting up" means, if by then we still have any doubts: "He said this to indicate the kind of death he was to die." It is this notion of a dying Messiah that the crowd cannot understand and promptly rejects. "We have heard from the law that the Messiah remains forever. How can you say that the Son of Man must be lifted up?" In other words, "How can you claim the Son of Man must die?"

Indeed! Is our idea of a "Messiah" so different today? To whom do we look for inspiration and help? What catches our eye, stirs our soul, and inspires our heart? Is it not the tall, statuesque man, whose clothing is just as impeccable as his manners? The photogenic supermodel, so sprightly, thin and lithe, who earns in one season more than some will ever save for retirement? The sports figures, strong and young, who compete valiantly in the Olympics and fill us with pride that we too are included in the human race they seem to define?

The hero, the star, the entrepreneur, the young, the proud, the beautiful; certainly there is nothing wrong with these things as such. It is God who has created them and made them good, and yet great danger lies in their appeal. John 12:39: "And so they could not believe, because Isaiah also said, 'He has blinded their eyes and hardened their heart, so that they might not look with their eyes, and understand with their heart and turn—and I would heal them.'" That is, God would heal them, but they cannot see God. We cannot understand the "heavenly things"—"theological" things—because our eyes are blinded with dazzling visions of worldly glamour. But there is healing. There is balm in Gilead yet.

"As Moses lifted up the serpent in the wilderness, so must the Son of Man be lifted up." In Num 21:4-9, we find another story of healing. Wandering in the wilderness, the people of Israel became impatient for the promised land. "Why have you brought us up out of Egypt to die?" they complained to Moses and to God. "There is no water and no food to speak of and even the food we get we don't like." God responded to this ingratitude by sending serpents in among the people, who are then bitten, and many die. In telling how God had done this, the story does not attribute to God something wicked, but testifies to God's justice and lordship over the history of Israel. Confronted with their sin, the people repented and pleaded with Moses to intercede on their behalf with God, which he did. In response, God told Moses to make a serpent and set it upon a pole. So Moses fashioned a serpent of bronze and we are told that after that, whenever an Israelite was bitten by a snake in the wilderness, "that person would look at the serpent of bronze and live."

Here then is another story about a people who are blind to the care and compassion of God, a God made vulnerable precisely because of a commitment made to this people. Because they lacked material things, they were unhappy with their hero Moses. However, their healing did not come from Moses or from any hero, but from their act of looking up toward a curious symbol, a symbol fashioned in the form of death, a symbol of death that nevertheless brought new life.

Even within the OT, this story is plainly bizarre. What of the second commandment—the prohibition against graven images? This bronze serpent seems a lot like that golden calf in Exod 32! Why would God command Moses to do something that seems to violate God's own law? Moreover, this serpent symbol appears to work almost magically. Under Israel's law, magic and magicians are also outlawed (e.g., Deut 18:9-14). And yet in Num 21 God required Moses to make a snake that—on its own? or, on God's behalf?—cured snake bite. And why a snake of all things? Was it not a snake that had been cursed by God in Gen 3 to crawl upon its belly all the days of its life and to be at enmity with the human race? Was it not the snake that symbolized eternal distance from God and human sin? In all these ways, the story from Numbers does not seem to fit very well within Israel's traditions and brings up troubling associations from within the broader context of the OT canon.

From a later period in Israel's history, however, we also read of a king named Hezekiah who came to the throne of Judah determined to avert the coming disaster predicted by a few faithful prophets—namely, that the nation's disobedience to God's laws will soon result in its defeat and domination by a foreign power. So Hezekiah implemented sweeping reforms in Judah's worship. In 2 Kgs 18 we are told: "He removed the hill-top altars, broke down the sacred pillars, and cut down the holy pole. He broke into pieces the bronze serpent that Moses had made, for until those days the people of Israel had made offerings to it; it was called *Nehushtan*." Here, hundreds of years after the wilderness wanderings, we find that the people of Israel had been making offerings to the bronze serpent and calling upon it by name. The symbol had become an image, an idol, and the reform-king Hezekiah dutifully ground it into dust.

Both of these stories echo in Israel's memory and take root in its Scripture: God's command for Moses to build the serpent and Hezekiah's God-given mandate to destroy it. The serpent had become a graven image which ultimately misdirected Israel's faith, even though it was originally designed to save God's people from mortal danger. "*Nehushtan*" is a tragic, accursed figure—apart from God and yet of God—a figure which could give life, but only as long as it served to lift up the eyes of Israel to God. No wonder, in all its strangeness, that this aspect of the Old Testament's witness provided a central motif for John. Like the bronze serpent of old, Jesus had been raised on a pole. Like Moses' serpent, he, too, was cursed according to the law. Like the serpent, Jesus gave new life.

Raised, yes; new life, yes; but, "cursed"? Yes, for "no one has ascended to heaven except the one who descended from heaven, the Son of Man" (John 3:13). The serpent tradition implies Jesus' full descent as well as his inevitable elevation. Deuteronomy 21:22-23 provides the ancient verdict: anyone hung on a tree is accursed of God. We suspect this text played an important role in the preaching of the early church from Paul's use of it in Gal 3:13-14 and Peter's words before the high priest in Acts 5:30-31: "The God of our ancestors raised up Jesus whom you had killed by hanging him on a tree. God exalted him at his right hand as Leader and Savior that he might give repentance to Israel and forgiveness of sins" (cf. Acts 10:39; 13:29). Here the implied question is ultimately the same as the explicit protest in John 12 with which we began: how can the Messiah die, especially in this shameful, undignified way—in fact, contrary to Scripture?

No wonder John perceived that something crucial about Jesus was foretold in the old tradition of the brazen serpent. No wonder John draws upon the OT brazenly to reveal a deeper dimension of God's character and purpose. It is not that John just "opted" to use this particular OT tradition, one among several, but rather that he was compelled, constrained, to cite this authoritative witness from Scripture which spoke to him so clearly of the Messiah he knew in Jesus Christ. The story of the brazen serpent told of another occasion on which God had used something which carried a curse to bring blessing. Here was another time God's justice was not compromised, but redirected to a figure outside God's favor in order that the people of God might be saved.

Only this time the figure outside God's favor is himself the Son of Man, the only Son of the Father. This sacrifice of love—the willingness of God the Father to allow God the Son to experience the dreadful curse of life apart from God, the willingness of God to take upon himself all the venom of our murmuring, wandering and rebellion—this sacrifice of love is perfectly expressed for John by the very hideousness of the serpent in the wilderness—brazen, cursed, and mounted.

This is what John would have us know: there is not one of us, he is saying, who has not been bitten by sin and its allure. We too murmur, grumble, and spend our lives rebelling against God in the wasteland. "Why have you taken us out of our comfortable lives, O God?" we protest. Of course, we were in slavery there—in the Egypt of our yesterdays—but the fleshpots of that former life continue to seem tantalizingly tasty. "Why do we not have better provisions for our journey?" we murmur. "Where are our heroes?" we grumble. "Have you brought us out to die in this wilderness? How can these things be?" Such complaints are truly as sharp as any serpent's tooth, but at the hour in which we feel their bite, the only antivenin is already "lifted up" within our midst—just not in the form we expected.

Consider again these words from the book of Isa 52:13-15 and 53:2-5:

> See, my servant shall prosper; he shall be exalted and lifted up, and shall be very high. Just as there were many who were astonished at him—so marred was his appearance, beyond human semblance . . . so shall he startle many nations . . . he had no form or majesty that we should look at him, nothing in his appearance that we should desire him. He was despised and rejected by others; a man of suffering and acquainted with infirmity; and as one from whom others hide their faces he was despised, and we held him of no account. Surely he has borne our infirmities and carried our diseases; yet we accounted him stricken, struck down by God, and afflicted. But he was wounded for our transgressions, crushed for our iniquities; upon him was the punishment that made us whole, and by his bruises we are healed.

Is it not this passage from Isaiah that best describes the full logic of John's OT allusion? By the wounds and bruises of Christ we are healed. Because he took upon himself our sin and our punishment we are made whole. In the marring of his appearance we may yet become fully who we really are.

So lift up your eyes to him—the Serpent in the Wilderness—and live! Whatever you have done—God has raised him up in power! Whatever shame you carry—God has laid upon him the curse of us all. However much you fear you are lost, perishing, or dying—he who had no cause to die has died that you may live.

So look to him! Christ is lifted up in tenderness and mercy, not in worldly power or prestige. Christ is lifted up in righteousness and peace, not in stratagems of greed or gain. Wherever there is truth and love, gentleness and sacrifice, Christ is there, but Christ crucified. Lift up your eyes to him and to his Cross and you shall surely live.

Yes, Nicodemus, these are heavenly things, theological things. How does the Gospel of John proceed next? "For God so loved the world that he gave his only Son, so that everyone who believes in him may not perish but may have eternal life" (John 3:16). The brazen serpent leads to the telling of the brazen gospel of Jesus Christ. In this telling is the only true hope for the life we seek. How are we to be teachers in Israel, if we do not understand such things?

BIBLIOGRAPHY

Adam, A.K.M., *Making Sense of New Testament Theology: "Modern" Problems and Prospects.* Macon, Georgia: Mercer University Press, 1995. Adam attacks the pretentiousness (but not the legitimacy) of historical criticism with its attempts to wrest the Bible from the control of the church. Through a discussion of modernity, New Testament theology (Gabler, Wrede, Stendahl), paradigms for interpretation, politics and the interpreter, the philosophical erosion of modernity, and future prospects, Adam's intent is to help us understand what to keep of the historical-critical perspective. He champions the need for a hermeneutics of theology and attempts to restore the Bible to the believing community.

Alexander, T. Desmond, et al., eds. *New Dictionary of Biblical Theology: Exploring the Unity and Diversity of Scripture*. Downers Grove: InterVarsity, 2000. This biblical reference work assumes the basic theological unity of Scripture and engages in dialogue with the whole range of contemporary scholarship. It includes an encyclopedia of important biblical-theological themes and articles on the theology of individual biblical books and on issues in biblical theology.

Augustine. *De doctrina Christiana.* Edited and translated by R. P. H. Green. Oxford: Clarendon, 1995. This great treatise on hermeneutics is indispensable for anyone who wishes to understand and practice theological exegesis. Concentrate on the theme that dominates the work: the journey of the soul to God. Augustine's *City of God* also deserves attention.

Barr, James. "Biblical Theology." in *The Interpreter's Dictionary of the Bible.* Supplementary Volume. Edited by Keith Crim. Nashville: Abingdon, 1976, 104-111. As a response to criticism that Stendahl's article in the first edition of this dictionary was idealistic and unrepresentative of what was going on in biblical theology, Barr's article distinguishes between two senses of "biblical theology" (the movement as opposed to a collection of individual studies and themes associated with theological interpretation) and then considers issues relevant to recent development.

______. *The Concept of Biblical Theology: an Old Testament Perspective.* Minneapolis: Fortress, 1999. Barr has interacted with issues dealing with biblical theology most of his career, often in ways quite critical of the efforts.

Barth Karl. *The Epistle to the Romans.* Translated from the sixth edition by Edwyn C. Hoskyns. London: Oxford University Press, 1968. This commentary is famous for its effort to bring theological interpretation back on the scene. Barth's prefaces, some lengthy, to the various editions of this commentary discuss method and the reactions to his approach and are well worth attention as one seeks to develop a procedure for interpreting Scripture theologically.

Bartholomew, Craig, Colin Greene, and Karl Moller, eds. *Renewing Biblical Interpretation.* Grand Rapids, Michigan: Zondervan, 2000. This collection of wide-ranging essays provides a helpful discussion of the current crisis in biblical interpretation, but focuses on the renewal of biblical theology. A consensus is not to be sought through easy compromise,

---

*This bibliography is primarily based on suggestions and comments by the participants in the symposium. Appreciation is expressed to Sarah Eix and James Amadon for their work in compiling and supplementing the contributions to create this bibliography.

but through courage to examine whether "hermeneutical experiments lead us closer to the biblical text rather than increasing our distance from it through endless abstraction." The essays engage the reader in a search for divine truth that is faithful to the challenge of the world today.

Bartlett, David L. "Story and History: Narratives and Claims." *Interp* 45 (1991): 229-240. This article encourages pastors to do their historical-critical homework alongside their literary and imaginative construal of texts when preparing a sermon. It addresses the study and history of biblical interpretation and looks at narratives and claims in preaching.

Braaten, Carl E. "Scripture, Church, and Dogma: An Essay on Theological Method." *Interp* 50 (1996): 142-155. Under the overarching umbrella of "doing theology under the authority of Scripture within the context of the church," this article identifies the two very different ways of doing theology by Jüngel and Pannenberg. It also addresses transcendence, the principle of referentiality, revelation and salvation, the authority of Scripture, and a Chalcedonian hermeneutic.

Braaten Carl E., and Robert W. Jenson, eds. *Reclaiming the Bible for the Church.* Grand Rapids: Eerdmans, 1995. The chapters of this book are papers delivered at a 1994 conference on the theme of reclaiming the Bible for the church. Contributers include: Elizabeth Achtemeier, Carl Braaten, Brevard Childs, Karl Donfried, Roy Harrisville, Thomas Hopko, Robert Jenson, Aidan Kavanagh, and Alister McGrath. Most address the gap between the historical-critical method and the church's dogmatic interpretation of biblical faith and discuss the hermeneutics best qualified to understand the Scriptures.

Brueggemann, Walter. *Deep Memory, Exuberent Hope.* Edited by Patrick Miller. Minneapolis, Fortress, 2000. See especially chapter 9, "The Role of Old Testament Theology in Interpretation."

Buber, Martin. *The Prophetic Faith.* New York: Harper & Row, 1960. This work of a great Jewish philosopher/theologian is a fascinating account of his perception of Israel's writing prophets as men of faith who continued and enriched the old Israelite concepts of the encounter with their God. Many highly provocative sketches of the individual prophets provide profound insights into "prophetic faith."

______. *Moses: The Revelation and the Covenant.* New York: Harper & Brothers, 1958. Buber's Moses is the attempt, against the prevailing scholarly fragmentation of the biblical traditions into sources and isolated units of legends, to provide a synthetic portrait of Moses as a definite individual who accomplished his work of revealing the God of the covenant with Israel, not just a monotheistic theory.

Carson, D. A., ed. *Biblical Interpretation and the Church: The Problem of Contextualization.* Nashville: Nelson, 1984. As an effort to construct "a biblical theology of the church that reflects the flavor of international Christians joined in reverent submission to the Scriptures, and that rejoices in cultural diversity," this collection of essays outlines the factors currently determining hermeneutical debate in cross-cultural contexts, such as the hermeneutical issues that surface in comparing the "kingdom-language" of current evangelicalism and "the kingdom of God" language of the Bible, the hermeneutical presuppositions of the church in African theology, the hermeneutics of the church in liberation theology, and the hermeneutical issues surrounding social justice.

______. "Current Issues in Biblical Theology: A New Testament Perspective," *BBR* 5 (1995) 17-41. Carson articulates the necessity of pressing towards "whole-bible theology" while still stressing the distinctions of individual corpora and probes the challenges to biblical theology today.

Childs, Brevard S. *Biblical Theology in Crisis.* Philadelphia: Westminster, 1970. Childs traces the history of the American biblical theology movement since the 1940s, examines its strengths and weaknesses, and offers an alternative approach that takes the canon more seriously. He illustrates his method by studying Ps 8 to demonstrate the theological significance of the different roles that a text can have within Scripture. He uses Exod 2 to show how history of interpretation is part of the exegetical discipline, and he explores the theological implications of Prov 7 with regard to sex. He concludes with an essay reflecting on the understanding of God in both testaments.

Childs, Brevard S. *Biblical Theology of the Old and New Testaments: Theological Reflection on the Christian Bible.* Minneapolis: Fortress, 1993. This is one of the more serious attempts to do a theology of both testaments. After discussing method and a brief history of the discipline through the church's history, Childs moves through both testaments to hear the "discrete witness" of each. Then after demonstrating his exegesis through treatment of Gen 22:1-19 and Matt 21:33-46, he treats several key theological topics such as God, election, Christology, etc.

______. *The Book of Exodus.* Philadelphia: Westminster, 1974. Unlike many commentaries, this one is "unabashedly theological" and is a good example of a comprehensive attempt to deal with historical-critical issues, but also to include the use of the OT by the NT, the impact of the church's exegesis, and the author's own theological reflection.

Coats, George W. *Moses: Heroic Man. Man of God.* Sheffield: JSOT Press, 1988. Emphasis is placed on the characteristics of the story of Moses that reveal two main trends: Moses is described as an active, heroic figure whose leadership represents God to the people, and as the dependent servant of God who is subservient to the actions of God and represents the people to God.

De Vries, Simon J. *The Achievements of Biblical Religion: A Prolegomena to Old Testament Theology.* Lanham, Md.: University Press of America, 1983. This is an important discussion and assessment of the theological interpretation of Scripture.

______. *From Old Revelation to New.* Grand Rapids: Eerdmans, 1995. This is a serious piece of scholarly research and provides a thorough study of the history of the development of eschatology in the OT.

Dubay, Thomas. *Authenticity: A Biblical Theology of Discernment.* San Francisco: Ignatius, 1977. This book outlines the biblical picture of discerning God's mind and will and seeks to offer an authentic understanding of how God and people interact. The author first raises problems associated with discernment, then expounds on what he believes discernment entails, what signals the Holy Spirit's action in one's life, and concludes with a section on the verifications and implications of proper discernment.

Dunn, James D. G. *The Theology of Paul the Apostle.* Grand Rapids: Eerdmans, 1998. Using primarily Paul's letter to the Romans as the foundation for constructing a fuller exposition of Paul's whole theology, Dunn's thematic treatment describes Paul's teaching on such topics as God, humankind, sin, Christology, salvation, the church, and the nature of the Christian life.

Dunn, James D. G., and James P. Mackey. *New Testament Theology in Dialogue: Christology and Ministry.* Philadelphia: Westminster, 1987. This is an interesting collaborative effort by a NT scholar and a systematic theologian. Each explains the task of his own theological discipline and then discusses Christology and church ministry as case studies.

Ex Auditu, 1 (1985), which provides a collection of significant articles on issues of intepretation and biblical theology and three articles focused on specific texts to demonstrate how to do theological interpretation. Among others, authors of articles include K. Froehlich, N. Nash, P. Hanson, G. Stanton, and D. Steinmetz. Volume 2 (1986), in addition to treating issues of church and state, has articles by P. Stuhlmacher and B. Meyer that are more general and methodological.

Fowl, Stephen E. *Engaging Scripture. A Model for Theological Interpretation.* Malden, Mass.: Blackwell, 1998. Concerned that contemporary Christian theologians and biblical scholars have bracketed out constructive theological convictions in the interest of disciplinary integrity and have lost the skills and habits that enabled earlier Christians to allow interpretation to shape and be shaped by Christian convictions and concerns, Fowl encourages scholars in both biblical and theological fields to work together and in conjunction with the Christian community. His central argument is that Christian interpretation of Scripture must involve an interaction of Christian convictions and scriptural interpretation. The authority of the Bible as the Scripture of Christians and biblical theology that serves faithful life and worship are both foundational for theological interpretation.

Fowl, Stephen E., ed. *The Theological Interpretation of Scripture: Classic and Contemporary Readings.* Cambridge, Mass.: Blackwell, 1997. This is an anthology of important writings that represent the issues and debates surrounding the integration of theological concerns and the interpretation of Scripture. Included are both historical readings which shed light on the modern conversation and recent essays which challenge the direction of the theological and biblical disciplines in the present and future. Varied examples of theological interpretation are included as exemplars. The intent is that as students read concrete examples of biblical theology, they learn to practice themselves.

Fretheim, Terence E. *The Suffering God: An Old Testament Perspective.* Philadelphia: Fortress, 1984. This is an important contribution to understanding the concept of God in the OT. It takes the anthropomorphic metaphors in much of the OT language of God seriously as expressions of God's decision to adopt the life of God's human creature into the core of God's own being.

Fretheim, Terence and Karlfried Froehlich. *The Bible as Word of God in a Postmodern Age.* Minneapolis: Fortress, 1998. The authors respond, in divergent ways, to the questions: What does it mean to say that Scripture has authority for Christian faith and life in light of contemporary forms of biblical criticism? How do we understand a biblical text to be the Word of God when the meaning of the text can vary, depending on the perspective of the reader/hearer? And, given the profound hermeneutical challenges of our time, how does Scripture serve as a guide in worship, doctrine, preaching, and ethical decision-making for the people of God?

Goldingay, John. *Theological Diversity and the Authority of the Old Testament.* Grand Rapids: Eerdmans, 1987. Goldingay considers how the theologian must wrestle with the diverse viewpoints evident in the OT, addresses the questions that diversity, contradiction, and the search for theological coherence raise, analyzes how even varied viewpoints are interrelated and function theologically, and ultimately shows how to move in a disciplined way from diversity in the OT to the coherence of one canon. He analyzes and demonstrates three different approaches to OT theology: the contextual or historical approach, of evaluative or critical approach, and the unifying or constructive approach.

Graef, Hilda. *Mary: A History of Doctrine and Devotion.* 2 vols. New York: Sheed and Ward, 1963-1965. This historical treatment of the devotion to Mary from a Catholic perspective also includes discussion of Protestant Reformers.

Green, Joel and Max Turner. *Between Two Horizons: Spanning New Testament Studies and Systematic Theology.* Grand Rapids: Eerdmans, 2000. This selection of essays intends to bridge the chasm between the disciplines of theology and biblical studies. The discussion embraces a variety of significant issues including the role of the author's intention and the role the "rule of faith."

Harrington, Wilfrid J. *The Path of Biblical Theology.* Dublin: Gill and Macmillan, 1973. This is a survey and summary of the work done in the theology of each testament and of the Bible as a whole. Section four is relevant to the theory of biblical theology and its place in the wider field of theology in general (and Roman Catholic dogmatic theology in particular). The book intends to present the purpose, scope, method, and range of biblical theology.

Hasel, Gerhard. *New Testament Theology: Basic Issues in the Current Debate.* Grand Rapids: Eerdmans, 1978. Recognizing the undeniable crisis in current NT theology and the deep historical and methodological problems that plague the discipline, Hasel begins with a historical survey of the development of NT theology, then introduces the reader to the issues in the current debate and to the relationship between the theologies of the testaments, and finally provides suggestions for doing NT theology. A bibliography is included.

______. *Old Testament Theology: Basic Issues in the Current Debate.* Revised edition. Grand Rapids: Eerdmans, 1972. Hasel offers a useful introduction to the intense debate regarding the nature, function, method, and scope of OT theology. By surveying the history of the discipline, he exposes the roots of the fundamental issues. Here, too, he addresses the relationship between the testaments and then offers basic proposals for doing OT Theology. A bibliography is included.

Hays, Richard B. "Scripture-Shaped Community: The Problem of Method in New Testament Ethics." *Interp* 44 (1990) 42-55. This article addresses the hermeneutical crisis regarding ethical questions in light of widely divergent versions of Christian morality. It looks at the task of NT ethics, guidelines for discernment, and guidelines for biblical authority. Reason and experience are insufficient to guide the self-sacrificial service to which the NT calls the church; practice and decisions must be disciplined by Scripture.

Heschel, Abraham J. *The Prophets*. New York: Harper & Row, 1962. This outstanding study of Hebrew prophecy by a Jewish interpreter take the nature of the God of the prophets equally seriously as the psychological state and the human situation of the prophets. The God of the prophets is the God of pathos who is moved and affected by what happens in the world, effecting in him joy and sorrow, pleasure and wrath. Correspondingly, the prophet shares in this pathos of God, communicating not only God's will and direction but participating in God's pathos.

Hubbard, Robert L. Jr., Robert K. Johnston, and Robert P. Meye. *Studies in Old Testament Theology*. Dallas: Word, 1992. These essays in honor of David Hubbard are authored mostly by leading evangelical scholars. The essays were arranged to explore each part of the Old Testament canon (Torah, Prophets, Writings) to determine what is said in each about God and the people of God. Additional essays analyze integrative and practical aspects of each division of the canon for theology and church life today.

Ingraffia, Brian D. *Postmodern Theory and Biblical Theology*. Cambridge: Cambridge University Press, 1995. Through an exegesis of the NT and wide reference to philosophers and theologians Ingraffia argues that biblical theology must be separated from Greek and modern metaphysics. He demonstrates how any attempted reconciliation between contemporary critical theory and biblical theology is radically incompatible. Drawing upon the writings of Luther, Kierkegaard, Barth, Bonhoeffer, Niebuhr, and Moltmann, he argues that an "either/or" must be articulated between postmodern theory and biblical theology.

Journal of Religion, 76.2 (1996). This issue of *Journal of Religion* provides several articles on the Bible and Christian Theology in an attempt to address the theological and methodological issues. Of two review articles, one surveys recent German OT theologies and the other the wisdom tradition in recent Christian theology.

Kim, Wonil, et al., eds. *Reading the Hebrew Bible for a New Millenium: Form, Concept and Theological Perspective*. Vol 1: *Theological and Hermeneutical Studies*. Harrisburg, Pa: Trinity Press International, 2000. This is a collection of essays that applies Rolf P. Knierim's methods of interpretation to Hebrew texts, esp. Josh 1-12 and Lev 15.

Kneirim, Rolf P. *The Task of Old Testament Theology: Substance, Method, and Cases*. Grand Rapids: Eerdmans, 1995. This collection of Kneirim's essays offers a comprehensive look at OT theology. The author treats issues such as methodology, hermeneutics, and linguistics, and also offers specific exegetical case studies as examples of OT theology.

Kraftchick, Steven J., Charles D. Myers, Jr., and Ben C. Ollenburger, eds. *Problems and Perspectives: Biblical Theology*. Nashville: Abingdon, 1995. These essays in honor of J. Christiaan Beker discuss the nature of biblical theology by treating the important issues: the relation of the testaments, the problems of faith and history, the means and goals of interpretation, and the existence of a centering theology.

Lung-kwong, Lo, ed. *Jesus, Paul, and John*. Hong Kong: Theology Division, Chung Chi College, The Chinese University of Hong Kong, 1999. This small book consists of three papers: a discussion of NT theology by C. K. Barrett; a view of Paul as pastor by A. Malherbe; and an article on the use of the Bible in Contextualizing Theology by K. Koyama.

Luther, Martin. *The Large Catechesim*. Translated by R. H. Fischer. Philadelphia: Fortress, 1959. See especially part one on the ten commandments as a model of theological interpretation.

Luz, Ulrich. *Matthew: A Commentary*. 2 vols. Translated by W. C. Linss, and James E. Crouch. Minneapolis: Augsburg/Fortress, 1989, 2001. This commentary, as yet complete only to ch. 20, is an example of a method of NT exegesis that deals with the effects of biblical texts on subsequent understanding in the history of the church. The commentary provides a treasure of texts through centuries of interpretation, but it by no means neglects the more traditional methods of interpretation.

Luz, Ulrich. *Matthew in History: Interpretation, Influence, and Effects.* Minneapolis: Fortress, 1994.This is a thorough exposition of the principles of an exegesis concerned with the "history of effects" of a biblical text on the subsequent understanding in the history of interpretation and an evaluation of the possibilities and limitations of this method.

Meyer, Ben F. *Critical Realism and the New Testament.* San Jose, Calif.: Pickwick, Second Printing, 2001. This is an important but neglected volume. Meyer embraces critical realism as a way to insist on the communicative intent of authors and texts, on historical consciousness, and on an openness to transcendence. Meyer views judgment as integral to the task of interpretation and discusses the relationships between reader, text, and referent. Insisting on both human and Christian authenticity he calls for interpreters who can meet the challenge of the text.

Morgan, Robert, ed. *The Nature of New Testament Theology.* Naperville, Il.: SCM, 1973. This book seeks to highlight the contributions of William Wrede and Adolf Schlatter to the field of New Testament Theology. The extensive introduction by Morgan highlights their respective contributions and is followed by Wrede's "The Task and Method of 'New Testament Theology' " and Schlatter's "The Theology of the New Testament and Dogmatics."

Murphy Roland, ed. *Theology, Exegesis and Proclamation.* New York: Herder and Herder 1971. This collection of articles examines the relationship between exegesis and dogmatic theology, exegesis and proclamation, and exegesis and the church. An examination of original sin provides a format for dealing with questions pertaining to the dialogue between exegetes and theologians.

Noble, Paul R. *The Canonical Approach: A Critical Reconstruction of the Hermeneutics of Brevard S. Childs.* Leiden: Brill, 1995. This work preserves the principles and objectives of Brevard Childs, treats the issues and problems raised by Childs' methodology, and searches for ways that they can be dealt with more satisfactorily. The discussion covers central issues in biblical methodology and hermeneutics.

O'Collins Gerald, and Daniel Kendall. *The Bible for Theology: Ten Principles for the Theological Use of Scripture.* New York: Paulist Press, 1997. O'Collins and Kendall sketch their presuppositions about the origins of Scripture and their interpretation and then elaborate upon and argue the relevance of ten principles that they recommend as guidelines for moving from Scripture to theology. This brief book is written for the educated nonspecialist and applies the principles to basic Christian doctrines.

Ollenburger, Ben C., ed. *So Wide a Sea: Essays on Biblical and Systematic Theology.* Elkhart, Ind.: Institute of Mennonite Studies, 1991. Recognizing the vastness of Scripture, itself "so wide a sea," and the enormous chasm that has emerged between biblical studies and systematic theology, this collection of essays treats theology's relation to the Bible. The discussion deals with fundamental disagreements about the definition, task, and legitimacy of biblical and systematic theology. Case studies are presented and focus is placed on the responsibility of the disciplines.

Ollenburger, Ben C., Elmer A. Martens, and Gerhard F. Hasel, eds. *The Flowering of Old Testament Theology: A Reader in Twentieth Century Old Testament Theology.* Winona Lake, Ind.: Eisenbrauns, 1992. This collection of essays provides a sweeping orientation to the issues, the progress, and the achievements in OT theology throughout the centuries. The volume includes a translation of Johann P. Gabler's pioneer statement, "An Oration on the Proper Distinction between Biblical and Dogmatic Theology with the Specific Objectives of Each," which distinguishes between systematic and biblical theology and sets the stage for future discussion.

O'Meara, Thomas. *Mary in Protestant and Catholic Theology.* New York: Sheed and Ward. 1966. In addition to Roman Catholic positions, O'Meara considers Luther, Calvin, and contemporary Protestant theologians.

Pedersen Sigfred. *New Directions in Biblical Theology: Papers of the Aarhus Conference.* Leiden: Brill, 1994. This volume contains papers, some in German, by mostly contintental NT scholars to showcase recent thinking on a variety of topics and aspects of NT theology.

Pelikan, Jaroslav. *Mary Through the Centuries: Her Place in the History of Culture.* New Haven: Yale University Press, 1996. While this work is less theological than one might have hoped, it nevertheless provides helpful information regarding the history of culture and the way Mary has been viewed.

Penchansky, David. *The Politics of Biblical Theology: A Postmodern Reading.* Macon, Georgia: Mercer University Press, 1995. The author emphasizes that community and culture inform the voice that we impose on biblical texts to affirm our deepest convictions. With an awareness of the reader's participation in the production of meaning, the author explores and confirms his own "hermeneutical suspicion" of postmodern terms closely integrated with the subjective, political dimension of the academy. After analyzing the Biblical Theology Movement and attacks on it, he offers his "more honest and self-conscious" way of reading the Bible.

Perdue, Leo G. *The Collapse of History: Reconstructing Old Testament Theology.* Minneapolis: Fortress, 1994. In addition to discussing the present and future states of OT theology, this book focuses on four areas in the attempt to understand OT theology: redemption and history; cosmology and anthropology; Scripture and metaphor; and story and imagination.

Rad, Gerhard von. *Old Testament Theology.* Translated by D. M. G. Stalker. 2 vols. New York: Harper & Brothers, 1962. Von Rad's work is still a standard on OT Theology, even if some of his methodological assumptions call for revision today.

Radner, Ephraim. *The End of the Church: A Pneumatology of Christian Division in the West.* Grand Rapids: Eerdmans, 1998. This work offers important insights into the practice of early Christian exegesis, as well as the theological horizon of biblical hermeneutics. It is a remarkable study of the consequences of Reformation schism and yields stunning insight into our current condition of exegetical aphasia. It is a difficult book that will be cited more often than read, but anyone who wishes to recover the potency and depth of precritical exegesis will have to come to terms with Radner's analysis.

Raisanen, Heikki. *Beyond New Testament Theology.* Philadelphia: Trinity Press International, 1990. A selective look at the history of NT theology that highlights different scholars from Gabler to the present. Like Wrede, Raisanen contends that the concept NT theology should be replaced with the "history of early Christian thought" (seen in the context of early Judaism), and critical philosophical/theological "reflection on the New Testament," as well as its influence on our history and its significance for contemporary life.

Reumann, John, ed. *The Promise and Practice of Biblical Theology.* Minneapolis: Fortress, 1991. This collection of essays provides a valuable introduction to the range of issues connected with biblical theology, both as regards method, modern religious and societal issues, and the life of the church. Reumann's introduction and afterward insightfully address questions about the nature and practice of biblical theology.

Reventlow, Henning Graf. *Problems of Biblical Theology in the Twentieth Century.* Philadelphia: Fortress, 1986. In addition to dealing with current debated issues about recovering a biblical theology Reventlow deals with controversial aspects of the relationship between the testaments. He argues a biblical theology of the entire Bible will be possible only with careful methodological engagement with the problems of the relationship between the testaments: the salvation history model, the typological approach, the *sensus plenior* debate, promise and furfillment, the superiority of the OT, Israel and the church, and the problem of the canon.

Robinson, H. Wheeler. *The Cross in the Old Testament.* Philadelphia: Westminster, 1955. This book contains three originally separate monographs of the author, on the cross of Job, on the Servant of God, and on Jeremiah. As the title of each part of the book indicates, the sufferings of the three exponents of Israelite faith in the OT are viewed as prefigurations of the suffering of Jesus Christ. Thus, the book is a contribution to the understanding of the inner unity of the testaments.

Sandys-Wunsch, John and Laurence Eldredge. "J. P. Gabler and the Distinction between Biblical and Dogmatic Theology: Translation, Commentary, and Discussion of his Originality." *SJT* 33 (1980): 133-158. The famous essay by Gabler is made available in this translation, and the commentary provides insight and helpful bibliographical and historical information.

Satterthwaite, Philip E. and David F. Wright, eds. *A Pathway into the Holy Scripture.* Grand Rapids: Eerdmans, 1994. This book contains a collection of papers given at the jubilee meeting of the Tyndale Fellowship for Biblical and Theological Research. The topics include a discussion of William Tyndale as biblical interpreter, surveys of current trends in OT and NT scholarship, treatments of biblical theology, hermeneutics, inspiration, and studies discussing the role of Scripture in the church in earlier periods and in the present day.

Scalise, Charles J. *Hermeneutics as Theological Prolegomena: A Canonical Approach.* Macon, Ga: Mercer University Press, 1994. Scalise responds to current challenges to the doctrine of revelation and the dominance of historical-critical study of the Bible by giving a carefully nuanced understanding of canonical hermeneutics, modifying and extending the interpretive methodology of Brevard Childs, and providing a new central theme for prolegomena to a postcritical evangelical theology.

Seitz, Christopher. *Word Without End: The Old Testament as Abiding Theological Witness.* Grand Rapids: Eerdmans, 1998. In this important book Seitz divides his work into three sections: the biblical theology of the OT and the issues that surround it; Isaiah as an exegetical example; and a section on OT theology and Christian practice.

Seitz, Christopher and Kathryn Greene-McCreight, eds. Theological Exegesis: Essays in Honor of Brevard S. Childs. This is a significant collection of essays dealing with Childs' canonical approach and with several texts and themes from both testaments.

Stendahl, Krister. "Biblical Theology, Contemporary." In *Interpreter's Dictionary of the Bible.* Edited by George Arthur Buttrick. Nashville: Abingdon, 1.418-432. This classic article on biblical theology has been discussed frequently for its distinction between what the text meant and what the text means. It still deserves serious reflection.

Stuckenbruck, Loren T. "Johann Philipp Gabler and the Delineation of Biblical Theology," *SJT* 52 (1999): 139-157. This helpful article seeks to situate Gabler historically and theologically so that one understands the developments that led to Gabler and the significance his ideas still have.

Stuhlmacher, Peter. *How to Do Biblical Theology.* Allison Park, Penn.: Pickwick Publications, Second Printing 1998. Convinced that the primary duty of biblical theology is to discover and develop the original historical meaning and the theological claims of the biblical texts, and concerned that the worlds of biblical scholarship and the church increasingly question the Word of God and its authority, Stuhlmacher considers what it means to speak with Paul of the "truth of the gospel" (Gal 2:14). He recognizes the righteousness of God as seen in Jesus' life and teaching and developed in Paul's theology as the central and unifying foundation for his biblical theology. A brief bibliography is included.

______. *Historical Criticism and Theological Interpretation of Scripture: Towards a Hermeneutics of Consent.* Translated by Roy A. Harrisville. Philadelphia: Fortress, 1977. Stuhlmacher recognizes the indispensability and the limits and problems of the historical-critical method. He argues for its expansion beyond Troeltsch's principles of criticism, analogy, and correlation, to include the principle of hearing which necessitates that a historical critic understand that history is open to transcendence. He argues for a hermeneutics of consent and an openness to an encounter with the truth of God coming to us from out of transcendence. What is especially significant to the discipline of biblical theology is Stuhlmacher's contention that it is the community, which has staked its very existence on this text, that must give definition to an interpreter's "hearing" and "consent."

Sun, Henry T. C., Keith L. Eades, James M. Robinson, and Garth I. Moller, eds. *Problems in Biblical Theology.* Grand Rapids: Eerdmans, 1997. This is a collection of 24 essays in honor of Rolf Kneirim. Topics include detailed exegetical studies of biblical texts, analyses of different theological methods and approaches, and the relation of OT exegesis, theology, and hermeneutics to current ways of interpretation and postmodern thought.

Tavard, George. *The Thousand Faces of the Virgin Mary*. Collegeville, Minn.: Liturgical, 1996. Tavard examines considerations of Mary from the NT to Vatican II, including the Protestant Reformation and Anglican theology.

Torrance Thomas F. *Divine Meaning: Studies in Patristic Hermeneutics*. Edinburgh T. & T. Clark, 1995. This book seeks to answer the question how the early Christians interpreted the Bible in the context of the philosophical and scientific thinking of their contemporary world. Particular attention is given to the way in which exploratory or "heuristic" science developed in the early centuries of the Christian church and became an integral part of biblical interpretation.

Tucker, Gene M., David L. Petersen, and Robert R. Wilson, eds. *Canon, Theology. and Old Testament Interpretation*. Philadelphia: Fortress, 1988. A collection of 20 essays in honor of Brevard Childs. The book is divided into four sections: canon and theology; the interpretation of the Torah and the Former Prophets; the interpretation of prophetic texts; and the interpretation of the writings.

VanGemeren, Willem A. *A Guide to Old Testament Theology and Exegesis: The Introductory Articles From the New International Dictionary of Old Testament Theology and Exegesis*. Grand Rapids: Zondervan, 1997. As the title implies, this book contains ten articles that deal with issues pertaining to the New International Dictionary of Old Testament Theology. Topics include hermeneutics, biblical theology, semantics, literary criticism, and canonical issues as they relate to the OT.

Vorgrimler, Herbert. *Dogmatic Vs. Biblical Theology*. London: Burns & Oates, 1964. A collection of nine essays written in non-technical language that seek to explore and further the relationship between dogmatic theology and biblical exegesis. The goal is to increase the connection between the two fields and the scholars that work within them.

Wainwright, Geoffrey, ed. *Keeping the Faith: Essays to Mark the Centenary of Lux Mundi*. Philadelphia: Fortress, 1988. The essays collected in this book are contributions to the task of doing biblical theology (of "interpreting the faith we have received") in the wake of the modern explosion of knowledge. The essays deal with a broad range of theological topics.

Watson, Francis. *Text, Church, and World: Biblical Interpretation in Theological Perspective*. Grand Rapids, Michigan: Eerdmans Publishing Company, 1994. Watson offers critical appreciation of recent hermeneutical work in the areas of literary, canonical, and feminist perspectives and makes his own hermeneutical proposals, always arguing for (and recognizing this as a minority position) the "primacy of theology within biblical interpretation." He calls for renewed dialogue with systematic theology and asserts that Christian theology is both a possible and relevant ecclesial discipline necessary for biblical interpretation. A bibliograhphy is included. See also his *Text and Truth: Redefining Biblical Theology*. Grand Rapids: Eerdmans, 1997.

Wolff, H. W. Hosea: *A Commentary on the Book of the Prophet Hosea*. Translated by G. Stansell. Philadelphia: Fortress, 1974. One of the most thorough and theologically sensitive expositions of the only writing prophet in the OT whose home was in the northern part of the divided kingdom who, nonetheless, greatly influenced later Judean prophecy.

Woodbridge, John D. and Thomas Edward McComiskey, eds. *Doing Theology in Today's World: Essays in Honor of Kenneth S. Kantzer*. Grand Rapids: Zondervan, 1991. This collection of essays provides dialogue with the "helping disciplines" of systematic theology, exegesis, church history, philosophy, and methodology. A variety of confessional perspectives is represented. The book concludes with Kantzer's approach to doing biblical theology today: a systematic biblical dogmatics.

Word and World, (1981); 3 (1983); and 13 (1993). These three issues of this journal are devoted to the process of biblical interpretation and theology. Vol. I deals with the Bible as Scripture and includes articles by R. Klein and W. Brueggemann. Vol. 3 deals with the relation of the testaments, and vol. 13 focuses on biblical interpretation for Christian ministry.

NORTH PARK THEOLOGICAL SEMINARY

SYMPOSIUM ON THE THEOLOGICAL INTERPRETATION OF SCRIPTURE

SEPTEMBER 29-OCTOBER 1, 2000

THE TASK OF INTERPRETING SCRIPTURE THEOLOGICALLY

THE PRESENTERS

STEPHEN CHAPMAN

Duke Divinity School (Worship Leader)

JAMES D. G. DUNN

University of Durham (New Testament)

KATHRYN GREENE-McCREIGHT

Smith College (Theology)

ROBERT L. HUBBARD, Jr.

North Park Theological Seminary (Old Testament)

ROLF P. KNIERIM

Claremont School of Theology and Claremont Graduate University (Hebrew Bible)

ULRICH MAUSER

Princeton Theological Seminary, emeritus (New Testament)

R. R. RENO

Creighton University (Theology)

KEVIN J. VANHOOZER

Trinity Evangelical Divinity School (Theology and Hermeneutics)

GEOFFREY WAINWRIGHT

Duke Divinity School (Theology)

THE RESPONDENTS

VINCENT BACOTE

Wheaton College

STEPHEN CHAPMAN

Duke Divinity School

CHARLES COSGROVE

Northern Baptist Theological Seminary

DAVID S. CUNNINGHAM

Seabury-Western Theological Seminary

PHILIP HEFNER

Lutheran School of Theology

TODD E. JOHNSON

Loyola University

JOHN McCARTHY

Loyola University

DAVID P. MOESSNER

University of Dubuque Theological Seminary

NORTH PARK THEOLOGICAL SEMINARY

SYMPOSIUM ON THE THEOLOGICAL INTERPRETATION OF SCRIPTURE

SEPTEMBER 29-OCTOBER 1, 2000

THE TASK OF INTERPRETING SCRIPTURE THEOLOGICALLY

PERSONS IN ATTENDANCE

James Amadon
Isolde Anderson
*Vincent Bacote
Daniel Bailey
Robert Boehm
Paul D. G. Bramer
John Bray
James K. Bruckner
LeRoy Carlson
Richard W. Carlson
*Stephen Chapman
Mary Chase-Ziolek
Janson Condren
*Charles Cosgrove
*David S. Cunningham
Jo Ann Deasy
*James D. G. Dunn
Sarah Eix
Bruce Fields
Linda Forbes
Christine Franzon
Carl Franzon
*Kathryn Greene-McCreight
Stephen Graham
Dikran Hadidian
Jean Hadidian
Bill Hansen
*Philip Hefner
*Robert L. Hubbard
Ken Johnson
*Todd Johnson
Larry Kamphausen
Katie Kamphausen
Lisa Kallen-Youngberg
*Rolf P. Knierim
Bo Lim
Matthew Lundgren
Don Madvig
John Madvig
Linda Mainey
Eric F. Mason
*Ulrich W. Mauser
*John McCarthy
Michael Miller
*David P. Moessner
F. Burton Nelson
James Nelson
Monty Newton
Dave Noreen
Carol M. Norén
Jerry Reed
*R. R. Reno

John Sanders
Phillis Sheppard
Juhie Shinn
Tim M. Sigler
Klyne Snodgrass
Phyllis Snodgrass
Carol Souliere
Louis Souliere
Luke Swanson
Carl L. Taylor
Daniel J. Treier
*Kevin Vanhoozer
*Geoffrey Wainwright
Lois Weborg
Wayne Weld
Jonathan Wilson
Kazu Wu

EX AUDITU

VOLUMES AVAILABLE

EX AUDITU Vol. 1 (1985) consists of selected articles presenting the issues inherent in the theological interpretation of Scripture.

EX AUDITU Vol. 2 (1986) discusses the theme: "Church and State Relationship." In addition there are two lead articles, one by Peter Stuhlmacher on "EX AUDITU and the Theological Interpretation of Holy Scripture," and the second by Ben F. Meyer on "The Primacy of Consent and the Uses of Suspicion."

EX AUDITU Vol.	3 (1987)	The theme:	"Creation."
EX AUDITU Vol.	4 (1988)	The theme:	"The Church and Israel (Romans 9-11)."
EX AUDITU Vol.	5 (1989)	The theme:	"What is Salvation?"
EX AUDITU Vol.	6 (1990)	The theme:	"Prophetic and/or Apocalyptic Eschatology."
EX AUDITU Vol	7 (1991)	The theme:	"Christology and Incarnation."
EX AUDITU Vol.	8 (1992)	The theme:	"Worship."
EX AUDITU Vol.	9 (1993)	The theme:	"Resurrection."
EX AUDITU Vol.	10 (1994)	The theme:	"The Church."
EX AUDITU Vol.	11 (1995)	The theme:	"Biblical Law and Liberty" (OP)
EX AUDITU Vol.	12 (1996)	The theme:	"Holy Spirit"
EX AUDITU Vol.	13 (1997)	The theme:	"What is a Human?"
EX AUDITU Vol.	14 (1998)	The Theme:	"The Theological Significance of the Earthly Jesus"
EX AUDITU Vol.	15 (1999)	The Theme:	"Idolatry and the Understanding of God
EX AUDITU Vol.	16 (2000)	The Theme:	"The Task of Interpreting Scripture Theologically"

EX AUDITU Vol. 17 (2001).
The theme will be: "Biblical Ethics"

To be published in April 2002

Pickwick Publications
215 Incline Way
San Jose, CA 95139-1526